The World's Best Poetry

Volume VIII

National Spirit

Poetry Anthology Press

The World's Best Poetry

Volume VIII

National Spirit

Edited by Bliss Carman

Prepared by
The Editorial Board, Granger Book Co., Inc.

 Poetry Anthology Press
Great Neck, New York

Library of Congress Catalog Card Number 80-84498
International Standard Book Number 0-89609-209-7
International Standard Book Number for
Foundation Volumes I-X, 0-89609-300-X

Manufactured in the U.S.À.

Poetry Anthology Press is a
division of Granger Book Co., Inc.

Granger Book Co. has no affiliation
with Columbia University Press or its
publication "Granger's Index to Poetry."

TABLE OF CONTENTS.

Preface

The publications of **Poetry Anthology Press** constitute a comprehensive conspectus of international verse in English designed to form the core of a library's poetry collection. Covering the entire range of poetic literature, these anthologies encompass all topics and national literatures.

Each collection, published in a multivolume continuing series format, is devoted to a major area of the whole undertaking and contains complete author, title, and first line indexes. Biographical data is also provided.

The World's Best Poetry, with coverage through the 19th century, is topically classified and arranged by subject matter. Supplements keep the 10 volume foundation collection current and complete.

Survey of American Poetry is an anthology of American verse arranged chronologically in 10 volumes. Each volume presents a significant period of American poetic history, from 1607 to date.

POEMS OF NATIONAL SPIRIT.

I.

PATRIOTISM.

WHAT CONSTITUTES A STATE?

WHAT constitutes a state?
Not high-raised battlement or labored mound,
  Thick wall or moated gate;
Not cities proud with spires and turrets crowned;
  Not bays and broad-armed ports,
Where, laughing at the storm, rich navies ride;
  Not starred and spangled courts,
Where low-browed baseness wafts perfume to
    pride.
  No:—men, high-minded men,
With powers as far above dull brutes endued
  In forest, brake, or den,
As beasts excel cold rocks and brambles rude,—
  Men who their duties know,
But know their rights, and, knowing, dare main-
    tain,
  Prevent the long-aimed blow,
And crush the tyrant while they rend the chain;
  These constitute a State;

And sovereign law, that State's collected will,
  O'er thrones and globes elate
Sits empress, crowning good, repressing ill.
  Smit by her sacred frown,
The fiend, Dissension, like a vapor sinks;
  And e'en the all-dazzling crown
Hides his faint rays, and at her bidding shrinks.
  Such was this heaven-loved isle,
Than Lesbos fairer and the Cretan shore!
  No more shall freedom smile?
Shall Britons languish, and be men no more?
  Since all must life resign,
Those sweet rewards which decorate the brave
  'T is folly to decline,
And steal inglorious to the silent grave.

SIR WILLIAM JONES.

BREATHES THERE THE MAN?

FROM "THE LAY OF THE LAST MINSTREL," CANTO VI.

BREATHES there the man with soul so dead
Who never to himself hath said,
  This is my own, my native land!
Whose heart has ne'er within him burned,
As home his footsteps he hath turned
  From wandering on a foreign strand?
If such there breathe, go, mark him well;
For him no minstrel raptures swell;
High though his titles, proud his name,
Boundless his wealth as wish can claim,
Despite those titles, power, and pelf,

The wretch, concentred all in self,
Living, shall forfeit fair renown,
And, doubly dying, shall go down
To the vile dust from whence he sprung,
Unwept, unhonored, and unsung.

SIR WALTER SCOTT.

MY COUNTRY.

THERE is a land, of every land the pride,
Beloved by Heaven o'er all the world beside,
Where brighter suns dispense serener light,
And milder moons imparadise the night;
A land of beauty, virtue, valor, truth,
Time-tutored age, and love-exalted youth:
The wandering mariner, whose eye explores
The wealthiest isles, the most enchanting shores,
Views not a realm so bountiful and fair,
Nor breathes the spirit of a purer air.
In every clime, the magnet of his soul,
Touched by remembrance, trembles to that pole;
For in this land of Heaven's peculiar race,
The heritage of nature's noblest grace,
There is a spot of earth supremely blest,
A dearer, sweeter spot than all the rest,
Where man, creation's tyrant, casts aside
His sword and sceptre, pageantry and pride,
While in his softened looks benignly blend
The sire, the son, the husband, brother, friend.
Here woman reigns; the mother, daughter, wife,
Strew with fresh flowers the narrow way of life:
In the clear heaven of her delightful eye

An angel-guard of love and graces lie;
Around her knees domestic duties meet,
And fireside pleasures gambol at her feet.
"Where shall that land, that spot of earth be
    found?"
Art thou a man?—a patriot?—look around;
O, thou shalt find, howe'er thy footsteps roam,
That land *thy* country, and that spot *thy* home!

Man, through all ages of revolving time,
Unchanging man, in every varying clime,
Deems his own land of every land the pride,
Beloved by Heaven o'er the world beside;
His home the spot of earth supremely blest,
A dearer, sweeter spot than all the rest.

JAMES MONTGOMERY.

FATHER AND MOTHER TONGUE.

Our Father Land! and wouldst thou know
    Why we should call it Father Land?
It is that Adam here below
    Was made of earth by Nature's hand;
And he our father, made of earth,
    Hath peopled earth on every hand;
And we, in memory of his birth,
    Do call our country Father Land.

At first, in Eden's bowers, they say,
    No sound of speech had Adam caught,
But whistled like a bird all day,—
    And maybe 't was for want of thought:
But Nature, with resistless laws,
    Made Adam soon surpass the birds;

She gave him lovely Eve because
If he 'd a wife they must *have words.*

And so the native land, I hold,
  By male descent is proudly mine;
The language, as the tale hath told,
  Was given in the female line.
And thus we see on either hand
  We name our blessings whence they 've
    sprung;
We call our country Father Land,
  We call our language Mother Tongue.

SAMUEL LOVER.

EAST, WEST, HOME 'S BEST.

FROM "THE TRAVELLER."

As some lone miser visiting his store,
Bends at his treasure, counts, recounts it o'er;
Hoards after hoards his rising raptures fill,
Yet still he sighs, for hoards are wanting still:
Thus to my breast alternate passions rise,
Pleased with each good that heaven to man sup-
    plies:
Yet oft a sigh prevails, and sorrows fall,
To see the sum of human bliss so small;
And oft I wish, amidst the scene to find
Some spot to real happiness consigned,
Where my worn soul, each wandering hope at
    rest,
May gather bliss to see my fellows blest.
But where to find that happiest spot below,

Who can direct, when all pretend to know?
The shuddering tenant of the frigid zone
Boldly proclaims that happiest spot his own,
Extols the treasures of his stormy seas,
And his long nights of revelry and ease;
The naked negro, planting at the line,
Boasts of his golden sands and palmy wine,
Basks in the glare, or stems the tepid wave,
And thanks his gods for all the good they gave.
Such is the patriot's boast where'er we roam,
His first, best country, ever is at home.
And yet, perhaps, if countries we compare,
And estimate the blessings which they share,
Though patriots flatter, still shall wisdom find
An equal portion dealt to all mankind,
As different good, by art or nature given,
To different nations, makes their blessings even.

OLIVER GOLDSMITH.

GIFTS.

"O World-God, give me Wealth!" the Egyptian
    cried.
His prayer was granted. High as heaven behold
Palace and Pyramid; the brimming tide
Of lavish Nile washed all his land with gold.
Armies of slaves toiled ant-wise at his feet,
World-circling traffic roared through mart and
    street,
His priests were gods, his spice-balmed kings en-
    shrined
Set death at naught in rock-ribbed charnels deep.

Seek Pharaoh's race to-day, and ye shall find
Rust and the moth, silence and dusty sleep.

" O World-God, give me Beauty!" cried the Greek.
His prayer was granted. All the earth became
Plastic and vocal to his sense; each peak,
Each grove, each stream, quick with Promethean
    flame,
Peopled the world with imaged grace and light.
The lyre was his, and his the breathing might
Of the immortal marble, his the play
Of diamond-pointed thought and golden tongue.
Go seek the sunshine race. Ye find to-day
A broken column and a lute unstrung.

" O World-God, give me Power!" the Roman
    cried.
His prayer was granted. The vast world was
    chained
A captive to the chariot of his pride,
The blood of myriad provinces was drained
To feed that fierce, insatiable red heart—
Invulnerably bulwarked every part
With serried legions and with close-meshed Code.
Within, the burrowing worm had gnawed its
    home:
A roofless ruin stands where once abode
The imperial race of everlasting Rome.

" O God-head, give me Truth!" the Hebrew cried.
His prayer was granted. He became the slave
Of the Idea, a pilgrim far and wide,
Cursed, hated, spurned, and scourged with none
    to save.

The Pharaohs knew him, and when Greece beheld,
His wisdom wore the hoary crown of Eld.
Beauty he hath forsworn, and wealth and power.
Seek him to-day, and find in every land.
No fire consumes him, neither floods devour;
Immortal through the lamp within his hand.

EMMA LAZARUS.

ENGLAND.

FROM " THE TIMEPIECE ": " THE TASK," BK. II.

ENGLAND, with all thy faults, I love thee still,—
My country! and, while yet a nook is left
Where English minds and manners may be found,
Shall be constrained to love thee.   Though thy
    clime
Be fickle, and thy year most part deformed
With dripping rains, or withered by a frost,
I would not yet exchange thy sullen skies,
And fields without a flower, for warmer France
With all her vines; nor for Ausonia's groves
Of golden fruitage and her myrtle bowers.
To shake thy senate, and from height sublime
Of patriot eloquence to flash down fire
Upon thy foes, was never meant my task:
But I can feel thy fortunes, and partake
Thy joys and sorrows with as true a heart
As any thunderer there.   And I can feel
Thy follies too; and with a just disdain
Frown at effeminates whose very looks
Reflect dishonor on the land I love.
How, in the name of soldiership and sense,

Should England prosper, when such things, as
    smooth
And tender as a girl, all essenced o'er
With odors, and as profligate as sweet,
Who sell their laurel for a myrtle wreath,
And love when they should fight,—when such as
    these
Presume to lay their hand upon the ark
Of her magnificent and awful cause?
Time was when it was praise and boast enough
In every clime, and travel where we might,
That we were born her children. Praise enough
To fill the ambition of a private man,
That Chatham's language was his mother tongue,
And Wolfe's great name compatriot with his own.

WILLIAM COWPER.

RULE, BRITANNIA.

FROM "ALFRED," ACT II. SC. 5.

WHEN Britain first, at Heaven's command,
    Arose from out the azure main,
This was the charter of the land,
    And guardian angels sung the strain:
      Rule, Britannia, rule the waves!
      For Britons never will be slaves.

The nations not so blest as thee
    Must in their turns to tyrants fall;
Whilst thou shalt flourish, great and free,
    The dread and envy of them all.
      Rule, Britannia! etc.

Still more majestic shalt thou rise,
  More dreadful from each foreign stroke;
As the loud blasts that tear the skies
  Serve but to root thy native oak.
    Rule, Britannia! etc.

Thee haughty tyrants ne'er shall tame;
  All their attempts to bend thee down
Will but arouse thy generous flame,
  And work their woe—but thy renown.
    Rule, Britannia! etc.

To thee belongs the rural reign;
Thy cities shall with commerce shine;
All thine shall be the subject main,
  And every shore it circles thine.
    Rule, Britannia! etc.

The Muses, still with Freedom found,
  Shall to thy happy coast repair;
Blest Isle! with matchless beauty crowned,
  And manly hearts to guard the fair.
    Rule, Britannia, rule the waves!
    For Britons never will be slaves.

                              JAMES THOMSON.

THE BOWMAN'S SONG.

FROM "THE WHITE COMPANY."

  WHAT of the bow?
The bow was made in England:
Of true wood, of yew wood,
  The wood of English bows;

So men who are free
Love the old yew-tree
And the land where the yew-tree grows.

What of the cord?
The cord was made in England:
A rough cord, a tough cord,
 A cord that bowmen love;
  So we 'll drain our jacks
  To the English flax
And the land where the hemp was wove.

What of the shaft?
The shaft was cut in England:
A long shaft, a strong shaft,
 Barbed and trim and true;
  So we 'll drink all together
  To the gray goose feather,
And the land where the gray goose flew.

What of the men?
The men were bred in England:
The bowman—the yeoman—
 The lads of dale and fell.
  Here 's to you—and to you!
  To the hearts that are true
And the land where the true hearts dwell.

SIR A. CONAN DOYLE.

THE ROAST BEEF OF OLD ENGLAND.

WHEN mighty roast beef was the Englishman's
 food,
It ennobled our hearts, and enrichèd our blood;

Our soldiers were brave, and our courtiers were
    good.
> *O, the Roast Beef of old England,*
> *And O, the old English Roast Beef!*

But since we have learned from effeminate France
To eat their ragouts, as well as to dance,
We are fed up with nothing but vain complai-
    sance.
> *O, the Roast Beef,* etc.

HENRY FIELDING.

———

Our fathers of old were robust, stout, and strong,
And kept open house with good cheer all day long,
Which made their plump tenants rejoice in this
    song.
> *O, the Roast Beef,* etc.

When good Queen Elizabeth sat on the throne,
Ere coffee and tea, and such slip-slops, were
    known,
The world was in terror, if e'en she did frown.
> *O, the Roast Beef,* etc.

In those days, if fleets did presume on the main,
They seldom or never returned back again;
As witness the vaunting Armada of Spain.
> *O, the Roast Beef,* etc.

O, then we had stomachs to eat and to fight,
And when wrongs were cooking, to set ourselves
    right;

But now we 're—hum?—I could, but—good
    night;
      O, the Roast Beef of old England,
      And O, the old English Roast Beef!

The last four stanzas added by RICHARD LOVERIDGE.

THE SNUG LITTLE ISLAND.

DADDY NEPTUNE, one day, to Freedom did say,
  If ever I lived upon dry land,
The spot I should hit on would be little Britain!
  Says Freedom, " Why, that 's my own island! "
    O, it 's a snug little island!
    A right little, tight little island!
    Search the globe round, none can be found
    So happy as this little island.

Julius Cæsar, the Roman, who yielded to no man,
  Came by water,—he couldn't come by land;
And Dane, Pict, and Saxon, their homes turned
    their backs on,
  And all for the sake of our island.
    O, what a snug little island!
    They 'd all have a touch at the island!
    Some were shot dead, some of them fled,
    And some stayed to live on the island.

Then a very great war-man, called Billy the Nor-
    man,
  Cried, " Drat it, I never liked my land.
It would be much more handy to leave this Nor-
    mandy,

And live on your beautiful island."
   Says he, " 'T is a snug little island;
   Sha'n't us go visit the island? "
Hop, skip, and jump, there he was plump,
   And he kicked up a dust in the island.

But party deceit helped the Normans to beat;
   Of traitors they managed to buy land;
By Dane, Saxon, or Pict, Britons ne'er had been
         licked,
   Had they stuck to the king of their island.
      Poor Harold, the king of our island!
      He lost both his life and his island!
      That's all very true: what more could he do?
      Like a Briton he died for his island!

The Spanish armada set out to invade—a,
   'T will sure, if they ever come nigh land.
They couldn't do less than tuck up Queen Bess,
   And take their full swing on the island.
      O the poor queen of the island!
      The Dons came to plunder the island;
      But snug in her hive the queen was alive,
      And " buzz " was the word of the island.

These proud puffed-up cakes thought to make
         ducks and drakes
   Of our wealth; but they hardly could spy land,
When our Drake had the luck to make their pride
         duck
   And stoop to the lads of the island!
      O, for the ships of the island!
      The good wooden walls of the island;

Devil or Don, let them come on;
And see how they 'd come off the island!

Since Freedom and Neptune have hitherto kept
time,
In each saying, " This shall be my land ";
Should the " Army of England," or all it could
bring, land,
We 'd show 'em some play for the island.
We 'd fight for our right to the island;
We 'd give them enough of the island;
Invaders should just—bite once at the dust,
But not a bit more of the island.

THOMAS DIBDIN.

THE JACOBITE ON TOWER HILL.

HE tripped up the steps with a bow and a smile,
Offering snuff to the chaplain the while,
A rose at his button-hole that afternoon—
'T was the tenth of the month, and the month it
was June.

Then shrugging his shoulders, he looked at the
man
With the mask and the axe, and a murmuring ran
Through the crowd, who below, were all pushing
to see
The gaoler kneel down, and receiving his fee.

He looked at the mob, as they roared, with a stare,
And took snuff again with a cynical air.
" I 'm happy to give but a moment's delight
To the flower of my country agog for a sight."
2

Then he looked at the block, and with scented
 cravat
Dusted room for his neck, gayly doffing his hat,
Kissed his hand to a lady, bent low to the crowd,
Then smiling, turned round to the headsman and
 bowed.

"God save King James!" he cried bravely and
 shrill,
And the cry reached the houses at foot of the hill,
" My friend with the axe, *à votre service,*" he said;
And ran his white thumb 'long the edge of the
 blade.

When the multitude hissed he stood firm as a rock;
Then kneeling, laid down his gay head on the
 block;
He kissed a white rose,—in a moment 't was red
With the life of the bravest of any that bled.

     GEORGE WALTER THORNBURY.

GOD SAVE THE KING.

God save our gracious king!
Long live our noble king!
 God save the king!
Send him victorious,
Happy and glorious,
Long to reign over us—
 God save the king!

O Lord our God, arise!
Scatter his enemies,
 And make them fall;

Confound their politics,
Frustrate their knavish tricks;
On him our hopes we fix,
God save us all!

Thy choicest gifts in store
On him be pleased to pour;
Long may he reign.
May he defend our laws,
And ever give us cause,
To sing with heart and voice—
God save the king!

HENRY CAREY.

VETERAN AND RECRUIT.

HE filled the crystal goblet
With golden-beaded wine:
" Come, comrades, now, I bid ye—
' To the true love of mine!'

" Her forehead 's pure and holy,
Her hair is tangled gold,
Her heart to me so tender,
To others' love is cold.

" So drain your glasses empty
And fill me another yet;
Two glasses at least for the dearest
And sweetest girl, Lisette."

Up rose a grizzled sergeant—
" My true love I give thee,
Three true loves blent in one love,
A soldier's trinity.

" Here 's to the flag we follow,
  Here 's to the land we serve,
And here 's to holy honor
  That doth the two preserve."

Then rose they up around him,
  And raised their eyes above,
And drank in solemn silence
  Unto the sergeant's love.

EDWARD WENTWORTH HAZEWELL.

THE PRIVATE OF THE BUFFS; * OR,
THE BRITISH SOLDIER IN CHINA.

["Some Seiks, and a private of the Buffs, having re-
mained behind with the grog-carts, fell into the hands of
the Chinese. On the next day they were brought before
the authorities and ordered to perform *Kotou.* The Seiks
obeyed, but Moyse, the English soldier, declared he would
not prostrate himself before any Chinaman alive, and was
immediately knocked upon the head, and his body thrown
upon a dunghill."—*China Correspondent of the London
Times.*]

LAST night, among his fellow roughs,
  He jested, quaffed, and swore;
A drunken private of the Buffs,
  Who never looked before.
To-day, beneath the foeman's frown,
  He stands in Elgin's place,
Ambassador from Britain's crown,
  And type of all her race.

Poor, reckless, rude, low-born, untaught,
  Bewildered, and alone,

* The "Buffs" are the East Kent Regiment.

A heart, with English instinct fraught,
  He yet can call his own.
Ay, tear his body limb from limb,
  Bring cord or axe or flame,
He only knows that not through him
  Shall England come to shame.

Far Kentish hop-fields round him seemed,
  Like dreams, to come and go;
Bright leagues of cherry-blossom gleamed,
  One sheet of living snow;
The smoke above his father's door
  In gray soft eddyings hung;
Must he then watch it rise no more,
  Doomed by himself so young?

Yes, honor calls!—with strength like steel
  He put the vision by;
Let dusky Indians whine and kneel,
  An English lad must die.
And thus, with eyes that would not shrink,
  With knee to man unbent,
Unfaltering on its dreadful brink,
  To his red grave he went.

Vain mightiest fleets of iron framed,
  Vain those all-shattering guns,
Unless proud England keep untamed
  The strong heart of her sons;
So let his name through Europe ring,—
  A man of mean estate,
Who died, as firm as Sparta's king,
  Because his soul was great.

SIR FRANCIS HASTINGS DOYLE.

THE TURK IN ARMENIA.

FROM "THE PURPLE EAST."

WHAT profits it, O England, to prevail
  In camp and mart and council, and bestrew.
With argosies thy oceans, and renew
With tribute levied on each golden gale
Thy treasuries, if thou canst hear the wail
  Of women martyred by the turbaned crew,
  Whose tenderest mercy was the sword that slew,
And lift no hand to wield the purging flail?
  We deemed of old thou held'st a charge from
    Him
Who watches girdled by his seraphim,
To smite the wronger with thy destined rod.
  Wait'st thou his sign? Enough, the unanswered
    cry
Of virgin souls for vengeance, and on high
The gathering blackness of the frown of God!

WILLIAM WATSON.

AVE IMPERATRIX.

SET in this stormy Northern sea,
  Queen of these restless fields of tide,
England! what shall men say of thee,
  Before whose feet the worlds divide?

The earth, a brittle globe of glass,
  Lies in the hollow of thy hand,
And through its heart of crystal pass,
  Like shadows through a twilight land,

The spears of crimson-suited war,
  The long white-crested waves of fight,
And all the deadly fires which are
  The torches of the lords of Night.

The yellow leopards, strained and lean,
  The treacherous Russian knows so well,
With gaping blackened jaws are seen
  To leap through hail of screaming shell.

The strong sea-lion of England's wars
  Hath left his sapphire cave of sea,
To battle with the storm that mars
  The star of England's chivalry.

The brazen-throated clarion blows
  Across the Pathan's reedy fen,
And the high steeps of Indian snows
  Shake to the tread of armèd men.

And many an Afghan chief, who lies
  Beneath his cool pomegranate-trees,
Clutches his sword in fierce surmise
  When on the mountain-side he sees

The fleet-foot Marri scout, who comes
  To tell how he hath heard afar
The measured roll of English drums
  Beat at the gates of Kandahar.

For southern wind and east wind meet
  Where, girt and crowned by sword and fire,

England with bare and bloody feet
  Climbs the steep road of wide empire.

O lonely Himalayan height,
  Gray pillar of the Indian sky,
Where saw'st thou last in clanging fight
  Our wingèd dogs of Victory?

The almond groves of Samarcand,
  Bokhara, where red lilies blow,
And Oxus, by whose yellow sand
  The grave white-turbaned merchants go;

And on from thence to Ispahan,
  The gilded garden of the sun,
Whence the long dusty caravan
  Brings cedar and vermilion;

And that dread city of Cabool
  Set at the mountain's scarpèd feet,
Whose marble tanks are ever full
  With water for the noonday heat,

Where through the narrow straight Bazaar
  A little maid Circasian
Is led, a present from the Czar
  Unto some old and bearded khan,—

Here have our wild war-eagles flown,
  And flapped wide wings in fiery fight;
But the sad dove, that sits alone
  In England—she hath no delight.

In vain the laughing girl will lean
  To greet her love with love-lit eyes:
Down in some treacherous black ravine,
  Clutching his flag, the dead boy lies.

And many a moon and sun will see
  The lingering wistful children wait
To climb upon their father's knee;
  And in each house made desolate

Pale women who have lost their lord
  Will kiss the relics of the slain—
Some tarnished epaulette—some sword—
  Poor toys to soothe such anguished pain.

For not in quiet English fields
  Are these, our brothers, lain to rest,
Where we might deck their broken shields
  With all the flowers the dead love best.

For some are by the Delhi walls,
  And many in the Afghan land,
And many where the Ganges falls
  Through seven mouths of shifting sand.

And some in Russian waters lie,
  And others in the seas which are
The portals to the East, or by
  The wind-swept heights of Trafalgar.

O wandering graves! O restless sleep!
  O silence of the sunless day!

O still ravine! O stormy deep!
  Give up your prey! Give up your prey!

And those whose wounds are never healed,
  Whose weary race is never won,
O Cromwell's England! must thou yield
  For every inch of ground a son?

Go! crown with thorns thy gold-crowned head,
  Change thy glad song to song of pain;
Wind and wild wave have got thy dead,
  And will not yield them back again.

Wave and wild wind and foreign shore
  Possess the flower of English land—
Lips that thy lips shall kiss no more,
  Hands that shall never clasp thy hand.

What profit now that we have bound
  The whole round world with nets of gold,
If hidden in our heart is found
  The care that groweth never old?

What profit that our galleys ride,
  Pine-forest like, on every main?
Ruin and wreck are at our side,
  Grim warders of the House of pain.

Where are the brave, the strong, the fleet?
  Where is our English chivalry?
Wild grasses are their burial-sheet,
  And sobbing waves their threnody.

O loved ones lying far away,
  What word of love can dead lips send?
O wasted dust! O senseless clay!
  Is this the end? is this the end?

Peace, peace! we wrong the noble dead
  To vex their solemn slumber so;
Though childless, and with thorn-crowned head,
  Up the steep road must England go,

Yet when this fiery web is spun,
  Her watchmen shall descry from far
The young Republic like a sun
  Rise from these crimson seas of war.

OSCAR WILDE.

AMERICA TO GREAT BRITAIN.

ALL hail; thou noble land,
  Our Fathers' native soil!
O, stretch thy mighty hand,
  Gigantic grown by toil,
O'er the vast Atlantic wave to our shore!
  For thou with magic might
  Canst reach to where the light
  Of Phœbus travels bright
    The world o'er!

The genius of our clime
  From his pine-embattled steep
Shall hail the guest sublime;
  While the Tritons of the deep

With their conchs the kindred league shall pro-
    claim.
        Then let the world combine,—
        O'er the main our naval line
        Like the Milky Way shall shine
            Bright in flame!

        Though ages long have passed
            Since our Fathers left their home,
        Their pilot in the blast,
            O'er untravelled seas to roam,
Yet lives the blood of England in our veins!
        And shall we not proclaim
        That blood of honest fame
        Which no tyranny can tame
            By its chains?

        While the language free and bold
            Which the Bard of Avon sung,
        In which our Milton told
            How the vault of heaven rung
When Satan, blasted, fell with his host;
        While this, with reverence meet,
        Ten thousand echoes greet,
        From rock to rock repeat
            Round our coast;

        While the manners, while the arts,
            That mould a nation's soul,
        Still cling around our hearts,—
            Between let Ocean roll,
Our joint communion breaking with the sun:
        Yet still from either beach

The voice of blood shall reach,
More audible than speech,
" We are One."

WASHINGTON ALLSTON.

HANDS ALL ROUND.

FIRST drink a health, this solemn night,
    A health to England, every guest:
That man 's the best cosmopolite
    Who loves his native country best.
May Freedom's oak for ever live
    With stronger life from day to day:
That man 's the best Conservative
    Who lops the moulded branch away.
        Hands all round!
    God the tyrant's hope confound!
To this great cause of Freedom drink, my friends,
And the great name of England, round and round.

A health to Europe's honest men!
    Heaven guard them from her tyrants' jails!
From wronged Poerio's noisome den,
    From iron limbs and tortured nails!
We curse the crimes of southern kings,
    The Russian whips and Austrian rods:
We likewise have our evil things,—
    Too much we make our ledgers, gods.
        Yet hands all round!
    God the tyrant's cause confound!
To Europe's better health we drink, my friends,
And the great name of England, round and round!

What health to France, if France be she,
  Whom martial progress only charms?
Yet tell her—better to be free
  Than vanquish all the world in arms.
Her frantic city's flashing heats
  But fire, to blast the hopes of men.
Why change the titles of your streets?
  You fools, you 'll want them all again.
      Hands all round!
  God the tyrant's cause confound!
To France, the wiser France, we drink, my friends,
And the great name of England, round and round.

Gigantic daughter of the West,
  We drink to thee across the flood!
We know thee and we love thee best;
  For art thou not of British blood?
Should war's mad blast again be blown,
  Permit not thou the tyrant powers
To fight thy mother here alone,
  But let thy broadsides roar with ours.
      Hands all round!
  God the tyrant's cause confound!
To our great kinsman of the West, my friends,
And the great name of England, round and round.

Oh rise, our strong Atlantic sons,
  When war against our freedom springs!
Oh, speak to Europe through your guns!
  They *can* be understood by kings.
You must not mix our Queen with those
  That wish to keep their people fools:

Our freedom's foemen are her foes;
  She comprehends the race she rules.
    Hands all round!
  God the tyrant's cause confound!
To our great kinsman in the West, my friends,
And the great cause of Freedom, round and round.

ALFRED, LORD TENNYSON.

RECESSIONAL.

GOD of our fathers, known of old,—
  Lord of our far-flung battle line,—
Beneath whose awful hand we hold
  Dominion over palm and pine,—
Lord God of Hosts, be with us yet,
Lest we forget,—lest we forget!

The tumult and the shouting dies,
  The captains and the kings depart:
Still stands thine ancient sacrifice,—
  An humble and a contrite heart.
Lord God of Hosts, be with us yet,
Lest we forget,—lest we forget!

Far-called, our navies melt away;
  On dune and headland sinks the fire.
Lo! all our pomp of yesterday
  Is one with Nineveh and Tyre!
Judge of the nations, spare us yet,
Lest we forget,—lest we forget!

If, drunk with sight of power, we loose
  Wild tongues that have not thee in awe,

Such boasting as the Gentiles use
  Or lesser breeds without the law,—
Lord God of Hosts, be with us yet,
Lest we forget,—lest we forget!

For heathen heart that puts her trust
  In reeking tube and iron shard,
All valiant dust that builds on dust,
  And guarding calls not thee to guard,
For frantic boasts and foolish word,
Thy mercy on thy people, Lord!
                  Amen.

RUDYARD KIPLING.

ENGLAND AND HER COLONIES.

SHE stands, a thousand-wintered tree,
  By countless morns impearled;
Her broad roots coil beneath the sea,
  Her branches sweep the world;
Her seeds, by careless winds conveyed,
  Clothe the remotest strand
With forests from her scatterings made,
New nations fostered in her shade,
  And linking land with land.

O ye by wandering tempest sown
  'Neath every alien star,
Forget not whence the breath was blown
  That wafted you afar!
For ye are still her ancient seed
  On younger soil let fall—

Children of Britain's island-breed,
To whom the Mother in her need
Perchance may one day call.

WILLIAM WATSON.

SCOTLAND.

FROM " THE LAY OF THE LAST MINSTREL," CANTO VI.

O CALEDONIA! stern and wild,
Meet nurse for a poetic child!
Land of brown heath and shaggy wood,
Land of the mountain and the flood,
Land of my sires! what mortal hand
Can e'er untie the filial band
That knits me to thy rugged strand?
Still, as I view each well-known scene,
Think what is now, and what hath been,
Seems, as to me, of all bereft,
Sole friends thy woods and streams were left;
And thus I love them better still,
Even in extremity of ill.
By Yarrow's stream still let me stray,
Though none should guide my feeble way;
Still feel the breeze down Ettrick break,
Although it chilled my withered cheek;
Still lay my head by Teviot stone,
Though there, forgotten and alone,
The bard may draw his parting groan.

SIR WALTER SCOTT.

3

THE BARD.

A PINDARIC ODE.

I

" RUIN seize thee, ruthless King!
   Confusion on thy banners wait;
Tho' fanned by Conquest's crimson wing,
   They mock the air with idle state,
Helm, nor hauberk's twisted mail,
Nor e'en thy virtues, Tyrant, shall avail
   To save thy secret soul from nightly fears,
   From Cambria's curse, from Cambria's tears!"
Such were the sounds that o'er the crested pride
   Of the first Edward scattered wild dismay,
As down the steep of Snowdon's shaggy side
   He wound with toilsome march his long array.
Stout Glo'ster stood aghast in speechless trance:
" To arms!" cried Mortimer, and couched his
      quiv'ring lance.

   On a rock, whose haughty brow
Frowns o'er cold Conway's foaming flood,
   Robed in the sable garb of woe,
With haggard eyes the poet stood:
(Loose his beard, and hoary hair
Streamed, like a meteor, to the troubled air)
And with a master's hand, and prophet's fire,
Struck the deep sorrows of his lyre.
" Hark how each giant oak, and desert cave,
   Sighs to the torrent's awful voice beneath!

O'er thee, O King! their hundred arms they wave,
  Revenge on thee in hoarser murmurs breathe;
Vocal no more, since Cambria's fatal day,
To high-born Hoel's harp, or soft Llewellyn's lay.

  " Cold is Cadwallo's tongue,
  That hushed the stormy main:
Brave Urien sleeps upon his craggy bed:
  Mountains, ye mourn in vain
  Modred, whose magic song
Made huge Plinlimmon bow his cloud-topt head.
  On dreary Arvon's shore they lie,
Smeared with gore, and ghastly pale;
Far, far aloof th' affrighted ravens sail;
  The famished eagle screams, and passes by.
Dear lost companions of my tuneful art,
  Dear as the light that visits these sad eyes,
Dear as the ruddy drops that warm my heart,
  Ye died amidst your dying country's cries—
No more I weep. They do not sleep.
  On yonder cliffs, a grisly band,
I see them sit, they linger yet,
  Avengers of their native land:
With me in dreadful harmony they join,
And weave with bloody hands the tissues of thy
    line.

II.

  " Weave the warp, and weave the woof,
The winding sheet of Edward's race.
  Give ample room, and verge enough
The characters of hell to trace.
Mark the year, and mark the night,

When Severn shall re-echo with affright
The shrieks of death, thro' Berkeley's roof that
    ring,
Shrieks of an agonizing king!
    She-wolf of France, with unrelenting fangs,
That tear'st the bowels of thy mangled mate,
    From thee be born, who o'er thy country hangs
The scourge of Heaven. What Terrors round him
    wait!
Amazement in his van, with Flight combined,
And Sorrow's faded form, and solitude behind.

    " Mighty victor, mighty lord!
Low on his funeral couch he lies!
    No pitying heart, no eye, afford
A tear to grace his obsequies.
Is the sable warrior fled?
Thy son is gone. He rests among the dead.
The swarm, that in thy noon-tide beam were born,
Gone to salute the rising morn.
Fair laughs the morn, and soft the zephyr blows.
    While proudly riding o'er the azure realm
In gallant trim the gilded vessel goes;
    Youth on the prow, and Pleasure at the helm;
Regardless of the sweeping whirlwind's sway,
That, hushed in grim repose, expects his evening
    prey.

    " Fill high the sparkling bowl,
The rich repast prepare,
    Reft of a crown, he yet may share the feast;
Close by the regal chair

Fell Thirst and Famine scowl
A baleful smile upon their baffled guest.
Heard ye the din of battle bray,
　Lance to lance, and horse to horse?
Long years of havoc, urged their destined
　　course,
And through the kindred squadrons mow their
　　way.
Ye towers of Julius, London's lasting shame,
With many a foul and midnight murder fed,
　Revere his consort's faith, his father's fame,
And spare the meek usurper's holy head.
Above, below, the rose of snow,
　Twined with her blushing foe, we spread:
The bristled Boar in infant-gore
　Wallows beneath the thorny shade.
Now, brothers, bending o'er the accursèd loom,
Stamp we our vengeance deep, and ratify his
　　doom.

III.

"Edward, lo! to sudden fate
(Weave we the woof. The thread is spun.)
　Half of thy heart we consecrate.
(The web is wove. The work is done.)
Stay, oh stay! nor thus forlorn
Leave me unblessed, unpitied, here to mourn:
In yon bright track, that fires the western skies,
They melt, they vanish from my eyes.
But oh! what solemn scenes on Snowdon's height
　Descending slow their glittering skirts unroll?
Visions of glory, spare my aching sight!
　Ye unborn ages, crowd not on my soul!

No more our long-lost Arthur we bewail.
All hail, ye genuine kings, Britannia's issue, hail!

" Girt with many a baron bold
Sublime their starry fronts they rear;
  And gorgeous dames, and statesmen old
In bearded majesty, appear.
In the midst a form divine!
Her eye proclaims her of the Briton line:
Her lion-port, her awe-commanding face,
Attempered sweet to virgin-grace.
What strings symphonious tremble in the air,
  What strains of vocal transport round her play!
Hear from the grave, great Taliessin, hear;
  They breathe a soul to animate thy clay.
Bright Rapture calls, and soaring as she sings,
Waves in the eye of heaven her many-colored
        wings.

" The verse adorn again,
  Fierce War, and faithful Love,
And Truth severe by fairy fiction drest.
  In buskined measure move
Pale Grief and pleasing Pain,
With Horror, tyrant of the throbbing breast.
  A voice, as of the cherub-choir,
Gales from blooming Eden bear;
And distant warblings lessen on my ear,
  That lost in long futurity expire.
Fond impious man, think'st thou yon sanguine
        cloud,
  Raised by thy breath, has quenched the orb of
        day?

To-morrow he repairs the golden flood,
And warms the nations with redoubled ray.
Enough for me; with joy I see
The different doom our fates assign.
Be thine Despair, and sceptred Care,
To triumph, and to die, are mine."
He spoke and headlong from the mountain's
height
Deep in the roaring tide he plunged to endless
night.

THOMAS GRAY.

MY HEART'S IN THE HIGHLANDS.

My heart's in the Highlands, my heart is not here;
My heart's in the Highlands a-chasing the deer;
Chasing the wild deer, and following the roe.
My heart's in the Highlands, wherever I go.
Farewell to the Highlands, farewell to the North,
The birthplace of valor, the country of worth;
Wherever I wander, wherever I rove,
The hills of the Highlands forever I love.

Farewell to the mountains high covered with
snow;
Farewell to the straths and green valleys below;
Farewell to the forests and wild-hanging woods;
Farewell to the torrents and loud-pouring floods.
My heart's in the Highlands, my heart is not here;
My heart's in the Highlands a-chasing the deer;
Chasing the wild deer, and following the roe.
My heart's in the Highlands wherever I go.

ROBERT BURNS.

HEATHER ALE: A GALLOWAY LEGEND.

From the bonny bells of heather
  They brewed a drink long-syne,
Was sweeter far than honey,
  Was stronger far than wine.
They brewed it and they drank it,
  And lay in a blessèd swound
For days and days together
  In the dwellings underground.

There rose a king in Scotland,
  A fell man to his foes,
He smote the Picts in battle,
  He hunted them like roes.
Over miles of the red mountain
  He hunted as they fled,
And strewed the dwarfish bodies
  Of the dying and the dead.

Summer came in the country,
  Red was the heather bell;
But the manner of the brewing
  Was none alive to tell.
In graves that were like children's
  On many a mountain head,
The Brewsters of the Heather
  Lay numbered with the dead.

The king in the red moorland
  Rode on a summer's day;

And the bees hummed, and the curlews
  Cried beside the way.
The king rode, and was angry;
  Black was his brow and pale,
To rule in a land of heather
  And lack the Heather Ale.

It fortuned that his vassals,
  Riding free on the heath,
Came on a stone that was fallen
  And vermin hid beneath.
Rudely plucked from their hiding,
  Never a word they spoke:
A son and his agèd father—
  Last of the dwarfish folk.

The king sat high on his charger,
  He looked on the little men;
And the dwarfish and swarthy couple
  Looked at the king again.
Down by the shore he had them;
  And there on the giddy brink—
" I will give you life, ye vermin,
  For the secret of the drink."

There stood the son and father
  And they looked high and low;
The heather was red around them,
  The sea rumbled below.
And up and spoke the father,
  Shrill was his voice to hear;
" I have a word in private,
  A word for the royal ear.

" Life is dear to the agèd,
  And honor a little thing;
I would gladly sell the secret,"
  Quoth the Pict to the King.
His voice was small as a sparrow's,
  And shrill and wonderful clear:
" I would gladly sell my secret,
  Only my son I fear.

" For life is a little matter,
  And death is nought to the young;
And I dare not sell my honor
  Under the eye of my son.
Take *him,* O king, and bind him,
  And cast him far in the deep;
And it 's I will tell the secret
  That I have sworn to keep."

They took the son and bound him,
  Neck and heels in a thong,
And a lad took him and swung him,
  And flung him far and strong,
And the sea swallowed his body,
  Like that of a child of ten;—
And there on the cliff stood the father,
  Last of the dwarfish men.

" True as the word I told you:
  Only my son I feared;
For I doubt the sapling courage
  That goes without the beard.
But now in vain is the torture,
  Fire shall never avail:

Here dies in my bosom
The secret of Heather Ale."

ROBERT LOUIS STEVENSON.

THE EXECUTION OF MONTROSE.

[James Graham, Marquis of Montrose, was executed in
Edinburgh, May 21, 1650. for an attempt to overthrow the
Commonwealth and restore Charles II.]

COME hither, Evan Cameron!
Come, stand behind my knee—
I hear the river roaring down
Toward the wintry sea.
There 's shouting on the mountain-side,
There 's war within the blast—
Old faces look upon me,
Old forms go trooping past.
I hear the pibroch wailing
Amidst the din of fight,
And my dim spirit wakes again
Upon the verge of night.

'T was I that led the Highland host
Through wild Lochaber's snows,
What time the plaided clans came down
To battle with Montrose.
I 've told thee how the Southrons fell
Beneath the broad claymore,
And how we smote the Campbell clan
By Inverlochy's shore.
I 've told thee how we swept Dundee,
And tamed the Lindsays' pride;

But never have I told thee yet
    How the great Marquis died.

A traitor sold him to his foes;—
    O deed of deathless shame!
I charge thee, boy, if e'er thou meet
    With one of Assynt's name—
Be it upon the mountain's side,
    Or yet within the glen,
Stand he in martial gear alone,
    Or backed by armèd men—
Face him as thou wouldst face the man
    Who wronged thy sire's renown;
Remember of what blood thou art,
    And strike the caitiff down!

They brought him to the Watergate,
    Hard bound with hempen span,
As though they held a lion there,
    And not a 'fenceless man.
They set him high upon a cart—
    The hangman rode below—
They drew his hands behind his back,
    And bared his noble brow.
Then, as a hound is slipped from leash,
    They cheered the common throng,
And blew the note with yell and shout,
    And bade him pass along.

It would have made a brave man's heart
    Grow sad and sick that day,
To watch the keen, malignant eyes
    Bent down on that array.

There stood the Whig west-country lords
  In balcony and bow;
There sat their gaunt and withered dames,
  And their daughters all a-row.
And every open window
  Was full as full might be
With black-robed Covenanting carles,
  That goodly sport to see!

But when he came, though pale and wan,
  He looked so great and high,
So noble was his manly front,
  So calm his steadfast eye;—
The rabble rout forbore to shout,
  And each man held his breath,
For well they knew the hero's soul
  Was face to face with death.
And then a mournful shudder
  Through all the people crept,
And some that came to scoff at him
  Now turned aside and wept.

But onward—always onward,
  In silence and in gloom,
The dreary pageant labored,
  Till it reached the house of doom.
Then first a woman's voice was heard
  In jeer and laughter loud,
And an angry cry and a hiss arose
  From the heart of the tossing crowd:
Then, as the Græme looked upward,
  He saw the ugly smile
Of him who sold his king for gold—
  The master-fiend Argyle!

The Marquis gazed a moment,
  And nothing did he say,
But the cheek of Argyle grew ghastly pale,
  And he turned his eyes away.
The painted harlot by his side,
  She shook through every limb,
For a roar like thunder swept the street,
  And hands were clenched at him;
And a Saxon soldier cried aloud,
  " Back, coward, from thy place!
For seven long years thou hast not dared
  To look him in the face."

Had I been there with sword in hand,
  And fifty Camerons by,
That day through high Dunedin's streets
  Had pealed the slogan-cry.
Not all their troops of trampling horse,
  Nor might of mailèd men—
Not all the rebels in the south
  Had borne us backward then!
Once more his foot on Highland heath
  Had trod as free as air,
Or I, and all who bore my name,
  Been laid around him there!

It might not be.   They placed him next
  Within the solemn hall,
Where once the Scottish kings were throned
  Amidst their nobles all.
But there was dust of vulgar feet
  On that polluted floor,
And perjured traitors filled the place
  Where good men sate before.

With savage glee came Warriston
  To read the murderous doom;
And then uprose the great Montrose
  In the middle of the room:

" Now, by my faith as belted knight
  And by the name I bear,
And by the bright St. Andrew's cross
  That waves above us there—
Yea, by a greater, mightier oath—
  And O that such should be!—
By that dark stream of royal blood
  That lies 'twixt you and me—
I have not sought in battle-field
  A wreath of such renown,
Nor dared I hope on my dying day
  To win the martyr's crown!

" There is a chamber far away
  Where sleep the good and brave,
But a better place ye have named for me
  Than by my father's grave.
For truth and right, 'gainst treason's might,
  This hand has always striven,
And ye raise it up for a witness still
  In the eye of earth and heaven.
Then nail my head on yonder tower—
  Give every town a limb—
And God who made shall gather them:
  I go from you to Him!"

The morning dawned full darkly,
  The rain came flashing down,

And the jagged streak of the levin bolt
   Lit up the gloomy town.
The thunder crashed across the heaven,
   The fatal hour was come;
Yet aye broke in, with muffled beat,
   The 'larum of the drum.
There was madness on the earth below
   And anger in the sky,
And young and old, and rich and poor,
   Came forth to see him die.

Ah God! that ghastly gibbet!
   How dismal 't is to see
The great tall spectral skeleton,
   The ladder and the tree!
Hark! hark! it is the clash of arms,—
   The bells begin to toll,—
" He is coming! he is coming!
   God's mercy on his soul! "
One last long peal of thunder,—
   The clouds are cleared away,
And the glorious sun once more looks down
   Amidst the dazzling day.

" He is coming! he is coming! "
   Like a bridegroom from his room
Came the hero from his prison
   To the scaffold and the doom.
There was glory on his forehead,
   There was lustre in his eye,
And he never walked to battle
   More proudly than to die.
There was color in his visage,
   Though the cheeks of all were wan;

And they marvelled as they saw him pass,
That great and goodly man!

He mounted up the scaffold,
And he turned him to the crowd;
But they dared not trust the people,
So he might not speak aloud.
But he looked upon the heavens,
And they were clear and blue,
And in the liquid ether
The eye of God shone through:
Yet a black and murky battlement
Lay resting on the hill,
As though the thunder slept within,—
All else was calm and still.

The grim Geneva ministers
With anxious scowl drew near,
As you have seen the ravens flock
Around the dying deer.
He would not deign them word nor sign,
But alone he bent the knee;
And veiled his face for Christ's dear grace
Beneath the gallows-tree.
Then, radiant and serene, he rose,
And cast his cloak away;
For he had ta'en his latest look
Of earth and sun and day.

A beam of light fell o'er him,
Like a glory round the shriven,

4

And he climbed the lofty ladder
  As it were the path to heaven.
Then came a flash from out the cloud,
  And a stunning thunder-roll;
And no man dared to look aloft,—
  Fear was on every soul.
There was another heavy sound,
  A hush, and then a groan;
And darkness swept across the sky,—
  The work of death was done!

WILLIAM EDMONDSTOUNE AYTOUN.

BORDER BALLAD.

March, march, Ettrick and Teviotdale!
  Why the de'il dinna ye march forward in order?
March, march, Eskdale and Liddesdale!
  All the Blue Bonnets are over the Border!
      Many a banner spread
      Flutters above your head,
Many a crest that is famous in story!—
      Mount and make ready, then,
      Sons of the mountain glen,
Fight for the queen and our old Scottish glory.

Come from the hills where your hirsels are graz-
    ing;
  Come from the glen of the buck and the roe;
Come to the crag where the beacon is blazing;
  Come with the buckler, the lance, and the bow.
      Trumpets are sounding;
      War-steeds are bounding;

Stand to your arms, and march in good order,
  England shall many a day
  Tell of the bloody fray,
When the Blue Bonnets came over the Border.

SIR WALTER SCOTT.

THE EXILE'S SONG.

OH! why left I my hame?
  Why did I cross the deep?
Oh! why left I the land
  Where my forefathers sleep?
I sigh for Scotia's shore,
  And I gaze across the sea,
But I canna get a blink
  O' my ain countrie.

The palm-tree waveth high,
  And fair the myrtle springs;
And, to the Indian maid,
  The bulbul sweetly sings.
But I dinna see the broom
  Wi' its tassels on the lee,
Nor hear the lintie's sang
  O' my ain countrie.

Oh! here no Sabbath bell
  Awakes the Sabbath morn,
Nor song of reapers heard
  Among the yellow corn:
For the tyrant's voice is here,
  And the wail of slaverie;

But the sun of freedom shines
In my ain countrie.

There 's a hope for every woe,
And a balm for every pain,
But the first joys o' our heart
Come never back again.
There 's a track upon the deep,
And a path across the sea:
But the weary ne'er return
To their ain countrie.

ROBERT GILFILLAN.

THE IRISHMAN.

THE savage loves his native shore,
Though rude the soil and chill the air;
Then well may Erin's sons adore
Their isle which nature formed so fair,
What flood reflects a shore so sweet
As Shannon great or pastoral Bann?
Or who a friend or foe can meet
So generous as an Irishman?

His hand is rash, his heart is warm,
But honesty is still his guide;
None more repents a deed of harm,
And none forgives with nobler pride;
He may be duped, but won't be dared—
More fit to practise than to plan;
He dearly earns his poor reward,
And spends it like an Irishman.

If strange or poor, for you he 'll pay,
   And guide to where you safe may be;
If you 're his guest, while e'er you stay,
   His cottage holds a jubilee.
His inmost soul he will unlock,
   And if he may *your* secrets scan,
Your confidence he scorns to mock,
   For faithful is an Irishman.

By honor bound in woe or weal,
   Whate 'er she bids he dares to do;
Try him with bribes—they won't prevail;
   Prove him in fire—you 'll find him true.
He seeks not safety, let his post
   Be where it ought in danger's van;
And if the field of fame be lost,
   It won't be by an Irishman.

Erin! loved land! from age to age,
   Be thou more great, more famed, and free,
May peace be thine, or shouldst thou wage
   Defensive war, cheap victory.
May plenty bloom in every field
   Which gentle breezes softly fan,
And cheerful smiles serenely gild
   The home of every Irishman.

                       JAMES ORR.

TURLOUGH MacSWEENEY.

A health to you, Piper,.
  And your pipes silver-tongued, clear and
  sweet in their crooning!

Full of the music they gathered at morn
  On your high heather hills from the lark on the
    wing,
From the blackbird at eve on the blossoming thorn,
  From the little green linnet whose plaining
    they sing,
And the joy and the hope in the heart of the
  Spring,
      O, Turlough MacSweeney!

Play us our Eire's most sorrowful songs,
  As she sits by her reeds near the wash of the
    wave,
That the coldest may thrill at the count of her
  wrongs,
    That the sword may flash forth from the scab-
      bard to save,
And the wide land awake at the wrath of the
  brave,
      O, Turlough MacSweeney!

Play as the bards played in days long ago,
  When O'Donnell, arrayed for the foray or feast,
With your kinsmen from Bannat and Fannat and
    Doe,
  With piping and harping, and blessing of priest,

Rode out in the blaze of the sun from the East,
  O, Turlough MacSweeney!

Play as they played in that rapturous hour
  When the clans heard in gladness his young fiery
    call
Who burst from the gloom of the Sassenach tower,
  And sped to the welcome in dear Donegal,
Then on to his hailing as chieftain of all—
    O, Turlough MacSweeney!

Play as they played, when, a trumpet of war,
  His voice for the rally, pealed up to the blue,
And the kerns from the hills and the glens and the
    scaur
Marched after the banner of conquering Hugh—
Led into the fray by a piper like you,
    O, Turlough MacSweeney!

And surely no note of such music shall fail,
  Wherever the speech of our Eire is heard,
To foster the hope of the passionate Gael,
  To fan the old hatred, relentless when stirred,
To strengthen our souls for the strife to be dared,
    O, Turlough MacSweeney!

May your pipes, silver-tongued, clear and sweet in
  their crooning,
Keep the magic they captured at dawning and
  even
From the blackbird at home, and the lark on its
  journey,

From the thrush on its spray, and the little green
*   linnet.*
>   *A health to you, Piper!*

>   ANNA MACMANUS (*Ethna Carbery*).

A SPINNING SONG.

My love to fight the Saxon goes,
    And bravely shines his sword of steel;
A heron's feather decks his brows,
    And a spur on either heel;
His steed is blacker than the sloe,
    And fleeter than the falling star;
Amid the surging ranks he'll go
    And shout for joy of war.
Twinkle, twinkle, pretty spindle; let the white
    wool drift and dwindle.
  Oh! we weave a damask doublet for my love's
    coat of steel.
Hark! the timid, turning treadle crooning soft,
    old-fashioned ditties
  To the low, slow murmur of the brown round
    wheel.

My love is pledged to Ireland's fight;
    My love would die for Ireland's weal,
To win her back her ancient right,
    And make her foemen reel.
Oh! close I'll clasp him to my breast
    When homeward from the war he comes;
The fires shall light the mountain's crest,
    The valley peal with drums.

Twinkle, twinkle, pretty spindle; let the white
  wool drift and dwindle.
  Oh! we weave a damask doublet for my love's
    coat of steel.
Hark! the timid, turning treadle crooning soft
  old-fashioned ditties
  To the low, slow murmur of the brown round
    wheel.

JOHN FRANCIS O'DONNELL.

THE WEARING OF THE GREEN.*

O PADDY dear, an' did you hear the news that's
  goin' round?
The shamrock is forbid by law to grow on Irish
  ground;
St. Patrick's Day no more we'll keep; his colors
  can't be seen:
For there's a cruel law agin' the wearin' of the
  green.
I met with Napper Tandy, and he tuk me by the
  hand,
And he said, "How's poor ould Ireland, and how
  does she stand?"
She's the most distressful country that ever yet
  was seen:
They are hangin' men and women there for wearin' of the green.

An' if the color we must wear is England's cruel
  red,

* Variation of an old street song of about 1798. Sung
in Dion Boucicault's play ' The Shan Van Voght."

Sure Ireland's sons will ne'er forget the blood that
they have shed.
Then pull the shamrock from your hat and cast it
on the sod,
And never fear, 't will take root there, though
under foot 't is trod.
When law can stop the blades of grass from grow-
in' as they grow,
And when the leaves in summer-time their color
dare not show,
Then I will change the color, too, I wear in my
caubeen;
But till that day, please God, I 'll stick to wearin' of the green.

But if at last our color should be torn from Ireland's heart,
Her sons with shame and sorrow from the dear
old isle will part:
I 've heard a whisper of a land that lies beyond
the sea,
Where rich and poor stand equal in the light of
freedom's day.
O Erin, must we leave you, driven by a tyrant's
hand?
Must we ask a mother's blessin' from a strange
and distant land?
Where the cruel cross of England shall nevermore be seen,
And where, please God, we 'll live and die still
wearin' of the green.

MY NATIVE LAND.

It chanced to me upon a time to sail
  Across the Southern ocean to and fro;
And, landing at fair isles, by stream and vale
  Of sensuous blessing did we ofttimes go.
And months of dreamy joys, like joys in sleep,
  Or like a clear, calm stream o'er mossy stone,
Unnoted passed our hearts with voiceless sweep,
  And left us yearning still for lands unknown.

And when we found one,—for 't is soon to find
  In thousand-isled Cathay another isle,—
For one short noon its treasures filled the mind,
  And then again we yearned, and ceased to smile.
And so it was from isle to isle we passed,
  Like wanton bees or boys on flowers or lips;
And when that all was tasted, then at last
  We thirsted still for draughts instead of sips.

I learned from this there is no Southern land
  Can fill with love the hearts of Northern men.
Sick minds need change; but, when in health they
    stand
  'Neath foreign skies, their love flies home agen.
And thus with me it was: the yearning turned
  From laden airs of cinnamon away,
And stretched far westward, while the full heart
    burned
  With love for Ireland, looking on Cathay!

My first dear love, all dearer for thy grief!
  My land, that has no peer in all the sea

For verdure, vale, or river, flower or leaf,—
  If first to no man else, thou 'rt first to me.
New loves may come with duties, but the first
  Is deepest yet,—the mother's breath and smiles;
Like that kind face and breast where I was nursed
  Is my poor land, the Niobe of isles.

JOHN BOYLE O'REILLY.

BLESS THE DEAR OLD VERDANT LAND.

Bless the dear old verdant land!
  Brother, wert thou born of it?
As thy shadow life doth stand
Twining round its rosy band,
Did an Irish mother's hand
  Guide thee in the morn of it?
Did a father's first command
  Teach thee love or scorn of it?

Thou who tread'st its fertile breast,
  Dost thou feel a glow for it?
Thou of all its charms possest,
Living on its first and best,
Art thou but a thankless guest
  Or a traitor foe for it,
If thou lovest, where 's the test?
  Wilt thou strike a blow for it?

Has the past no goading sting
  That can make thee rouse for it?
Does thy land's reviving spring,
Full of buds and blossoming,

Fail to make thy cold heart cling,
　　Breathing lover's vows for it?
With the circling ocean's ring
　　Thou wert made a spouse for it.

Hast thou kept as thou shouldst keep
　　Thy affections warm for it,
Letting no cold feeling creep
Like an ice-breath o'er the deep,
Freezing to a stony sleep
　　Hopes the heart would form for it,
Glories that like rainbows peep
　　Through the darkening storm for it?

Son of this down-trodden land,
　　Aid us in the fight for it.
We seek to make it great and grand,
Its shipless bays, its naked strand,
By canvas-swelling breezes fanned:
　　Oh, what a glorious sight for it,
The past expiring like a brand
　　In morning's rosy light for it!

Think, this dear old land is thine,
　　And thou a traitor slave of it:
Think how the Switzer leads his kine,
When pale the evening star doth shine;
His song has home in every line,
　　Freedom in every stave of it;
Think how the German loves his Rhine
　　And worships every wave of it!

Our own dear land is bright as theirs,
　　But oh! our hearts are cold for it;

Awake! we are not slaves, but heirs.
Our fatherland requires our cares,
Our speech with men, with God our prayers;
    Spurn blood-stained Judas gold for it:
Let us do all that honor dares—
    Be earnest, faithful, bold for it!

DENIS FLORENCE MAC CARTHY.

IRELAND.

[1847.]

THEY are dying! they are dying! where the golden
        corn is growing;
They are dying! they are dying! where the
        crowded herds are lowing:
They are gasping for existence where the streams
        of life are flowing,
And they perish of the plague where the breeze of
        health is blowing!

God of justice! God of power!
    Do we dream? Can it be,
In this land, at this hour,
    With the blossom on the tree,
In the gladsome month of May,
When the young lambs play,
When Nature looks around
    On her waking children now,
The seed within the ground,
    The bud upon the bough?
Is it right, is it fair,

That we perish of despair
In this land, on this soil,
  Where our destiny is set,
Which we cultured with our toil,
  And watered with our sweat?
We have ploughed, we have sown
But the crop was not our own;
We have reaped, but harpy hands
Swept the harvest from our lands;
We were perishing for food,
When lo! in pitying mood,
Our kindly rulers gave
The fat fluid of the slave,
While our corn filled the manger
Of the war-horse of the stranger!

God of mercy! must this last?
  Is this land preordained,
For the present and the past
  And the future, to be chained,—
  To be ravaged, to be drained,
To be robbed, to be spoiled,
  To be hushed, to be whipt,
  Its soaring pinions clipt,
And its every effort foiled?

Do our numbers multiply
But to perish and to die?
  Is this all our destiny below,—
That our bodies, as they rot,
May fertilize the spot
  Where the harvests of the stranger grow?

If this be, indeed, our fate,
Far, far better now, though late,
That we seek some other land and try some other
    zone;
The coldest, bleakest shore
Will surely yield us more
Than the storehouse of the stranger that we dare
    not call our own.

Kindly brothers of the West,
Who from Liberty's full breast
Have fed us, who are orphans beneath a step-
    dame's frown,
Behold our happy state,
And weep your wretched fate
That you share not in the splendors of our em-
    pire and our crown!

Kindly brothers of the East,—
Thou great tiaraed priest,
Thou sanctified Rienzi of Rome and of the
    earth,—
Or thou who bear'st control
Over golden Istambol,
Who felt for our misfortunes and helped us in
    our dearth,—

Turn here your wondering eyes,
Call your wisest of the wise,
Your muftis and your ministers, your men of
    deepest lore;
Let the sagest of your sages
Ope our island's mystic pages,

And explain unto your highness the wonders of
our shore.

A fruitful, teeming soil,
Where the patient peasants toil
Beneath the summer's sun and the watery winter
sky;
Where they tend the golden grain
Till it bends upon the plain,
Then reap it for the stranger, and turn aside to
die;

Where they watch their flocks increase,
And store the snowy fleece
Till they send it to their masters to be woven o'er
the waves;
Where, having sent their meat
For the foreigner to eat,
Their mission is fulfilled, and they creep into
their graves.

'T is for this they are dying where the golden
corn is growing,
'T is for this they are dying where the crowded
herds are lowing,
'T is for this they are dying where the streams of
life are flowing,
And they perish of the plague where the breeze of
health is blowing!

DENIS FLORENCE MAC CARTHY.

5

IRELAND.

A SEASIDE PORTRAIT.

A GREAT, still Shape, alone,
   She sits (her harp has fallen) on the sand,
And sees her children, one by one, depart:—
Her cloak (that hides what sins beside her own!)
   Wrapped fold on fold about her. Lo,
     She comforts her fierce heart,
As wailing some, and some gay-singing go,
With the far vision of that Greater Land
     Deep in the Atlantic skies,
     Saint Brandan's Paradise!
     Another Woman there,
     Mighty and wondrous fair,
Stands on her shore-rock:—one uplifted hand
     Holds a quick-piercing light
     That keeps long sea-ways bright;
She beckons with the other, saying " Come,
     O landless, shelterless,
Sharp-faced with hunger, worn with long dis-
     tress:—
     Come hither, finding home!
Lo, my new fields of harvest, open, free,
   By winds of blessing blown,
Whose golden corn-blades shake from sea to sea—
Fields without walls that all the people own! "

JOHN JAMES PIATT.

EXILE OF ERIN.

THERE came to the beach a poor exile of Erin,
   The dew on his thin robe was heavy and chill;
For his country he sighed, when at twilight re-
     pairing
   To wander alone by the wind-beaten hill.
But the day-star attracted his eye's sad devotion,
For it rose o'er his own native isle of the ocean,
Where once, in the fire of his youthful emotion,
   He sang the bold anthem of Erin go bragh.

Sad is my fate! said the heart-broken stranger;
   The wild deer and wolf to a covert can flee,
But I have no refuge from famine and danger,
   A home and a country remain not to me.
Never again in the green sunny bowers
Where my forefathers lived shall I spend the sweet
     hours,
Or cover my harp with the wild-woven flowers,
   And strike to the numbers of Erin go bragh!

Erin, my country! though sad and forsaken,
   In dreams I revisit thy sea-beaten shore;
But, alas! in a far foreign land I awaken,
   And sigh for the friends who can meet me no
     more!
O cruel fate! wilt thou never replace me
In a mansion of peace, where no perils can chase
     me?
Never again shall my brothers embrace me?
   They died to defend me, or live to deplore!

Where is my cabin door, fast by the wildwood?
  Sisters and sire, did ye weep for its fall?
Where is the mother that looked on my child-
    hood?
  And where is the bosom-friend, dearer than all?
O my sad heart! long abandoned by pleasure,
Why did it dote on a fast-fading treasure?
Tears, like the rain-drop, may fall without meas-
  ure,
  But rapture and beauty they cannot recall.

Yet, all its sad recollections suppressing,
  One dying wish my lone bosom can draw,—
Erin, an exile bequeaths thee his blessing!
  Land of my forefathers, Erin go bragh!
Buried and cold, when my heart stills her motion,
Green be thy fields, sweetest isle of the ocean!
And thy harp-striking bards sing aloud with de-
  votion,—
  Erin mavourneen, Erin go bragh! *

THOMAS CAMPBELL.

AFTER DEATH.

SHALL mine eyes behold thy glory, O my country?
  Shall mine eyes behold thy glory?
Or shall the darkness close around them, ere the
  sun-blaze breaks at last upon thy story?
When the nations ope for thee their queenly cir-
  cle, as a sweet new sister hail thee,

* Ireland my darling, Ireland forever!

Shall these lips be sealed in callous death and
  silence, that have known but to bewail thee?
Shall the ear be deaf that only loved thy praises,
  when all men their tribute bring thee?
Shall the mouth be clay that sang thee in thy
  squalor, when all poets' mouths shall sing
  thee?

Ah, the harpings and the salvos and the shoutings
  of thy exiled sons returning!
I should hear, though dead and mouldered, and
  the grave-damps should not chill my bosom's
  burning.

Ah, the tramp of feet victorious! I should hear
  them 'mid the shamrocks and the mosses,
And my heart should toss within the shroud and
  quiver as a captive dreamer tosses.

I should turn and rend the cere-clothes round me,
  giant sinews I should borrow—
Crying, " O my brothers, I have also loved her in
  her loneliness and sorrow.

" Let me join with you the jubilant procession;
  let me chant with you her story;
Then contented I shall go back to the shamrocks,
  now mine eyes have seen her glory! "

                              FRANCES ISABEL PARNELL.

CANADA NOT LAST.

At Venice.

Lo Venice, gay with color, lights and song,
　Calls from St. Mark's with ancient voice and
　　strange:
I am the Witch of Cities! glide along
　My silver streets that never wear by change
Of years: forget the years, and pain, and wrong,
And ever sorrow reigning men among.
　Know I can soothe thee, please and marry thee
To my illusions. Old and siren strong,
　I smile immortal, while the mortals flee
Who whiten on to death in wooing me.

At Florence.

Say, what more fair by Arno's bridgèd gleam
　Than Florence, viewed from San Miniato's slope
At eventide, when west along the stream
　The last of day reflects a silver hope!—
Lo, all else softened in the twilight beam:—
The city's mass blent in one hazy cream,
　The brown Dome 'midst it, and the Lily tower,
And stern Old Tower more near, and hills that
　　seem
　Afar, like clouds to fade, and hills of power
　On this side greenly dark with cypress, vine and
　　bower.

At Rome.

End of desire to stray I feel would come
　Though Italy were all fair skies to me,

Though France's fields went mad with flowery
    foam
  And Blanc put on a special majesty,
Not all could match the growing thought of home
Nor tempt to exile. Look I not on Rome—
  This ancient, modern, mediæval queen—
Yet still sigh westward over hill and dome,
  Imperial ruin and villa's princely scene
  Lovely with pictured saints and marble gods
    serene.

REFLECTION.

Rome, Florence, Venice—noble, fair and quaint,
  They reign in robes of magic round me here;
But fading, blotted, dim, a picture faint,
  With spell more silent, only pleads a tear.
Plead not! Thou hast my heart, O picture dim!
  I see the fields, I see the autumn hand
Of God upon the maples! Answer Him
  With weird, translucent glories, ye that stand
Like spirits in scarlet and in amethyst!
I see the sun break over you: the mist
  On hills that lift from iron bases grand
  Their heads superb!—the dream, it is my na-
    tive land.

WILLIAM DOUW SCHUYLER-LIGHTHALL.

CANADA.

O CHILD of Nations, giant-limbed,
  Who stand'st among the nations now,
Unheeded, unadored, unhymned,
  With unanointed brow:

How long the ignoble sloth, how long
    The trust in greatness not thine own?
Surely the lion's brood is strong
    To front the world alone!

How long the indolence, ere thou dare
    Achieve thy destiny, seize thy fame;
Ere our proud eyes behold thee bear
    A nation's franchise, nation's name?

The Saxon force, the Celtic fire,
    These are thy manhood's heritage!
Why rest with babes and slaves?   Seek higher
    The place of race and age.

I see to every wind unfurled
    The flag that bears the Maple-Wreath;
Thy swift keels furrow round the world
    Its blood-red folds beneath;

Thy swift keels cleave the furthest seas;
    Thy white sails swell with alien gales;
To stream on each remotest breeze
    The black smoke of thy pipes exhales.

O Falterer, let thy past convince
    Thy future: all the growth, the gain,
The fame since Cartier knew thee, since
    Thy shores beheld Champlain!

Montcalm and Wolfe! Wolfe and Montcalm!
    Quebec, thy storied citadel

Attest in burning song and psalm
How here thy heroes fell!

O Thou that bor'st the battle's brunt
At Queenstown, and at Lundy's Lane:
On whose scant ranks but iron front
The battle broke in vain!

Whose was the danger, whose the day,
From whose triumphant throats the cheers,
At Chrysler's Farm, at Chateauguay,
Storming like clarion-bursts our ears?

On soft Pacific slopes,—beside
Strange floods that northward rave and fall,
Where chafes Acadia's chainless tide,—
Thy sons await thy call.

They wait; but some in exile, some
With strangers housed, in stranger lands;
And some Canadian lips are dumb
Beneath Egyptian sands.

O mystic Nile! Thy secret yields
Before us; thy most ancient dreams
Are mixed with far Canadian fields
And murmur of Canadian streams.

But thou, my Country, dream not thou!
Wake, and behold how night is done,—
How on thy breast, and o'er thy brow,
Bursts the uprising sun!

CHARLES G. D. ROBERTS.

WHAT IS THE GERMAN'S FATHERLAND?

WHAT is the German's fatherland?
Is it Prussia, or the Swabian's land?
Is it where the grape glows on the Rhine?
Where sea-gulls skim the Baltic's brine?
    Oh no! more grand
    Must be the German's fatherland!

What is the German's fatherland?
Bavaria, or the Styrian's land?
Is it where the Master's cattle graze?
Is it the Mark where forges blaze?
    Oh no! more grand
    Must be the German's fatherland!

What is the German's fatherland?
Westphalia?   Pomerania's strand?
Where the sand drifts along the shore?
Or where the Danube's surges roar?
    Oh no! more grand
    Must be the German's fatherland!

What is the German's fatherland?
Now name for me that mighty land!
Is it Switzerland? or Tyrols, tell;—
The land and people pleased me well!
    Oh no! more grand
    Must be the German's fatherland!

What is the German's fatherland?
Now name for me that mighty land!

Ah! Austria surely it must be,
So rich in fame and victory.
  Oh no! more grand
 Must be the German's fatherland!

What is the German's fatherland?
Tell me the name of that great land!
Is it the land which princely hate
Tore from the Emperor and the State?
  Oh no! more grand
 Must be the German's fatherland!

What is the German's fatherland?
Now name at last that mighty land!
" Where'er resounds the German tongue,
Where'er its hymns to God are sung!"
  That is the land,
 Brave German, that thy fatherland!

That is the German's fatherland!
Where binds like oak the claspèd hand,
Where truth shines clearly from the eyes,
And in the heart affection lies.
  Be this the land,
 Brave German, this thy fatherland!

That is the German's fatherland!
Where scorn shall foreign trifles brand,
Where all are foes whose deeds offend,
Where every noble soul's a friend:
  Be this the land,
 All Germany shall be the land!

All Germany that land shall be:
Watch o'er it, God, and grant that we,
With German hearts, in deed and thought,
May love it truly as we ought.
      Be this the land,
  All Germany shall be the land!

From the German of ERNST MORITZ ARNDT.

PATRIOTIC SONG.

God, who gave iron, purposed ne'er
    That man should be a slave:
Therefore the sabre, sword, and spear
    In his right hand He gave.
Therefore He gave him fiery mood,
    Fierce speech, and free-born breath,
That he might fearlessly the feud
    Maintain through life and death.

Therefore will we what God did say,
    With honest truth maintain,
And ne'er a fellow-creature slay,
    A tyrant's pay to gain!
But he shall fall by stroke of brand
    Who fights for sin and shame,
And not inherit German land
    With men of German name.

O Germany, bright fatherland!
    O German love, so true!
Thou sacred land, thou beauteous land,
    We swear to thee anew!

Outlawed, each knave and coward shall
  The crow and raven feed;
But we will to the battle all—
  Revenge shall be our meed.

Flash forth, flash forth, whatever can,
  To bright and flaming life!
Now all ye Germans, man for man,
  Forth to the holy strife!
Your hands lift upward to the sky—
  Your heart shall upward soar—
And man for man, let each one cry,
  Our slavery is o'er!

Let sound, let sound, whatever can,
  Trumpet and fife and drum,
This day our sabres, man for man,
  To stain with blood we come;
With hangman's and with Frenchmen's blood,
  O glorious day of ire,
That to all Germans soundeth good—
  Day of our great desire!

Let wave, let wave, whatever can,
  Standard and banner wave!
Here will we purpose, man for man,
  To grace a hero's grave.
Advance, ye brave ranks, hardily—
  Your banners wave on high;
We'll gain us freedom's victory,
  Or freedom's death we'll die!

From the German of ERNST MORITZ ARNDT.

MEN AND BOYS.

THE storm is out; the land is roused;
Where is the coward who sits well housed?
Fie on thee, boy, disguised in curls,
Behind the stove, 'mong gluttons and girls!
   A graceless, worthless wight thou must be;
   No German maid desires thee,
   No German song inspires thee,
   No German Rhine-wine fires thee.
      Forth in the van,
      Man by man,
   Swing the battle-sword who can!

When we stand watching, the livelong night,
Through piping storms, till morning light,
Thou to thy downy bed canst creep,
And there in dreams of rapture sleep.
   A graceless, worthless wight, etc.

When, hoarse and shrill, the trumpet's blast,
Like the thunder of God, makes our heart beat
    fast,
Thou in the theatre lov'st to appear,
Where trills and quavers tickle the ear.
   A graceless, worthless wight, etc.

When the glare of noonday scorches the brain,
When our parchèd lips seek water in vain,
Thou canst make champagne corks fly

At the groaning tables of luxury.
  A graceless, worthless wight, etc.

When we, as we rush to the strangling fight,
Send home to our true-loves a long " Good-night,"
Thou canst hie thee where love is sold,
And buy thy pleasure with paltry gold.
  A graceless, worthless wight, etc.

When lance and bullet come whistling by,
And death in a thousand shapes draws nigh,
Thou canst sit at thy cards, and kill
King, queen, and knave with thy spadille.
  A graceless, worthless wight, etc.

If on the red field our bell should toll,
Then welcome be death to the patriot's soul!
Thy pampered flesh shall quake at its doom,
And crawl in silk to a hopeless tomb.
  A pitiful exit thine shall be;
  No German maid shall weep for thee,
  No German song shall they sing for thee,
  No German goblets shall ring for thee.
      Forth in the van,
      Man for man,
Swing the battle-sword who can!

From the German of KARL THEODOR KÖRNER.
Translation of CHARLES TIMOTHY BROOKS.

THE WATCH ON THE RHINE.*

A voice resounds like thunder-peal,
'Mid dashing waves and clang of steel:—
" The Rhine, the Rhine, the German Rhine!
Who guards to-day my stream divine? "

Chorus.

Dear Fatherland, no danger thine:
Firm stand thy sons to watch the Rhine!

They stand, a hundred thousand strong,
Quick to avenge their country's wrong;
With filial love their bosoms swell,
They 'll guard the sacred landmark well!

The dead of a heroic race
From heaven look down and meet their gaze;
They swear with dauntless heart, " O Rhine,
Be German as this breast of mine!"

While flows one drop of German blood,
Or sword remains to guard thy flood,
While rifle rests in patriot hand,—
No foe shall tread thy sacred strand!

Our oath resounds, the river flows,
In golden light our banner glows;

* Written by a manufacturer of Wurtemburg in 1840,
when France was threatening the left bank of the Rhine.
It was set to music by Carl Wilhelm, and during the
Franco-Prussian war of 1871 was adopted as the national
folk-hymn and rallying cry of the army.

Our hearts will guard thy stream divine:
The Rhine, the Rhine, the German Rhine!

Dear Fatherland, no danger thine:
Firm stand thy sons to watch the Rhine!

From the German of MAX SCHNECKENBURGER.

PROEM.

FROM " THE KALEVALA " (*Land of heroes*), THE
NATIONAL EPIC OF FINLAND.*

MASTERED by desire impulsive,
By a mighty inward urging,
I am ready now for singing,
Ready to begin the chanting
Of our nation's ancient folk-song,
Handed down from bygone ages.
In my mouth the words are melting,
From my lips the tones are gliding,
From my tongue they wish to hasten;
When my willing teeth are parted,
When my ready mouth is opened,
Songs of ancient wit and wisdom
Hasten from me not unwilling.

Golden friend, and dearest brother,
Brother dear of mine in childhood,
Come and sing with me the stories,
Come and chant with me the legends,
Legends of the times forgotten,

* Aside from its national significance "The Kalevala"
is interesting from the fact of its having been taken as the
model in rhythm and style for Longfellow's "Hiawatha,"
the epic of the American Indian.

6

Since we now are here together,
Come together from our roamings.
Seldom do we come for singing,
Seldom to the one, the other,
O'er this cold and cruel country,
O'er the poor soil of the Northland.
Let us clasp our hands together,
That we thus may best remember.
Join we now in merry singing,
Chant we now the oldest folk-lore,
That the dear ones all may hear them,
That the well-inclined may hear them,
Of this rising generation.
These are words in childhood taught me,
Songs preserved from distant ages;
Legends they that once were taken
From the belt of Wainamoinen,
From the forge of Ilmarinen,
From the sword of Kaukomieli,
From the bow of Youkahainen,
From the pastures of the Northland,
From the meads of Kalevala.
These my dear old father sang me
When at work with knife and hatchet:
These my tender mother taught me
When she twirled the flying spindle,
When a child upon the matting
By her feet I rolled and tumbled.
    Incantations were not wanting
Over Sampo and o'er Louhi,
Sampo growing old in singing,
Louhi ceasing her enchantment.
In the songs died wise Wipunen,

At the games died Lemminkainen.
There are many other legends,
Incantations that were taught me,
That I found along the wayside,
Gathered in the fragrant copses,
Blown me from the forest branches,
Culled among the plumes of pine-trees,
Scented from the vines and flowers,
Whispered to me as I followed
Flocks in land of honeyed meadows,
Over hillocks green and golden,
After sable-haired Murikki,
And the many-colored Kimmo.
Many runes the cold has told me,
Many lays the rain has brought me,
Other songs the winds have sung me;
Many birds from many forests,
Oft have sung me lays in concord;
Waves of sea, and ocean billows,
Music from the many waters,
Music from the whole creation,
Oft have been my guide and master.
Sentences the trees created,
Rolled together into bundles,
Moved them to my ancient dwelling,
On the sledges to my cottage,
Tied them to my garret rafters,
Hung them on my dwelling-portals,
Laid them in a chest of boxes,
Boxes lined with shining copper.
Long they lay within my dwelling
Through the chilling winds of winter,
In my dwelling-place for ages.

Shall I bring these songs together?
From the cold and frost collect them?
Shall I bring this nest of boxes,
Keepers of these golden legends,
To the table in my cabin,
Underneath the painted rafters,
In this house renowned and ancient?
Shall I now these boxes open,
Boxes filled with wondrous stories?
Shall I now the end unfasten
Of this ball of ancient wisdom?
These ancestral lays unravel?
Let me sing an old-time legend,
That shall echo forth the praises
Of the beer that I have tasted,
Of the sparkling beer of barley.
Bring to me a foaming goblet
Of the barley of my fathers,
Lest my singing grow too weary,
Singing from the water only.
Bring me too a cup of strong beer;
It will add to our enchantment,
To the pleasure of the evening,
Northland's long and dreary evening,
For the beauty of the day-dawn,
For the pleasures of the morning,
The beginning of the new day.

From the FINNISH.
Translation of JOHN MARTIN CRAWFORD.

PARTING LOVERS.

SIENNA.

I LOVE thee, love thee, Giulio!
  Some call me cold, and some demure,
And if thou hast ever guessed that so
  I love thee . . . well;—the proof was poor,
  And no one could be sure.

Before thy song (with shifted rhymes
  To suit my name) did I undo
The persian? If it moved sometimes,
  Thou hast not seen a hand push through
  A flower or two.

My mother listening to my sleep
  Heard nothing but a sigh at night,—
The short sigh rippling on the deep,—
  When hearts run out of breath and sigh
  Of men, to God's clear light.

When others named thee, . . . thought thy brows
  Were straight, thy smile was tender, . . .
    " Here
He comes between the vineyard-rows!"—
  I said not " Ay,"—nor waited, Dear,
  To feel thee step too near.

I left such things to bolder girls,
  Olivia or Clotilda. Nay,

When that Clotilda through her curls
  Held both thine eyes in hers one day,
  I marvelled, let me say.

I could not try the woman's trick:
  Between us straightway fell the blush
Which kept me separate, blind, and sick.
  A wind came with thee in a flush,
  As blow through Horeb's bush.

But now that Italy invokes
  Her young men to go forth and chase
The foe or perish,—nothing chokes
  My voice, or drives me from the place:
  I look thee in the face.

I love thee! it is understood,
  Confest: I do not shrink or start:
No blushes: all my body's blood
  Has gone to greaten this poor heart,
  That, loving, we may part.

Our Italy invokes the youth
  To die if need be. Still there's room,
Though earth is strained with dead, in truth.
  Since twice the lilies were in bloom
  They had not grudged a tomb.

And many a plighted maid and wife
  And mother, who can say since then
" My country," cannot say through life
  " My son," " my spouse," " my flower of men,"
  And not weep dumb again.

Heroic males the country bears,
  But daughters give up more than sons.
Flags wave, drums beat, and unawares
  You flash your souls out with the guns,
    And take your heaven at once!

But we,—we empty heart and home
  Of life's life, love! we bear to think
You 're gone, . . . to feel you may not come, . . .
  To hear the door-latch stir and clink
    Yet no more you, . . . nor sink.

Dear God! when Italy is one
  And perfected from bound to bound, . . .
Suppose (for my share) earth 's undone
  By one grave in 't! as one small wound
    May kill a man, 't is found!

What then? If love's delight must end,
  At least we 'll clear its truth from flaws.
I love thee, love thee, sweetest friend!
  Now take my sweetest without pause,
    To help the nation's cause.

And thus of noble Italy
  We 'll both be worthy. Let her show
The future how we made her free,
  Not sparing life, nor Giulio,
    Nor this . . . this heart-break. Go!

        ELIZABETH BARRETT BROWNING.

AMERICA.

O MOTHER of a mighty race,
Yet lovely in thy youthful grace!
The elder dames, thy haughty peers,
Admire and hate thy blooming years;
 With words of shame
And taunts of scorn they join thy name.

For on thy cheeks the glow is spread
That tints thy morning hills with red;
Thy step,—the wild deer's rustling feet
Within thy woods are not more fleet;
 Thy hopeful eye
Is bright as thine own sunny sky.

Ay, let them rail, those haughty ones,
While safe thou dwellest with thy sons.
They do not know how loved thou art,
How many a fond and fearless heart
 Would rise to throw
Its life between thee and the foe.

They know not, in their hate and pride,
What virtues with thy children bide,—
How true, how good, thy graceful maids
Make bright, like flowers, the valley shades;
 What generous men
Spring, like thine oaks, by hill and glen;

What cordial welcomes greet the guest
By thy lone rivers of the west;

How faith is kept, and truth revered,
And man is loved, and God is feared,
    In woodland homes,
And where the ocean border foams.

There 's freedom at thy gates, and rest
For earth's down-trodden and opprest,
A shelter for the hunted head,
For the starved laborer toil and bread.
    Power, at thy bounds,
Stops, and calls back his baffled hounds.

O fair young mother! on thy brow
Shall sit a nobler grace than now.
Deep in the brightness of thy skies,
The thronging years in glory rise,
    And, as they fleet,
Drop strength and riches at thy feet.

Thine eye, with every coming hour,
Shall brighten, and thy form shall tower;
And when thy sisters, elder born,
Would brand thy name with words of scorn,
    Before thine eye
Upon their lips the taunt shall die.

                    WILLIAM CULLEN BRYANT.

COLUMBIA.

COLUMBIA, Columbia, to glory arise,
The queen of the world, and the child of the skies!
Thy genius commands thee; with rapture behold,
While ages on ages thy splendors unfold.

Thy reign is the last and the noblest of time,
Most fruitful thy soil, most inviting thy clime;
Let the crimes of the East ne'er encrimson thy
     name,
Be freedom and science and virtue thy fame.

To conquest and slaughter let Europe aspire;
Whelm nations in blood, and wrap cities in fire;
Thy heroes the rights of mankind shall defend,
And triumph pursue them, and glory attend.
A world is thy realm; for a world be thy laws
Enlarged as thine empire, and just as thy cause;
On Freedom's broad basis that empire shall rise,
Extend with the main, and dissolve with the skies.

Fair Science her gates to thy sons shall unbar,
And the East see thy morn hide the beams of her
     star;
New bards and new sages unrivalled shall soar
To fame unextinguished when time is no more;
To thee, the last refuge of virtue designed,
Shall fly from all nations the best of mankind;
Here, grateful to Heaven, with transport shall
     bring
Their incense, more fragrant than odors of spring.
Nor less shall thy fair ones to glory ascend,
And genius and beauty in harmony blend;
The graces of form shall awake pure desire,
And the charms of the soul ever cherish the fire;
Their sweetness unmingled, their manners refined,
And virtue's bright image, enstamped on the mind,
With peace and soft rapture shall teach life to
     glow,
And light up a smile on the aspect of woe.

Thy fleets to all regions thy power shall display,
The nations admire, and the ocean obey;
Each shore to thy glory its tribute unfold,
And the East and the South yield their spices and
  gold.
As the dayspring unbounded thy splendor shall
  flow,
And earth's little kingdoms before thee shall bow,
While the ensigns of union, in triumph unfurled,
Hush the tumult of war, and give peace to the
  world.

Thus, as down a lone valley, with cedars o'er-
  spread,
From war's dread confusion, I pensively strayed,—
The gloom from the face of fair heaven retired;
The wind ceased to murmur, the thunders ex-
  pired;
Perfumes, as of Eden, flowed sweetly along,
And a voice, as of angels, enchantingly sung:
" Columbia, Columbia, to glory arise,
The queen of the world, and the child of the
  skies!"

                    TIMOTHY DWIGHT.

ON THE PROSPECT OF PLANTING ARTS AND LEARNING IN AMERICA.

THE Muse, disgusted at an age and clime
  Barren of every glorious theme,
In distant lands now waits a better time,
  Producing subjects worthy fame.

In happy climes, where from the genial sun
    And virgin earth such scenes ensue,
The force of art by nature seems outdone,
    And fancied beauties by the true:

In happy climes, the seat of innocence,
    Where nature guides and virtue rules,
Where men shall not impose for truth and sense
    The pedantry of courts and schools:

There shall be sung another golden age,
    The rise of empire and of arts,
The good and great inspiring epic rage,
    The wisest heads and noblest hearts.

Not such as Europe breeds in her decay:
    Such as she bred when fresh and young,
When heavenly flame did animate her clay,
    By future poets shall be sung.

Westward the course of empire takes its way;
    The first four acts already past,
A fifth shall close the drama with the day;
    Time's noblest offspring is the last.

BISHOP GEORGE BERKELEY.

ENGLAND TO AMERICA.

Nor force nor fraud shall sunder us! O ye
    Who north or south, or east or western land,
    Native to noble sounds, say truth for truth,
Freedom for freedom, love for love, and God
    For God; O ye who in eternal youth

Speak with a living and creative flood
This universal English, and do stand
Its breathing book; live worthy of that grand
Heroic utterance—parted, yet a whole,
    Far, yet unsevered,—children brave and free
Of the great Mother tongue, and ye shall be
Lords of an empire wide as Shakespeare's soul,
    Sublime as Milton's immemorial theme,
And rich as Chaucer's speech, and fair as Spen-
    ser's dream.

                    SYDNEY DOBELL.

OUR STATE.

THE south-land boasts its teeming cane,
The prairied west its heavy grain,
And sunset's radiant gates unfold
On rising marts and sands of gold!

Rough, bleak, and hard, our little State
Is scant of soil, of limits strait;
Her yellow sands are sands alone,
Her only mines are ice and stone!

From autumn frost to April rain,
Too long her winter woods complain;
From budding flower to falling leaf,
Her summer time is all too brief.

Yet, on her rocks, and on her sands,
And wintry hills, the school-house stands;
And what her rugged soil denies
The harvest of the mind supplies.

The riches of the commonwealth
Are free, strong minds, and hearts of health;
And more to her than gold or grain
The cunning hand and cultured brain.

For well she keeps her ancient stock,
The stubborn strength of Pilgrim Rock;
And still maintains, with milder laws,
And clearer light, the good old cause!

Nor heeds the sceptic's puny hands,
While near her school the church-spire stands;
Nor fears the blinded bigot's rule,
While near her church-spire stands the school.

JOHN GREENLEAF WHITTIER.

THE REPUBLIC.

FROM "THE BUILDING OF THE SHIP."

THOU, too, sail on, O Ship of State!
Sail on, O UNION, strong and great!
Humanity with all its fears,
With all the hopes of future years,
Is hanging breathless on thy fate!
We know what Master laid thy keel,
What Workmen wrought thy ribs of steel,
Who made each mast, and sail, and rope,
What anvils rang, what hammers beat,
In what a forge and what a heat
Were shaped the anchors of thy hope!
Fear not each sudden sound and shock,
'T is of the wave and not the rock;

'T is but the flapping of the sail,
And not a rent made by the gale!
In spite of rock and tempest's roar,
In spite of false lights on the shore,
Sail on, nor fear to breast the sea!
Our hearts, our hopes, are all with thee,
Our hearts, our hopes, our prayers, our tears,
Our faith triumphant o'er our fears,
Are all with thee,—are all with thee!

HENRY WADSWORTH LONGFELLOW.

AMERICA.

[1832.]

My country, 't is of thee,
Sweet land of liberty,
    Of thee I sing;
Land where my fathers died,
Land of the pilgrims' pride,
From every mountain-side
    Let freedom ring.

My native country, thee,
Land of the noble free,—
    Thy name I love;
I love thy rocks and rills,
Thy woods and templed hills;
My heart with rapture thrills
    Like that above.

Let music swell the breeze,
And ring from all the trees,
    Sweet freedom's song;

Let mortal tongues awake,
Let all that breathe partake,
Let rocks their silence break,—
    The sound prolong.

Our fathers' God, to Thee,
Author of liberty,
    To Thee I sing;
Long may our land be bright
With freedom's holy light;
Protect us by thy might,
    Great God our King.

SAMUEL FRANCIS SMITH.

"OLD IRONSIDES."

[On the proposed breaking up of the United States frigate "Constitution."]

AY, tear her tattered ensign down!
    Long has it waved on high,
And many an eye has danced to see
    That banner in the sky;
Beneath it rung the battle-shout,
    And burst the cannon's roar:
The meteor of the ocean air
    Shall sweep the clouds no more!

Her deck, once red with heroes' blood,
    Where knelt the vanquished foe,
When winds were hurrying o'er the flood
    And waves were white below,
No more shall feel the victor's tread,
    Or know the conquered knee:

The harpies of the shore shall pluck
  The eagle of the sea!

O better that her shattered hulk
  Should sink beneath the wave!
Her thunders shook the mighty deep,
  And there should be her grave:
Nail to the mast her holy flag,
  Set every threadbare sail,
And give her to the god of storms,
  The lightning and the gale!

OLIVER WENDELL HOLMES.

MEN OF THE NORTH AND WEST.

[APRIL, 1861.]

MEN of the North and West,
  Wake in your might.
Prepare, as the rebels have done,
  For the fight!
You cannot shrink from the test;
Rise! Men of the North and West!

They have torn down your banner of stars;
  They have trampled the laws;
They have stifled the freedom they hate,
  For no cause!
Do you love it or slavery best?
Speak! Men of the North and West!

They strike at the life of the State:
  Shall the murder be done?

They cry: " We are two! "   And you?
  " We are one! "
You must meet them, then, breast to breast;
On! Men of the North and West!

Not with words; they laugh them to scorn,
  And tears they despise;
But with swords in your hands, and death
  In your eyes!
Strike home! leave to God all the rest;
Strike! Men of the North and West!
RICHARD HENRY STODDARD.

OUR COUNTRY'S CALL.

[1861.]

LAY down the axe, fling by the spade;
  Leave in its track the toiling plough;
The rifle and the bayonet-blade
  For arms like yours were fitter now;
And let the hands that ply the pen
  Quit the light task, and learn to wield
The horseman's crookèd brand, and rein
  The charger on the battle-field.

Our country calls; away! away!
  To where the blood-stream blots the green;
Strike to defend the gentlest sway
  That Time in all his course has seen.
See, from a thousand coverts—see
  Spring the armed foes that haunt her track;
They rush to smite her down, and we
  Must beat the banded traitors back.

Ho! sturdy as the oaks ye cleave,
   And moved as soon to fear and flight,
Men of the glade and forest! leave
   Your woodcraft for the field of fight.
The arms that wield the axe must pour
   An iron tempest on the foe;
His serried ranks shall reel before
   The arm that lays the panther low.

And ye who breast the mountain storm
   By grassy steep or highland lake,
Come, for the land ye love, to form
   A bulwark that no foe can break.
Stand, like your own gray cliffs that mock
   The whirlwind; stand in her defence:
The blast as soon shall move the rock,
   As rushing squadrons bear ye thence.

And ye whose homes are by her grand
   Swift rivers, rising far away,
Come from the depth of her green land
   As mighty in your march as they;
As terrible as when the rains
   Have swelled them over bank and bourne,
With sudden floods to drown the plains
   And sweep along the woods uptorn.

And ye who throng beside the deep,
   Her ports and hamlets of the strand,
In number like the waves that leap
   On his long-murmuring marge of sand,
Come, like that deep, when, o'er his brim,
   He rises, all his floods to pour,

And flings the proudest barks that swim,
    A helpless wreck against his shore.

Few, few were they whose swords of old
    Won the fair land in which we dwell;
But we are many, we who hold
    The grim resolve to guard it well.
Strike for that broad and goodly land,
    Blow after blow, till men shall see
That Might and Right move hand in hand,
    And Glorious must their triumph be.

WILLIAM CULLEN BRYANT.

A CRY TO ARMS.

[1861.]

Ho, woodsmen of the mountain-side!
    Ho, dwellers in the vales!
Ho, ye who by the chafing tide
    Have roughened in the gales!
Leave barn and byre, leave kin and cot,
    Lay by the bloodless spade;
Let desk and case and counter rot,
    And burn your books of trade!

The despot roves your fairest lands;
    And till he flies or fears,
Your fields must grow but armèd bands,
    Your sheaves be sheaves of spears!
Give up to mildew and to rust
    The useless tools of gain,
And feed your country's sacred dust
    With floods of crimson rain!

Come with the weapons at your call—
  With musket, pike, or knife;
He wields the deadliest blade of all
  Who lightest holds his life.
The arm that drives its unbought blows
  With all a patriot's scorn,
Might brain a tyrant with a rose
  Or stab him with a thorn.

Does any falter? Let him turn
  To some brave maiden's eyes,
And catch the holy fires that burn
  In those sublunar skies.
Oh, could you like your women feel,
  And in their spirit march,
A day might see your lines of steel
  Beneath the victor's arch!

What hope, O God! would not grow warm
  When thoughts like these give cheer?
The lily calmly braves the storm,
  And shall the palm-tree fear?
No! rather let its branches court
  The rack that sweeps the plain;
And from the lily's regal port
  Learn how to breast the strain.

Ho, woodsmen of the mountain-side!
  Ho, dwellers in the vales!
Ho, ye who by the roaring tide
  Have roughened in the gales!

Come, flocking gayly to the fight,
From forest, hill, and lake;
We battle for our country's right,
And for the lily's sake!

HENRY TIMROD.

THE NATION'S PRAYER.

[1861].

I.

BEFORE Thy Throne we bow:
O God, our shield be Thou
From Treason's rage!
In faith we look to Thee,
Our strength in Heav'n we see,
Defender of the free,
In ev'ry age.

II.

Our follies we confess:
O God, forgive and bless!
Let Mercy's light
Illumine this dark hour,
When war clouds o'er us lower,
And Thine eternal power
Defend the right!

III.

Our Pilgrim fathers sleep,
The ocean, broad and deep,
Beside their graves.
When Thine archangel cries,
Forbid that they should rise

To crowns in Paradise
    From soil of slaves!

IV.

Protect our armies, Lord,
And when they draw the sword
    In freedom's name,
Strike Thou for them the blow,
Overwhelm the vaunting foe,
And bury Treason low,
    In deathless shame!

V.

Let Liberty arise,
Her glory fill the skies,
    The world be free!
Let all adore Thy name,
And children lisp Thy fame—
Let earth and heav'n proclaim
    The jubilee!

                        CRAMMOND KENNEDY.

MY MARYLAND.

[1861.]

THE despot's heel is on thy shore,
                Maryland!
His torch is at thy temple door,
                Maryland!
Avenge the patriotic gore
That flecked the streets of Baltimore,
And be the battle queen of yore,
    Maryland, My Maryland!

Hark to thy wandering son's appeal,
        Maryland!
My mother State, to thee I kneel,
        Maryland!
For life and death, for woe and weal,
Thy peerless chivalry reveal,
And gird thy beauteous limbs with steel,
    Maryland, My Maryland!

Thou wilt not cower in the dust,
        Maryland!
Thy beaming sword shall never rust,
        Maryland!
Remember Carroll's sacred trust,
Remember Howard's warlike thrust,
And all thy slumberers with the just,
    Maryland, My Maryland!

Come, 't is the red dawn of the day,
        Maryland!
Come with thy panoplied array,
        Maryland!
With Ringgold's spirit for the fray,
With Watson's blood at Monterey,
With fearless Lowe and dashing May,
    Maryland, My Maryland!

Dear mother, burst the tyrant's chain,
        Maryland!
Virginia should not call in vain,
        Maryland!
She meets her sisters on the plain:
" Sic semper!" 't is the proud refrain

That baffles minions back amain,
  Maryland, My Maryland!

Come, for thy shield is bright and strong,
  Maryland!
Come, for thy dalliance does thee wrong,
  Maryland!
Come to thine own heroic throng,
That stalks with liberty along,
And give a new key to thy song,
  Maryland, My Maryland!

I see the blush upon thy cheek,
  Maryland!
But thou wast ever bravely meek,
  Maryland!
But lo! there surges forth a shriek
From hill to hill, from creek to creek;
Potomac calls to Chesapeake,
  Maryland, My Maryland!

Thou wilt not yield the Vandal toll,
  Maryland!
Thou wilt not crook to his control,
  Maryland!
Better the fire upon thee roll,
Better the shot, the blade, the bowl,
Than crucifixion of the soul,
  Maryland, My Maryland!

I hear the distant thunder hum,
  Maryland!
The Old Line's bugle, fife, and drum,
  Maryland!

She is not dead, nor deaf, nor dumb—
Huzza! she spurns the Northern scum;
She breathes, she burns—she'll come! she'll
    come!
  Maryland, My Maryland!

            JAMES RYDER RANDALL.

———

DIXIE.

[1861.]

SOUTHRONS, hear your country call you!
Up, lest worse than death befall you!
To arms! To arms! To arms, in Dixie!
Lo! all the beacon-fires are lighted,—
Let all hearts be now united!
  To arms! To arms! To arms, in Dixie!
    Advance the flag of Dixie!
      Hurrah! hurrah!
For Dixie's land we take our stand,
    And live or die for Dixie!
      To arms! To arms!
    And conquer peace for Dixie!
      To arms! To arms!
    And conquer peace for Dixie!

Hear the Northern thunders mutter!
Northern flags in South winds flutter!
Send them back your fierce defiance!
Stamp upon the accursed alliance!

Fear no danger! Shun no labor!
Lift up rifle, pike, and sabre!

Shoulder pressing close to shoulder,
Let the odds make each heart bolder!

How the South's great heart rejoices
At your cannons' ringing voices!
For faith betrayed, and pledges broken,
Wrongs inflicted, insults spoken.

Strong as lions, swift as eagles,
Back to their kennels hunt these beagles!
Cut the unequal bonds asunder!
Let them hence each other plunder!

Swear upon your country's altar
Never to submit or falter,
Till the spoilers are defeated,
Till the Lord's work is completed.

Halt not till our Federation
Secures among earth's powers its station!
Then at peace, and crowned with glory,
Hear your children tell the story!

If the loved ones weep in sadness,
Victory soon shall bring them gladness,—
            To arms!
Exultant pride soon banish sorrow,
Smiles chase tears away to-morrow.
      To arms! To arms! To arms, in Dixie!
          Advance the flag of Dixie!
              Hurrah! hurrah!
For Dixie's land we take our stand,

And live or die for Dixie!
　　To arms! To arms!
And conquer peace for Dixie!
　　To arms! To arms!
And conquer peace for Dixie!

ALBERT PIKE.

THE FLAG GOES BY.

HATS off!
Along the street there comes
A blare of bugles, a ruffle of drums,
A flash of color beneath the sky:
Hats off!
The flag is passing by!

Blue and crimson and white it shines,
Over the steel-tipped, ordered lines.
Hats off!
The colors before us fly;
But more than the flag is passing by.

Sea-fights and land-fights, grim and great,
Fought to make and to save the State:
Weary marches and sinking ships;
Cheers of victory on dying lips;

Days of plenty and years of peace;
March of a strong land's swift increase;
Equal justice, right and law,
Stately honor and reverend awe;

Sign of a nation, great and strong
To ward her people from foreign wrong:

Pride and glory and honor,—all
Live in the colors to stand or fall.

Hats off!
Along the street there comes
A blare of bugles, a ruffle of drums;
And loyal hearts are beating high:
Hats off!
The flag is passing by!

HENRY HOLCOMB BENNETT.

THE BRAVE AT HOME.

THE maid who binds her warrior's sash
 With smile that well her pain dissembles,
The while beneath her drooping lash
 One starry tear-drop hangs and trembles,
Though Heaven alone records the tear,
 And Fame shall never know her story,
Her heart has shed a drop as dear
 As e'er bedewed the field of glory!

The wife who girds her husband's sword,
 Mid little ones who weep or wonder,
And bravely speaks the cheering word,
 What though her heart be rent asunder,
Doomed nightly in her dreams to hear
 The bolts of death around him rattle,
Hath shed as sacred blood as e'er
 Was poured upon the field of battle!

The mother who conceals her grief
 While to her breast her son she presses,

Then breathes a few brave words and brief,
  Kissing the patriot brow she blesses,
With no one but her secret God
  To know the pain that weighs upon her,
Sheds holy blood as e'er the sod
  Received on Freedom's field of honor!

THOMAS BUCHANAN READ.

II.

FREEDOM.

THE PLACE WHERE MAN SHOULD DIE.

How little recks it where men lie,
　　When once the moment's past
In which the dim and glazing eye
　　Has looked on earth its last,—
Whether beneath the sculptured urn
　　The coffined form shall rest,
Or in its nakedness return
　　Back to its mother's breast!

Death is a common friend or foe,
　　As different men may hold,
And at his summons each must go,
　　The timid and the bold;
But when the spirit, free and warm,
　　Deserts it, as it must,
What matter where the lifeless form
　　Dissolves again to dust?

The soldier falls 'mid corses piled
　　Upon the battle-plain,

Where reinless war-steeds gallop wild
   Above the mangled slain;
But though his corse be grim to see,
   Hoof-trampled on the sod,
What recks it, when the spirit free
   Has soared aloft to God?

The coward's dying eyes may close
   Upon his downy bed,
And softest hands his limbs compose,
   Or garments o'er them spread.
But ye who shun the bloody fray,
   When fall the mangled brave,
Go—strip his coffin-lid away,
   And see him in his grave!

'T were sweet, indeed, to close our eyes,
   With those we cherish near,
And, wafted upwards by their sighs,
   Soar to some calmer sphere.
But whether on the scaffold high,
   Or in the battle's van,
The fittest place where man can die
   Is where he dies for man!

            MICHAEL JOSEPH BARRY.

LIBERTY.

WHAT man is there so bold that he should say,
" Thus, and thus only, would I have the Sea "?
For whether lying calm and beautiful,
Clasping the earth in love, and throwing back

The smile of Heaven from waves of amethyst;
Or whether, freshened by the busy winds,
It bears the trade and navies of the world
To ends of use or stern activity;
Or whether, lashed by tempests, it gives way
To elemental fury, howls and roars
At all its rocky barriers, in wild lust
Of ruin drinks the blood of living things,
And strews its wrecks o'er leagues of desolate
    shore,—
Always it is the Sea, and men bow down
Before its vast and varied majesty.

So all in vain will timorous ones essay
To set the metes and bounds of Liberty.
For Freedom is its own eternal law:
It makes its own conditions, and in storm
Or calm alike fulfils the unerring Will.
Let us not then despise it when it lies
Still as a sleeping lion, while a swarm
Of gnat-like evils hover round its head;
Nor doubt it when in mad, disjointed times
It shakes the torch of terror, and its cry
Shrills o'er the quaking earth, and in the flame
Of riot and war we see its awful form
Rise by the scaffold, where the crimson axe
Rings down its grooves the knell of shuddering
    kings.
For ever in thine eyes, O Liberty,
Shines that high light whereby the world is saved,
And though thou slay us, we will trust in thee!

JOHN HAY.

8

PATIENCE.

FROM "POEMS OF FREEDOM."

BE patient, O be patient! Put your ear against
    the earth;
Listen there how noiselessly the germ o' the seed
    has birth;
How noiselessly and gently it upheaves its little
    way
Till it parts the scarcely-broken ground, and the
    blade stands up in the day.

Be patient, O be patient! the germs of mighty
    thought
Must have their silent undergrowth, must under-
    ground be wrought;
But, as sure as ever there 's a Power that makes
    the grass appear,
Our land shall be green with Liberty, the blade-
    time shall be here.

Be patient, O be patient! go and watch the wheat-
    ears grow,
So imperceptibly that ye can mark nor change nor
    throe:
Day after day, day after day till the ear is fully
    grown;
And then again day after day, till the ripened
    field is brown.

Be patient, O be patient! though yet our hopes
    are green,

The harvest-field of Freedom shall be crowned
    with the sunny sheen.
Be ripening, be ripening! mature your silent way
Till the whole broad land is tongued with fire on
    Freedom's harvest day.

WILLIAM JAMES LINTON.

THE ANTIQUITY OF FREEDOM.

HERE are old trees, tall oaks and gnarled pines,
That stream with gray-green mosses; here the
    ground
Was never trenched by spade, and flowers spring
    up
Unsown, and die ungathered. It is sweet
To linger here, among the flitting birds,
And leaping squirrels, wandering brooks, and
    winds
That shake the leaves, and scatter, as they pass,
A fragrance from the cedars, thickly set
With pale blue berries. In these peaceful
    shades—
Peaceful, unpruned, immeasurably old—
My thoughts go up the long dim path of years,
Back to the earliest days of liberty.

Oh FREEDOM! thou art not, as poets dream,
A fair young girl, with light and delicate limbs,
And wavy tresses gushing from the cap
With which the Roman master crowned his slave
When he took off the gyves. A bearded man,
Armed to the teeth, art thou; one mailèd hand

Grasps the broad shield, and one the sword; thy
    brow,
Glorious in beauty though it be, is scarred
With tokens of old wars; thy massive limbs
Are strong with struggling.   Power at thee has
    launched
His bolts, and with his lightnings smitten thee;
They could not quench the life thou hast from
    heaven.
Merciless power has dug thy dungeon deep,
And his swart armorers, by a thousand fires,
Have forged thy chain; yet, while he deems thee
    bound,
The links are shivered, and the prison walls
Fall outward: terribly thou springest forth,
As springs the flame above a burning pile,
And shoutest to the nations, who return
Thy shoutings, while the pale oppressor flies.

Thy birthright was not given by human hands:
Thou wert twin-born with man.   In pleasant
    fields,
While yet our race was few, thou sat'st with him,
To tend the quiet flock and watch the stars,
And teach the reed to utter simple airs.
Thou by his side, amid the tangled wood,
Didst war upon the panther and the wolf,
His only foes; and thou with him didst draw
The earliest furrows on the mountain side,
Soft with the deluge.   Tyranny himself,
Thy enemy, although of reverend look,
Hoary with many years, and far obeyed,
Is later born than thou; and as he meets

The grave defiance of thine elder eye,
The usurper trembles in his fastnesses.

Thou shalt wax stronger with the lapse of years,
But he shall fade into a feebler age;
Feebler, yet subtler. He shall weave his snares,
And spring them on thy careless steps, and clap
His withered hands, and from their ambush call
His hordes to fall upon thee. He shall send
Quaint maskers, forms of fair and gallant mien,
To catch thy gaze, and uttering graceful words
To charm thy ear; while his sly imps, by stealth,
Twine around thee threads of steel, light thread
    on thread,
That grow to fetters; or bind down thy arms
With chains concealed in chaplets. Oh! not yet
May'st thou unbrace thy corselet, nor lay by
Thy sword; nor yet, O Freedom! close thy lids
In slumber; for thine enemy never sleeps,
And thou must watch and combat till the day
Of the new earth and heaven. But wouldst thou
    rest
Awhile from tumult and the frauds of men,
These old and friendly solitudes invite
Thy visit. They, while yet the forest trees
Were young upon the unviolated earth,
And yet the moss-stains on the rock were new,
Beheld thy glorious childhood, and rejoiced.

WILLIAM CULLEN BRYANT.

HALLOWED GROUND.

What 's hallowed ground? Has earth a clod
Its Maker meant not should be trod
By man, the image of his God,
    Erect and free,
Unscourged by Superstition's rod
    To bow the knee?

That 's hallowed ground where, mourned and
    missed,
The lips repose our love has kissed;—
But where 's their memory's mansion? Is 't
    Yon churchyard's bowers?
No! in ourselves their souls exist,
    A part of ours.

A kiss can consecrate the ground
Where mated hearts are mutual bound:
The spot where love's first links were wound,
    That ne'er are riven,
Is hallowed down to earth's profound,
    And up to heaven!

For time makes all but true love old;
The burning thoughts that then were told
Run molten still in memory's mould;
    And will not cool
Until the heart itself be cold
    In Lethe's pool.

What hallows ground where heroes sleep?
'T is not the sculptured piles you heap!
In dews that heavens far distant weep
    Their turf may bloom;
Or Genii twine beneath the deep
    Their coral tomb.

But strew his ashes to the wind
Whose sword or voice has served mankind,—
And is he dead, whose glorious mind
    Lifts thine on high?—
To live in hearts we leave behind
    Is not to die.

Is 't death to fall for Freedom's right?
He 's dead alone that lacks her light!
And murder sullies in heaven's sight
    The sword he draws:—
What can alone ennoble fight?
    A noble cause!

Give that,—and welcome War to brace
Her drums, and rend heaven's reeking space!
The colors planted face to face,
    The charging cheer,
Though Death's pale horse lead on the chase,
    Shall still be dear.

And place our trophies where men kneel
To Heaven!—but Heaven rebukes my zeal!
The cause of Truth and human weal,
    O God above!
Transfer it from the sword's appeal
    To Peace and Love.

Peace, Love! the cherubim, that join
Their spread wings o'er Devotion's shrine,
Prayers sound in vain, and temples shine,
 Where they are not,—
The heart alone can make divine
 Religion's spot.

To incantations dost thou trust,
And pompous rites in domes august?
See mouldering stones and metal's rust
 Belie the vaunt,
That man can bless one pile of dust
 With chime or chant.

The ticking wood-worm mocks thee, man!
Thy temples,—creeds themselves grow wan!
But there 's a dome of nobler span,
 A temple given
Thy faith, that bigots dare not ban,—
 Its space is heaven!

Its roof, star-pictured Nature's ceiling,
Where, trancing the rapt spirit's feeling,
And God himself to man revealing,
 The harmonious spheres
Make music, though unheard their pealing
 By mortal ears.

Fair stars! are not your beings pure?
Can sin, can death, your worlds obscure?
Else why so swell the thoughts at your
 Aspect above?

Ye must be heavens that make us sure
　　Of heavenly love!

And in your harmony sublime
I read the doom of distant time;
That man's regenerate soul from crime
　　Shall yet be drawn,
And reason on his mortal clime
　　Immortal dawn.

What 's hallowed ground? 'T is what gives birth
To sacred thoughts in souls of worth!—
Peace! Independence! Truth! go forth
　　Earth's compass round;
And your high-priesthood shall make earth
　　All hallowed ground.

THOMAS CAMPBELL.

THE WOLF AND THE DOG.

A PROWLING wolf, whose shaggy skin
(So strict the watch of dogs had been)
　　Hid little but his bones,
Once met a mastiff dog astray.
A prouder, fatter, sleeker Tray
　　No human mortal owns.
　　Sir Wolf, in famished plight,
Would fain have made a ration
Upon his fat relation:
　　But then he first must fight;
And well the dog seemed able
To save from wolfish table
　　His carcass snug and tight.

So then in civil conversation
The wolf expressed his admiration
Of Tray's fine case. Said Tray politely,
" Yourself, good sir, may be as sightly;
Quit but the woods, advised by me:
For all your fellows here, I see,
Are shabby wretches, lean and gaunt,
Belike to die of haggard want.
With such a pack, of course it follows,
One fights for every bit he swallows.
    Come then with me, and share
On equal terms our princely fare."
        " But what with you
        Has one to do? "
Inquires the wolf. " Light work indeed,"
Replies the dog: "you only need
To bark a little now and then,
To chase off duns and beggar-men,
To fawn on friends that come or go forth,
Your master please, and so forth ;
    For which you have to eat
    All sorts of well-cooked meat—
Cold pullets, pigeons, savory messes—
Besides unnumbered fond caresses."
    The wolf, by force of appetite,
    Accepts the terms outright,
    Tears glistened in his eyes;
    But faring on, he spies
A galled spot on the mastiff's neck.
" What's that? " he cries. " Oh, nothing but
    a speck."
" A speck? "—" Ay, ay: 't is not enough to pain
    me:

Perhaps the collar's mark by which they chain
    me."
  " Chain! chain you! What! run you not, then,
    Just where you please and when?"
  " Not always, sir; but what of that?"
  " Enough for me, to spoil your fat!
It ought to be a precious price
Which could to servile chains entice;
For me, I 'll shun them while I 've wit."
So ran Sir Wolf, and runneth yet.

From the French of JEAN DE LA FONTAINE.
Translation of ELIZUR WRIGHT.

RIENZI TO THE ROMANS.

FROM " RIENZI."

FRIENDS!

I come not here to talk. Ye know too well
The story of our thraldom. We are slaves!
The bright sun rises to his course, and lights
A race of slaves! he sets, and his last beam
Falls on a slave! Not such as, swept along
By the full tide of power, the conqueror leads
To crimson glory and undying fame,
But base, ignoble slaves!—slaves to a horde
Of petty tyrants, feudal despots; lords
Rich in some dozen paltry villages,
Strong in some hundred spearmen, only great
In that strange spell,—a name! Each hour, dark
    fraud,
Or open rapine, or protected murder,
Cries out against them. But this very day

An honest man, my neighbor (*pointing to* PAOLO),
  —there he stands,—
Was struck—struck like a dog—by one who wore
The badge of Ursini! because, forsooth,
He tossed not high his ready cap in air,
Nor lifted up his voice in servile shouts,
At sight of that great ruffian! Be we men,
And suffer such dishonor? men, and wash not
The stain away in blood? Such shames are com-
  mon.
I have known deeper wrongs. I, that speak to ye,
I had a brother once, a gracious boy,
Full of all gentleness, of calmest hope,
Of sweet and quiet joy; there was the look
Of Heaven upon his face which limners give
To the beloved disciple. How I loved
That gracious boy! younger by fifteen years,
Brother at once and son! He left my side;
A summer bloom on his fair cheeks, a smile
Parting his innocent lips. In one short hour
The pretty, harmless boy was slain! I saw
The corse, the mangled corse, and then I cried
For vengeance! Rouse ye, Romans! Rouse ye,
  slaves!
Have ye brave sons?—Look in the next fierce
  brawl
To see them die! Have ye fair daughters?—Look
To see them live, torn from your arms, distained,
Dishonored; and, if ye dare call for justice,
Be answered by the lash! Yet this is Rome,
That sat on her seven hills, and from her throne
Of beauty ruled the world! Yet we are Romans!
Why, in that elder day, to be a Roman

Was greater than a king! And once again—
Hear me, ye walls, that echoed to the tread
Of either Brutus!—once again, I swear,
The eternal city shall be free; her sons shall walk
    with princes.

            MARY RUSSELL MITFORD.

FALLEN GREECE.

FROM "THE GIAOUR."

CLIME of the unforgotten brave!
Whose land, from plain to mountain-cave,
Was Freedom's home or Glory's grave!
Shrine of the mighty! can it be
That this is all remains of thee?
Approach, thou craven, crouching slave;
    Say, is not this Thermopylæ?
These waters blue that round you lave,
    O servile offspring of the free,—
Pronounce what sea, what shore is this?
The gulf, the rock of Salamis!
These scenes, their story not unknown,
Arise, and make again your own;
Snatch from the ashes of your sires
The embers of their former fires;
And he who in the strife expires
Will add to theirs a name of fear
That Tyranny shall quake to hear,
And leave his sons a hope, a fame,
They too will rather die than shame;
For Freedom's battle once begun,
Bequeathed by bleeding sire to son,

Though baffled oft is ever won.
Bear witness, Greece, thy living page;
Attest it, many a deathless age:
While kings, in dusty darkness hid,
Have left a nameless pyramid,
Thy heroes, though the general doom
Hath swept the column from their tomb,
A mightier monument command,
The mountains of their native land!
There points thy Muse to stranger's eye
The graves of those that cannot die!
'T were long to tell, and sad to trace,
Each step from splendor to disgrace:
Enough,—no foreign foe could quell
Thy soul, till from itself it fell;
Yes! self-abasement paved the way
To villain-bonds and despot sway.

What can he tell who treads thy shore?
  No legend of thine olden time,
No theme on which the Muse might soar,
High as thine own in days of yore,
  When man was worthy of thy clime.
The hearts within thy valleys bred,
The fiery souls that might have led
  Thy sons to deeds sublime,
Now crawl from cradle to the grave,
Slaves—nay, the bondsmen of a slave,
  And callous save to crime.

LORD BYRON.

GREECE ENSLAVED.

FROM "CHILDE HAROLD," CANTO II.

FAIR Greece! sad relic of departed worth!
Immortal, though no more; though fallen,
    great!
Who now shall lead thy scattered children forth,
And long-accustomed bondage uncreate?
Not such thy sons who whilom did await,
The hopeless warriors of a willing doom,
In bleak Thermopylæ's sepulchral strait,—
O, who that gallant spirit shall resume,
Leap from Eurotas' banks, and call thee from the
    tomb?

Spirit of Freedom! when on Phyle's brow
Thou sat'st with Thrasybulus and his train,
Couldst thou forebode the dismal hour which
    now
Dims the green beauties of thine Attic plain?
Not thirty tyrants now enforce the chain,
But every carle can lord it o'er thy land;
Nor rise thy sons, but idly rail in vain,
Trembling beneath the scourge of Turkish hand,
From birth till death enslaved; in word, in deed,
    unmanned.

In all save form alone, how changed! and who
That marks the fire still sparkling in each eye,
Who but would deem their bosoms burned anew

With thy unquenchèd beam, lost Liberty!
And many dream withal the hour is nigh
That gives them back their fathers' heritage;
For foreign arms and aid they fondly sigh,
Nor solely dare encounter hostile rage,
Or tear their name defiled from Slavery's mournful page.

Hereditary bondsmen! know ye not,
Who would be free themselves must strike the blow?
By their right arms the conquest must be wrought?
Will Gaul or Muscovite redress ye? No!
True, they may lay your proud despoilers low,
But not for you will Freedom's altars flame.
Shades of the Helots! triumph o'er your foe!
Greece! change thy lords, thy state is still the same;
Thy glorious day is o'er, but not thy years of shame!

.   .   .   .   .

And yet how lovely in thine age of woe,
Land of lost gods and godlike men, art thou!
Thy vales of evergreen, thy hills of snow,
Proclaim thee Nature's varied favorite now.
Thy fanes, thy temples to thy surface bow,
Commingling slowly with heroic earth,
Broke by the share of every rustic plough:
So perish monuments of mortal birth,
So perish all in turn, save well-recorded worth;

Save where some solitary column mourns
Above its prostrate brethren of the cave;
Save where Tritonia's airy shrine adorns
Colonna's cliff, and gleams along the wave;
Save o'er some warrior's half-forgotten grave,
Where the gray stones and long-neglected grass
Ages, but not oblivion, feebly brave,
While strangers only not regardless pass,
Lingering like me, perchance, to gaze, and sigh
    " Alas! "

Yet are thy skies as blue, thy crags as wild,
Sweet are thy groves, and verdant are thy
    fields,
Thine olive ripe as when Minerva smiled,
And still his honeyed wealth Hymettus
    yields;
There the blithe bee his fragrant fortress
    builds,
The free-born wanderer of thy mountain air;
Apollo still thy long, long summer gilds,
Still in his beam Mendeli's marbles glare:
Art, Glory, Freedom fail, but Nature still is fair.

Where'er we tread, 't is haunted, holy ground;
No earth of thine is lost in vulgar mould,
But one vast realm of wonder spreads around,
And all the Muse's tales seem truly told,
Till the sense aches with gazing to behold
The scenes our earliest dreams have dwelt upon:
Each hill and dale, each deepening glen and
    wold,
9

Defies the power which crushed thy temples
    gone:
Age shakes Athena's tower, but spares gray Mara-
    thon.

LORD BYRON.

SONG OF THE GREEK POET.

FROM "DON JUAN," CANTO III.

THE isles of Greece, the isles of Greece!
  Where burning Sappho loved and sung,
Where grew the arts of war and peace,
  Where Delos rose, and Phœbus sprung!
Eternal summer gilds them yet;
But all, except their sun, is set.

The Scian and the Teian muse,
  The hero's harp, the lover's lute,
Have found the fame your shores refuse;
  Their place of birth alone is mute
To sounds which echo further west
Than your sires' Islands of the Blest.

The mountains look on Marathon,
  And Marathon looks on the sea:
And musing there an hour alone,
  I dreamed that Greece might still be free;
For, standing on the Persians' grave,
I could not deem myself a slave.

A king sat on the rocky brow
  Which looks o'er sea-born Salamis;

And ships, by thousands, lay below,
    And men in nations—all were his!
He counted them at break of day—
    And when the sun set, where were they?

And where are they? and where art thou,
    My country? On thy voiceless shore
The heroic lay is tuneless now,
    The heroic bosom beats no more!
And must thy lyre, so long divine,
Degenerate into hands like mine?

'T is something in the dearth of fame,
    Though linked among a fettered race,
To feel at least a patriot's shame,
    Even as I sing, suffuse my face;
For what is left the poet here?
For Greeks a blush—for Greece a tear.

Must we but weep o'er days more blest?
    Must we but blush? Our fathers bled.
Earth! render back from out thy breast
    A remnant of our Spartan dead!
Of the three hundred grant but three,
To make a new Thermopylæ!

What! silent still? and silent all?
    Ah no!—the voices of the dead
Sound like a distant torrent's fall,
    And answer, " Let one living head,
But one, arise—we come, we come! "
'T is but the living who are dumb.

In vain,—in vain; strike other chords;
　Fill high the cup with Samian wine!
Leave battles to the Turkish hordes,
　And shed the blood of Scio's vine!
Hark! rising to the ignoble call,
How answers each bold Bacchanal!

You have the Pyrrhic dance as yet,—
　Where is the Pyrrhic phalanx gone?
Of two such lessons, why forget
　The nobler and the manlier one?
You have the letters Cadmus gave,—
Think ye he meant them for a slave?

Fill high the bowl with Samian wine!
　We will not think of themes like these!
It made Anacreon's song divine:
　He served, but served Polycrates,—
A tyrant; but our masters then
Were still, at least, our countrymen.

The tyrant of the Chersonese
　Was freedom's best and bravest friend;
That tyrant was Miltiades!
　O that the present hour would lend
Another despot of the kind!
Such chains as his were sure to bind.

Fill high the bowl with Samian wine!
　On Suli's rock and Parga's shore
Exists the remnant of a line
　Such as the Doric mothers bore;

And there perhaps some seed is sown
The Heracleidan blood might own.

Trust not for freedom to the Franks,—
    They have a king who buys and sells:
In native swords, and native ranks,
    The only hope of courage dwells;
But Turkish force, and Latin fraud,
Would break your shield, however broad.

Fill high the bowl with Samian wine!
    Our virgins dance beneath the shade,—
I see their glorious black eyes shine;
    But, gazing on each glowing maid,
My own the burning tear-drop laves,
To think such breasts must suckle slaves.

Place me on Sunium's marbled steep,
    Where nothing, save the waves and I,
May hear our mutual murmurs sweep;
    There, swan-like, let me sing and die.
A land of slaves shall ne'er be mine,—
Dash down yon cup of Samian wine!

                              LORD BYRON.

TO ALTHEA FROM PRISON.

WHEN Love with unconfinèd wings
    Hovers within my gates,
And by divine Althea brings
    To whisper at my grates;
When I lie tangled in her hair
    And fettered with her eye,

The birds that wanton in the air
Know no such liberty.

When flowing cups pass swiftly round
With no allaying Thames,
Our careless heads with roses crowned,
Our hearts with loyal flames;
When thirsty grief in wine we steep,
When healths and draughts go free,
Fishes that tipple in the deep
Know no such liberty.

When, like committed linnets, I
With shriller throat shall sing
The mercy, sweetness, majesty
And glories of my King;
When I shall voice aloud, how good
He is, how great should be,
Enlargèd winds that curl the flood
Know no such liberty.

Stone walls do not a prison make,
Nor iron bars a cage;
Minds innocent and quiet take
That for an hermitage:
If I have freedom in my love,
And in my soul am free,
Angels alone, that soar above,
Enjoy such liberty.

RICHARD LOVELACE.

SLAVERY.

FROM " THE TIMEPIECE " : " THE TASK," BK. II.

O FOR a lodge in some vast wilderness,
Some boundless contiguity of shade,
Where rumor of oppression and deceit,
Of unsuccessful or successful war,
Might never reach me more! My ear is pained,
My soul is sick, with every day's report
Of wrong and outrage with which earth is filled.
There is no flush in man's obdúrate heart;
It does not feel for man; the natural bond
Of brotherhood is served as the flax,
That falls asunder at the touch of fire.
He finds his fellow guilty of a skin
Not colored like his own, and, having power
To enforce the wrong, for such a worthy cause
Dooms and devotes him as his lawful prey.
Lands intersected by a narrow frith
Abhor each other. Mountains interposed
Make enemies of nations, who had else
Like kindred drops been mingled into one.
Thus man devotes his brother, and destroys;
And, worse than all, and most to be deplored
As human nature's broadest, foulest blot,
Chains him, and tasks him, and exacts his sweat
With stripes, that Mercy, with a bleeding heart,
Weeps, when she sees inflicted on a beast.
Then what is man? And what man, seeing this,
And having human feelings, does not blush,
And hang his head, to think himself a man?

I would not have a slave to till my ground,
To carry me, to fan me while I sleep,
And tremble when I wake, for all the wealth
That sinews bought and sold have ever earned.
No; dear as freedom is, and in my heart's
Just estimation prized above all price,
I had much rather be myself the slave,
And wear the bonds, than fasten them on him.
We have no slaves at home.—Then why abroad?
And they themselves, once ferried o'er the wave
That parts us, are emancipate and loosed.
Slaves cannot breathe in England; if their lungs
Receive our air, that moment they are free;
They touch our country, and their shackles fall.
That's noble, and bespeaks a nation proud
And jealous of the blessing. Spread it then,
And let it circulate through every vein
Of all your empire; that, where Britain's power
Is felt, mankind may feel her mercy too.

WILLIAM COWPER.

SONG OF THE WESTERN MEN.

[After the English Revolution of 1688, all bishops were
compelled to swear allegiance to William and Mary.
Seven of them, adherents of James II., refused and were
imprisoned for treason,—the "Non-Jurors." Trelawney
of Cornwall was one.]

A GOOD sword and a trusty hand,
  A merry heart and true,
King James's men shall understand
  What Cornish lads can do.

And have they fixed the where and when,
  And shall Trelawney die?
Then twenty thousand Cornish men
  Will know the reason why.
What! will they scorn Tre, Pol, and Pen?
  And shall Trelawney die?
Then twenty thousand under ground
  Will know the reason why.

Out spake the captain brave and bold,
  A merry wight was he:
" Though London's Tower were Michael's hold,
  We 'll set Trelawney free.
We 'll cross the Tamar hand to hand,
  The Exe shall be no stay;
We 'll side by side from strand to strand,
  And who shall bid us nay?
What! will they scorn Tre, Pol, and Pen?
  And shall Trelawney die?
Then twenty thousand Cornish men
  Will know the reason why.

" And when we come to London wall
  We 'll shout with it in view,
' Come forth, come forth, ye cowards all!
  We 're better men than you!
Trelawney, he 's in keep and hold,
  Trelawney, he may die;
But here 's twenty thousand Cornish bold
  Will know the reason why!'
What! will they scorn Tre, Pol, and Pen?
  And shall Trelawney die?
Then twenty thousand under ground
  Will know the reason why."

ROBERT STEPHEN HAWKER.

THE HARP THAT ONCE THROUGH TARA'S HALLS.

The harp that once through Tara's halls
    The soul of music shed,
Now hangs as mute on Tara's walls
    As if that soul were fled.
So sleeps the pride of former days,
    So glory's thrill is o'er,
And hearts that once beat high for praise
    Now feel that pulse no more!

No more to chiefs and ladies bright
    The harp of Tara swells;
The chord alone that breaks at night
    Its tale of ruin tells.
Thus Freedom now so seldom wakes,
    The only throb she gives
Is when some heart indignant breaks,
    To show that still she lives.

                  THOMAS MOORE.

AS BY THE SHORE AT BREAK OF DAY.

As by the shore, at break of day,
A vanquished chief expiring lay,
Upon the sands, with broken sword,
    He traced his farewell to the free;
And there the last unfinished word
    He dying wrote, was " Liberty! "

At night a sea-bird shrieked the knell
Of him who thus for freedom fell:
The·words he wrote, ere evening came,
    Were covered by the sounding sea;—
So pass away the cause and name
Of him who dies for liberty!

THOMAS MOORE.

THE HILLS WERE MADE FOR FREEDOM.

WHEN freedom from her home was driven,
    'Mid vine-clad vales of Switzerland,
She sought the glorious Alps of heaven,
And there, 'mid cliffs by lightnings riven,
    Gathered her hero-band.

And still outrings her freedom-song,
    Amid the glaciers sparkling there,
At Sabbath bell, as peasants throng
Their mountain fastnesses along,
    Happy, and free as air.

The hills were made for freedom; they
    Break at a breath the tyrant's rod;
Chains clank in valleys; there the prey
Writhes 'neath Oppression's heel alway:
    Hills bow to none but God!

WILLIAM GOLDSMITH BROWN.

SWITZERLAND.

FROM " WILLIAM TELL."

ONCE Switzerland was free! With what a pride
I used to walk these hills,—look up to heaven,
And bless God that it was so! It was free
From end to end, from cliff to lake 't was free!
Free as our torrents are, that leap our rocks,
And plough our valleys, without asking leave;
Or as our peaks, that wear their caps of snow
In very presence of the regal sun!
How happy was I in it then! I loved
Its very storms. Ay, often have I sat
In my boat at night, when, midway o'er the lake,
The stars went out, and down the mountain gorge
The wind came roaring,—I have sat and eyed
The thunder breaking from his cloud, and smiled
To see him shake his lightnings o'er my head,
And think—I had no master save his own!

JAMES SHERIDAN KNOWLES.

MAKE WAY FOR LIBERTY!

[Battle of Sempach, fourteenth century.]

"MAKE way for Liberty!"—he cried;
Made way for Liberty, and died!
   In arms the Austrian phalanx stood,
A living wall, a human wood!
A wall, where every conscious stone
Seemed to its kindred thousands grown;

A rampart all assaults to bear,
Till time to dust their frames should wear;
A wood like that enchanted grove
In which with fiends Rinaldo strove,
Where every silent tree possessed
A spirit prisoned in its breast,
Which the first stroke of coming strife
Would startle into hideous life:
So dense, so still, the Austrians stood,
A living wall, a human wood!
Impregnable their front appears,
All horrent with projected spears,
Whose polished points before them shine,
From flank to flank, one brilliant line,
Bright as the breakers' splendors run
Along the billows to the sun.

Opposed to these, a hovering band
Contended for their native land:
Peasants, whose new-found strength had broke
From manly necks the ignoble yoke,
And forged their fetters into swords,
On equal terms to fight their lords,
And what insurgent rage had gained
In many a mortal fray maintained:
Marshalled once more at Freedom's call,
They came to conquer or to fall,
Where he who conquered, he who fell,
Was deemed a dead, or living, Tell!
Such virtues had that patriot breathed,
So to the soil his soul bequeathed,
That wheresoe'er his arrows flew
Heroes in his own likeness grew,

And warriors sprang from every sod
Which his awakening footstep trod.

And now the work of life and death
Hung on the passing of a breath;
The fire of conflict burned within,
The battle trembled to begin:
Yet, while the Austrians held their ground,
Point for attack was nowhere found;
Where'er the impatient Switzers gazed,
The unbroken line of lances blazed:
That line 't were suicide to meet,
And perish at their tyrants' feet,—
How could they rest within their graves,
And leave their homes the homes of slaves?
Would they not feel their children tread
With clanging chains above their head?

It must not be: this day, this hour,
Annihilates the oppressor's power;
All Switzerland is in the field,
She will not fly, she cannot yield,—
She must not fall; her better fate
Here gives her an immortal date.
Few were the numbers she could boast;
But every freeman was a host,
And felt as though himself were he
On whose sole arm hung victory.

It did depend on *one* indeed;
Behold him,—Arnold Winkelried!
There sounds not to the trump of fame
The echo of a nobler name.

Unmarked he stood amid the throng,
In rumination deep and long,
Till you might see, with sudden grace,
The very thought come o'er his face,
And by the motion of his form
Anticipate the bursting storm,
And by the uplifting of his brow
Tell where the bolt would strike, and how.

But 't was no sooner thought than done,
The field was in a moment won:—

"Make way for Liberty!" he cried,
Then ran, with arms extended wide,
As if his dearest friend to clasp;
Ten spears he swept within his grasp.

"Make way for Liberty!" he cried;
Their keen points met from side to side;
He bowed amongst them like a tree,
And thus made way for Liberty.

Swift to the breach his comrades fly;
"Make way for Liberty!" they cry,
And through the Austrian phalanx dart,
As rushed the spears through Arnold's heart;
While, instantaneous as his fall,
Rout, ruin, panic, scattered all:
An earthquake could not overthrow
A city with a surer blow.

Thus Switzerland again was free;
Thus Death made way for Liberty!

JAMES MONTGOMERY.

POLAND.

FROM "THE PLEASURES OF HOPE," PART I.

O SACRED Truth! thy triumph ceased awhile,
And Hope, thy sister, ceased with thee to smile,
When leagued Oppression poured to Northern
    wars
Her whiskered pandours and her fierce hussars,
Waved her dread standard to the breeze of morn,
Pealed her loud drum, and twanged her trumpet
    horn;
Tumultuous horror brooded o'er her van,
Presaging wrath to Poland—and to man!
  Warsaw's last champion from her height sur-
    veyed,
Wide o'er the fields, a waste of ruin laid;
"O Heaven!" he cried, "my bleeding country
    save!—
Is there no hand on high to shield the brave?
Yet, though destruction sweep these lovely plains,
Rise, fellow-men! our country yet remains!
By that dread name, we wave the sword on high,
And swear for her to live—with her to die!"
  He said, and on the rampart-heights arrayed
His trusty warriors, few, but undismayed;
Firm-paced and slow, a horrid front they form,
Still as the breeze, but dreadful as the storm;
Low murmuring sounds along their banners fly,
Revenge, or death,—the watchword and reply;
Then pealed the notes, omnipotent to charm,
And the loud tocsin tolled their last alarm!—

In vain, alas! in vain, ye gallant few!
From rank to rank your volleyed thunder flew:—
O, bloodiest picture in the book of Time!
Sarmatia fell, unwept, without a crime;
Found not a generous friend, a pitying foe,
Strength in her arms, nor mercy in her woe!
Dropped from her nerveless grasp the shattered
  spear,
Closed her bright eye, and curbed her high career;
Hope, for a season, bade the world farewell,
And Freedom shrieked—as Kosciusko fell!

THOMAS CAMPBELL.

THE MARSEILLAISE.

YE sons of freedom, wake to glory!
  Hark! hark! what myriads bid you rise!
Your children, wives, and grandsires hoary,
  Behold their tears and hear their cries!
Shall hateful tyrants, mischiefs breeding,
    With hireling hosts, a ruffian band,
    Affright and desolate the land,
While peace and liberty lie bleeding?
    To arms! to arms! ye brave!
    The avenging sword unsheathe;
    March on! march on! all hearts resolved
    On victory or death.

Now, now the dangerous storm is rolling,
  Which treacherous kings confederate raise;
The dogs of war, let loose, are howling,
  And lo! our fields and cities blaze;

10

And shall we basely view the ruin,
    While lawless force, with guilty stride,
    Spreads desolation far and wide,
With crimes and blood his hands imbruing?
    To arms! to arms! ye brave, etc.

O Liberty! can man resign thee,
    Once having felt thy generous flame?
Can dungeons, bolts, or bars confine thee?
    Or whips thy noble spirit tame?
Too long the world has wept, bewailing
    That falsehood's dagger tyrants wield,
    But freedom is our sword and shield,
And all their arts are unavailing.
    To arms! to arms! ye brave, etc,

From the French of CLAUDE JOSEPH ROUGET DE LISLE.

A COURT LADY.

HER hair was tawny with gold, her eyes with purple were dark,
Her cheeks' pale opal burnt with a red and restless spark.

Never was lady of Milan nobler in name and in race;
Never was lady of Italy fairer to see in the face.

Never was lady on earth more true as woman and wife,
Larger in judgment and instinct, prouder in manners and life.

She stood in the early morning, and said to her
    maidens, " Bring
That silken robe made ready to wear at the court
    of the king.

" Bring me the clasps of diamonds, lucid, clear
    of the mote,
Clasp me the large at the waist, and clasp me
    the small at the throat.

" Diamonds to fasten the hair, and diamonds to
    fasten the sleeves,
Laces to drop from their rays, like a powder of
    snow from the eaves."

Gorgeous she entered the sunlight which gathered
    her up in a flame,
While straight, in her open carriage, she to the
    hospital came.

In she went at the door, and gazing, from end to
    end,
" Many and low are the pallets, but each is the
    place of a friend."

Up she passed through the wards, and stood at a
    young man's bed :
Bloody the band on his brow, and livid the droop
    of his head.

" Art thou a Lombard, my brother? Happy art
    thou ! " she cried,
And smiled like Italy on him : he dreamed in her
    face and died.

Pale with his passing soul, she went on still to a
   second:
He was a grave, hard man, whose years by dungeons were reckoned.

Wounds in his body were sore, wounds in his life
   were sorer.
" Art thou a Romagnole? " Her eyes drove lightnings before her.

" Austrian and priest had joined to double and
   tighten the cord
Able to bind thee, O strong one,—free by the
   stroke of a sword.

" Now be grave for the rest of us, using the life
   overcast
To ripen our wine of the present (too new) in
   glooms of the past."

Down she stepped to a pallet where lay a face
   like a girl's,
Young, pathetic with dying,—a deep black hole in
   the curls.

" Art thou from Tuscany, brother? and seest thou,
   dreaming in pain,
Thy mother stand in the piazza, searching the list
   of the slain? "

Kind as a mother herself, she touched his cheeks
   with her hands:
" Blessèd is she who has borne thee, although she
   should weep as she stands."

On she passed to a Frenchman, his arm carried
   off by a ball:
Kneeling, . . "O more than my brother! how
   shall I thank thee for all?

"Each of the heroes round us has fought for his
   land and line,
But *thou* hast fought for a stranger, in hate of a
   wrong not thine.

"Happy are all free peoples, too strong to be dis-
   possessed;
But blessèd are those among nations who dare to
   be strong for the rest!"

Ever she passed on her way, and came to a couch
   where pined
One with a face from Venetia, white with a hope
   out of mind.

Long she stood and gazed, and twice she tried at
   the name,
But two great crystal tears were all that faltered
   and came.

Only a tear for Venice?—she turned as in passion
   and loss,
And stooped to his forehead and kissed it, as if she
   were kissing the cross.

Faint with that strain of heart, she moved on then
   to another,
Stern and strong in his death. "And dost thou
   suffer, my brother?"

Holding his hands in hers:—" Out of the Piedmont lion
Cometh the sweetness of freedom! sweetest to live
or to die on."

Holding his cold, rough hands,—" Well, O, well
have ye done
In noble, noble Piedmont, who would not be noble
alone."

Back he fell while she spoke.   She rose to her
feet with a spring,—
" That was a Piedmontese! and this is the Court
of the King."

ELIZABETH BARRETT BROWNING.

THE LANDING OF THE PILGRIM FATHERS IN NEW ENGLAND.

THE breaking waves dashed high
　　On a stern and rock-bound coast,
And the woods against a stormy sky
　　Their giant branches tossed;

And the heavy night hung dark
　　The hills and waters o'er,
When a band of exiles moored their bark
　　On the wild New England shore.

Not as the conqueror comes,
　　They, the true-hearted, came;
Not with the roll of the stirring drums,
　　And the trumpet that sings of fame:

Not as the flying come,
    In silence and in fear;—
They shook the depths of the desert gloom
    With their hymns of lofty cheer.

Amidst the storm they sang,
    And the stars heard, and the sea;
And the sounding aisles of the dim woods rang
    To the anthem of the free.

The ocean eagle soared
    From his nest by the white wave's foam,
And the rocking pines of the forest roared,—
    This was their welcome home.

There were men with hoary hair
    Amidst that pilgrim-band:
Why had they come to wither there,
    Away from their childhood's land?

There was woman's fearless eye,
    Lit by her deep love's truth;
There was manhood's brow serenely high,
    And the fiery heart of youth.

What sought they thus afar?
    Bright jewels of the mine?
The wealth of the seas, the spoils of war?—
    They sought a faith's pure shrine!

Ay, call it holy ground,
    The soil where first they trod;
They have left unstained what there they found,—
    Freedom to worship God.

                              FELICIA HEMANS.

THE AMERICAN FLAG.

WHEN Freedom, from her mountain height,
    Uufurled her standard to the air,
She tore the azure robe of night,
    And set the stars of glory there!
She mingled with its gorgeous dyes
The milky baldric of the skies,
And striped its pure, celestial white
With streakings of the morning light;
Then, from his mansion in the sun,
She called her eagle-bearer down,
And gave into his mighty hand
The symbol of her chosen land!

Majestic monarch of the cloud!
    Who rear'st aloft thy regal form,
To hear the tempest trumping loud,
And see the lightning lances driven,
    When strive the warriors of the storm,
And rolls the thunder-drum of heaven,—
Child of the Sun! to thee 't is given
    To guard the banner of the free,
To hover in the sulphur smoke,
To ward away the battle-stroke,
And bid its blendings shine afar,
Like rainbows on the cloud of war,
    The harbingers of victory!

Flag of the brave! thy folds shall fly,
The sign of hope and triumph high!

When speaks the signal-trumpet tone,
And the long line comes gleaming on,
Ere yet the life-blood, warm and wet,
Has dimmed the glistening bayonet,
Each soldier's eye shall brightly turn
To where thy sky-born glories burn,
And, as his springing steps advance,
Catch war and vengeance from the glance.

And when the cannon-mouthings loud
Heave in wild wreaths the battle shroud,
And gory sabres rise and fall
Like shoots of flame on midnight's pall,
Then shall thy meteor glances glow,
    And cowering foes shall shrink beneath
Each gallant arm that strikes below
    That lovely messenger of death.

Flag of the seas! on ocean wave
Thy stars shall glitter o'er the brave;
When death, careering on the gale,
Sweeps darkly round the bellied sail,
And frighted waves rush wildly back
Before the broadside's reeling rack,
Each dying wanderer of the sea
Shall look at once to heaven and thee,
And smile to see thy splendors fly
In triumph o'er his closing eye.

Flag of the free heart's hope and home,
    By angel hands to valor given!
Thy stars have lit the welkin dome,
    And all thy hues were born in heaven.

Forever float that standard sheet!
Where breathes the foe but falls before us,
With Freedom's soil beneath our feet,
And Freedom's banner streaming o'er us!

JOSEPH RODMAN DRAKE.

THE STAR–BANGLED BANNER.*

O, SAY, can you see by the dawn's early light
What so proudly we hailed at the twilight's last
gleaming?—
Whose broad stripes and bright stars, through the
clouds of the fight
O'er the ramparts we watched, were so gallantly
streaming!
And the rocket's red glare, the bombs bursting in
air,
Gave proof through the night that our flag was
still there;
O! say, does that star-spangled banner yet wave
O'er the land of the free, and the home of the
brave?

On that shore, dimly seen through the mists of the
deep,
Where the foe's haughty host in dread silence re-
poses,
What is that which the breeze, o'er the towering
steep,
As it fitfully blows, now conceals, now discloses?

* Begun during the attack on Fort McHenry, by a British
fleet, which on the night of Sept. 12, 1814, unsuccessfully
bombarded that fort from the river Chesapeake; the
author, an envoy from the city of Baltimore, having been
detained as a prisoner on the fleet.

Now it catches the gleam of the morning's first
beam,
In full glory reflected now shines on the stream;
'T is the star-spangled banner! O, long may it
wave
O'er the land of the free, and the home of the
brave!

And where is that band who so vauntingly swore
That the havoc of war and the battle's confusion
A home and a country should leave us no more?
Their blood has washed out their foul footsteps'
pollution.
No refuge could save the hireling and slave
From the terror of flight, or the gloom of the
grave;
And the star-spangled oanner in triumph doth
wave
O'er the land of the free, and the home of the
brave!

O! thus be it ever, when freemen shall stand
Between their loved homes and the war's deso-
lation!
Blest with vict'ry and peace, may the Heaven-
rescued land
Praise the Power that hath made and preserved
us a nation.
Then conquer we must, when our cause it is just,
And this be our motto. "*In God is our trust:*"
And the star-spangled banner in triumph shall
wave
O'er the land of the free, and the home of the
brave.

FRANCIS SCOTT KEY.

NEW ENGLAND'S DEAD.

NEW ENGLAND's dead! New England's dead!
  On every hill they lie;
On every field of strife, made red
  By bloody victory.
Each valley, where the battle poured
  Its red and awful tide,
Beheld the brave New England sword
  With slaughter deeply dyed.
Their bones are on the northern hill,
  And on the southern plain,
By brook and river, lake and rill,
  And by the roaring main.

The land is holy where they fought,
  And holy where they fell;
For by their blood that land was bought,
  The land they loved so well,
Then glory to that valiant band,
The honored saviours of the land!

O, few and weak their numbers were,—
  A handful of brave men;
But to their God they gave their prayer,
  And rushed to battle then.
The God of battles heard their cry,
And sent to them the victory.

They left the ploughshare in the mold,
Their flocks and herds without a fold,

The sickle in the unshorn grain,
The corn, half-garnered, on the plain,
And mustered, in their simple dress,
For wrongs to seek a stern redress,
To right those wrongs, come weal, come woe,
To perish, or o'ercome their foe.

And where are ye, O fearless men?
  And where are ye to-day?
I call:—the hills reply again
  That ye have passed away;
That on old Bunker's lonely height,
  In Trenton, and in Monmouth ground,
The grass grows green, the harvest bright
  Above each soldier's mound.
The bugle's wild and warlike blast
  Shall muster them no more;
An army now might thunder past,
  And they heed not its roar.
The starry flag, 'neath which they fought
  In many a bloody day,
From their old graves shall rouse them not,
  For they have passed away.

ISAAC M'LELLAN.

THE REFORMER.

ALL grim and soiled and brown and tan,
  I saw a Strong One, in his wrath,
Smiting the godless shrines of man
  Along his path.

The Church beneath her trembling dome
  Essayed in vain her ghostly charm:

Wealth shook within his gilded home
　　With strange alarm.

Fraud from his secret chambers fled
　　Before the sunlight bursting in:
Sloth drew her pillow o'er her head
　　To drown the din.

"Spare," Art implored, "yon holy pile;
　　That grand old time-worn turret spare:"
Meek Reverence, kneeling in the aisle
　　Cried out, "Forbear!"

Gray-bearded Use, who, deaf and blind,
　　Groped for his old accustomed stone,
Leaned on his staff, and wept to find
　　His seat o'erthrown.

Young Romance raised his dreamy eyes,
　　O'erhung with paly locks of gold,—
"Why smite," he asked in sad surprise,
　　"The fair, the old?"

Yet louder rang the Strong One's stroke,
　　Yet nearer flashed his axe's gleam;
Shuddering and sick of heart I woke,
　　As from a dream.

I looked: aside the dust-cloud rolled,—
　　The Waster seemed the Builder too;
Upspringing from the ruined Old
　　I saw the New.

'T was but the ruin of the bad,—
  The wasting of the wrong and ill;
Whate'er of good the old time had
    Was living still.

Calm grew the brows of him I feared,
  The frown which awed me passed away,
And left behind a smile which cheered
    Like breaking day.

The grain grew green on battle-plains,
  O'er swarded war-mounds grazed the cow;
The slave stood forging from his chains
    The spade and plough.

Where frowned the fort, pavilions gay
  And cottage windows, flower-entwined,
Looked out upon the peaceful bay
    And hills behind.

Through vine-wreathed cups with wine once red.
  The lights on brimming crystal fell,
Drawn, sparkling, from the rivulet head
    And mossy well.

Through prison-walls, like Heaven-sent hope,
  Fresh breezes blew, and sunbeams strayed,
And with the idle gallows-rope
    The young child played.

Where the doomed victim in his cell
  Had counted o'er the weary hours,

Glad school-girls, answering to the bell,
  Came crowned with flowers.

Grown wiser for the lesson given,
  I fear no longer, for I know
That where the share is deepest driven
  The best fruits grow.

The outworn rite, the old abuse,
  The pious fraud transparent grown,
The good held captive in the use
  Of wrong alone,—

These wait their doom, from that great law
  Which makes the past time serve to-day;
And fresher life the world shall draw
  From their decay.

O backward-looking son of time!
  The new is old, the old is new,
The cycle of a change sublime
  Still sweeping through.

So wisely taught the Indian seer;
  Destroying Seva, forming Brahm,
Who wake by turn Earth's love and fear,
  Are one, the same.

Idly as thou, in that old day
  Thou mournest, did thy sire repine;
So, in his time, thy child grown gray
  Shall sigh for thine.

But life shall on and upward go;
   The eternal step of Progress beats
To that great anthem, calm and slow,
   Which God repeats.

Take heart!—the Waster builds again,—
   A charmèd life old Goodness hath;
The tares may perish,—but the grain
   Is not for death.

God works in all things; all obey
   His first propulsion from the night:
Wake thou and watch!—the world is gray
   With morning light!

JOHN GREENLEAF WHITTIER.

FREEDOM OF THE MIND.

WRITTEN WHILE IN PRISON FOR DENOUNCING THE
DOMESTIC SLAVE-TRADE.

High walls and huge the body may confine,
   And iron gates obstruct the prisoner's gaze,
And massive bolts may baffle his design,
   And vigilant keepers watch his devious ways;
But scorns the immortal mind such base control:
   No chains can bind it and no cell enclose.
Swifter than light it flies from pole to pole,
   And in a flash from earth to heaven it goes.
It leaps from mount to mount; from vale to vale
   It wanders, plucking honeyed fruits and
      flowers;
It visits home to hear the fireside tale
   And in sweet converse pass the joyous hours;
'T is up before the sun, roaming afar,
And in its watches wearies every star.

11   WILLIAM LLOYD GARRISON.

THE PRESENT CRISIS.

WHEN a deed is done for Freedom, through the
    broad earth's aching breast
Runs a thrill of joy prophetic, trembling on from
    east to west,
And the slave, where'er he cowers, feels the soul
    within him climb
To the awful verge of manhood, as the energy
    sublime
Of a century bursts full-blossomed on the thorny
    stem of Time.

Through the walls of hut and palace shoots the
    instantaneous throe,
When the travail of the Ages wrings earth's sys-
    tems to and fro;
At the birth of each new Era, with a recognizing
    start,
Nation wildly looks at nation, standing with mute
    lips apart,
And glad Truth's yet mightier man-child leaps be-
    neath the Future's heart.

So the Evil's triumph sendeth, with a terror and
    a chill,
Under continent to continent, the sense of coming
    ill,
And the slave, where'er he cowers, feels his sym-
    pathies with God
In hot tear-drops ebbing earthward, to be drunk
    up by the sod,
Till a corpse crawls round unburied, delving in
    the nobler clod.

For mankind are one in spirit, and an instinct
  bears along,
Round the earth's electric circle, the swift flush
  of right or wrong;
Whether conscious or unconscious, yet Humanity's vast frame
Through its ocean-sundered fibres feels the gush
  of joy or shame;—
In the gain or loss of one race all the rest have
  equal claim.

Once to every man and nation comes the moment
  to decide,
In the strife of Truth with Falsehood, for the
  good or evil side;
Some great cause, God's new Messiah, offering
  each the bloom or blight,
Parts the goats upon the left hand, and the sheep
  upon the right,
And the choice goes by forever 'twixt that darkness and that light.

Hast thou chosen, O my people, on whose party
  thou shalt stand,
Ere the Doom from its worn sandals shakes the
  dust against our land?
Though the cause of Evil prosper, yet 't is Truth
  alone is strong,
And, albeit she wander outcast now, I see around
  her throng
Troops of beautiful, tall angels, to enshield her
  from all wrong.

Backward look across the ages and the beacon-
moments see,
That, like peaks of some sunk continent, jut
through Oblivion's sea;
Not an ear in court or market for the low foreboding cry
Of those Crises, God's stern winnowers, from
whose feet earth's chaff must fly;
Never shows the choice momentous till the judgment hath passed by.

Careless seems the great Avenger; history's pages
but record
One death-grapple in the darkness 'twixt old sys-
tems and the Word;
Truth forever on the scaffold, Wrong forever on
the throne,—
Yet that scaffold sways the Future, and, behind
the dim unknown,
Standeth God within the shadow, keeping watch
above his òwn.

We see dimly in the Present what is small and
what is great,
Slow of faith, how weak an arm may turn the iron
helm of fate,
But the soul is still oracular; amid the market's
din,
List the ominous stern whisper from the Delphic
cave within,—
" They enslave their children's children who make
compromise with sin."

Slavery, the earthborn Cyclops, fellest of the giant
  brood,
Sons of brutish Force and Darkness, who have
  drenched the earth with blood,
Famished in his self-made desert, blinded by our
  purer day,
Gropes in yet unblasted regions for his miserable
  prey;—
Shall we guide his gory fingers where our helpless
  children play?

Then to side with Truth is noble when we share
  her wretched crust,
Ere her cause bring fame and profit, and 't is prosperous to be just;
Then it is the brave man chooses, while the coward
  stands aside,
Doubting in his abject spirit, till his Lord is cru-
  cified,
And the multitude make virtue of the faith they
  had denied.

Count me o'er earth's chosen heroes,—they were
  souls that stood alone,
While the men they agonized for hurled the con-
  tumelious stone,
Stood serene, and down the future saw the golden
  beam incline
To the side of perfect justice, mastered by their
  faith divine,
By one man's plain truth to manhood and to God's
  supreme design.

By the light of burning heretics Christ's bleeding
    feet I track,
Toiling up new Calvaries ever with the cross that
    turns not back,
And these mounts of anguish number how each
    generation learned
One new word of that grand *Credo* which in
    prophet-hearts hath burned
Since the first man stood God-conquered with his
    face to heaven upturned.

For Humanity sweeps onward : where to-day the
    martyr stands,
On the morrow crouches Judas with the silver in
    his hands;
Far in front the cross stands ready and the crack-
    ling fagots burn,
While the hooting mob of yesterday in silent awe
    return
To glean up the scattered ashes into History's
    golden urn.

'T is as easy to be heroes as to sit the idle slaves
Of a legendary virtue carved upon our fathers'
    graves,
Worshippers of light ancestral make the present
    light a crime;—
Was the Mayflower launched by cowards, steered
    by men behind their time?
Turn those tracks toward Past or Future, that
    make Plymouth rock sublime?

They were men of present valor, stalwart old
    iconoclasts,

Unconvinced by axe or gibbet that all virtue was
   the Past's;
But we make their truth our falsehood, thinking
   that hath made us free,
Hoarding it in mouldy parchments, while our tender spirits flee
The rude grasp of that Impulse which drove them
   across the sea.

They have rights who dare maintain them; we are
   traitors to our sires,
Smothering in their holy ashes Freedom's new-
   lit altar-fires;
Shall we make their creed our jailer?   Shall we,
   in our haste to slay,
From the tombs of the old prophets steal the
   funeral lamps away
To light up the martyr-fagots round the prophets
   of to-day?

New occasions teach new duties; Time makes ancient good uncouth;
They must upward still, and onward, who would
   keep abreast of Truth;
Lo, before us gleam her camp-fires! we ourselves
   must Pilgrims be,
Launch our Mayflower, and steer boldly through
   the desperate winter sea,
Nor attempt the Future's portal with the Past's
   blood-rusted key.
   December, 1845.

                    JAMES RUSSELL LOWELL.

THE LITTLE CLOUD.*

[1853.]

As when, on Carmel's sterile steep,
  The ancient prophet bowed the knee,
And seven times sent his servant forth
  To look toward the distant sea;

There came at last a little cloud,
  Scarce larger than the human hand,
Spreading and swelling till it broke
  In showers on all the herbless land;

And hearts were glad, and shouts went up,
  And praise to Israel's mighty God,
As the sear hills grew bright with flowers,
  And verdure clothed the valley sod,—

Even so our eyes have waited long;
  But now a little cloud appears,
Spreading and swelling as it glides
  Onward into the coming years.

Bright cloud of Liberty! full soon,
  Far stretching from the ocean strand,
Thy glorious folds shall spread abroad,
  Encircling our beloved land.

* Arousing of Anti-Slavery agitation, when it was proposed in Congress to abolish the 'Missouri Compromise"
and throw open the Territories to slavery if their people
should so vote.

Like the sweet rain on Judah's hills,
  The glorious boon of love shall fall,
And our bond millions shall arise,
  As at an angel's trumpet-call.

Then shall a shout of joy go up,—
  The wild, glad cry of freedom come
From hearts long crushed by cruel hands,
  And songs from lips long sealed and dumb;

And every bondman's chain be broke,
  And every soul that moves abroad
In this wide realm shall know and feel
  The blessèd Liberty of God.

JOHN HOWARD BRYANT.

BROWN OF OSSAWATOMIE.

JOHN BROWN OF OSSAWATOMIE spake on his dying
  day:
"I will not have to shrive my soul a priest in
  Slavery's pay;
But let some poor slave-mother whom I have
  striven to free,
With her children, from the gallows-stair put up
  a prayer for me!"

John Brown of Ossawatomie, they led him out to
  die;
And lo! a poor slave-mother with her little child
  pressed nigh:
Then the bold, blue eye grew tender, and the old
  .harsh face grew mild,

As he stooped between the jeering ranks and
    kissed the negro's child!

The shadows of his stormy life that moment fell
    apart,
And they who blamed the bloody hand forgave
    the loving heart;
That kiss from all its guilty means redeemed the
    good intent,
And round the grisly fighter's hair the martyr's
    aureole bent!

Perish with him the folly that seeks through evil
    good!
Long live the generous purpose unstained with
    human blood!
Not the raid of midnight terror, but the thought
    which underlies;
Not the borderer's pride of daring, but the Chris-
    tian's sacrifice.

Nevermore may yon Blue Ridges the Northern
    rifle hear,
Nor see the light of blazing homes flash on the
    negro's spear;
But let the free-winged angel Truth their guarded
    passes scale,
To teach that right is more than might, and jus-
    tice more than mail!

So vainly shall Virginia set her battle in array;
In vain her trampling squadrons knead the win-
    ter snow with clay!

She may strike the pouncing eagle, but she dares
not harm the dove;
And every gate she bars to Hate shall open wide
to Love!

JOHN GREENLEAF WHITTIER.

WORDS FOR THE "HALLELUJAH CHORUS."

JOHN BROWN's body lies a-moldering in the grave,
John Brown's body lies slumbering in his grave—
But John Brown's soul is marching with the
brave,
His soul is marching on.

Glory, glory, hallelujah!
Glory, glory, hallelujah!
Glory, glory, hallelujah!
His soul is marching on.

He has gone to be a soldier in the Army of the
Lord;
He is sworn as a private in the ranks of the
Lord,—
He shall stand at Armageddon with his brave old
sword,
When Heaven is marching on.

He shall file in front where the lines of battle
form,
He shall face to front when the squares of battle
form—
Time with the column, and charge in the storm,
Where men are marching on.

Ah, foul Tyrants! do ye hear him where he comes?
Ah, black traitor! do ye know him as he comes,
In thunder of the cannon and roll of the drums,
    As we go marching on?

Men may die, and molder in the dust—
Men may die, and arise again from dust,
Shoulder to shoulder, in the ranks of the Just,
    When Heaven is marching on.

      Glory, glory, hallelujah!
      Glory, glory, hallelujah!
      Glory, glory, hallelujah!
      His soul is marching on.
          HENRY HOWARD BROWNELL.

BATTLE-HYMN OF THE REPUBLIC.

MINE eyes have seen the glory of the coming of
    the Lord:
He is trampling out the vintage where the grapes
    of wrath are stored;
He hath loosed the fateful lightning of his terri-
    ble swift sword:
    His truth is marching on.

I have seen him in the watch-fires of a hundred
    circling camps;
They have builded him an altar in the evening
    dews and damps;
I can read his righteous sentence by the dim and
    flaring lamps:
    His day is marching on.

I have read a fiery gospel, writ in burnished rows
    of steel:
" As ye deal with my contemners, so with you my
    grace shall deal;
Let the Hero, born of woman, crush the serpent
    with his heel,
      Since God is marching on."

He has sounded forth the trumpet that shall never
    call retreat;
He is sifting out the hearts of men before his
    judgment-seat:
O, be swift, my soul, to answer him! be jubilant,
    my feet!
      Our God is marching on.

In the beauty of the lilies Christ was born across
    the sea,
With a glory in his bosom that transfigures you
    and me;
As he died to make men holy, let us die to make
    men free,
      While God is marching on.

JULIA WARD HOWE.

JOHN CHARLES FRÉMONT.*

THY error, Frémont, simply was to act
A brave man's part, without the statesman's tact,
And, taking counsel but of common sense,
To strike at cause as well as consequence.

* Fremont's proclamation of martial law in Missouri, in
August, 1861, declaring free all slaves of Rebels, was re-
ceived with ardor by the North, but annulled by President
Lincoln as premature.

O, never yet since Roland wound his horn
At Roncesvalles has a blast been blown
Far-heard, wide-echoed, startling as thine own,
Heard from the van of freedom's hope forlorn!
It had been safer, doubtless, for the time,
To flatter treason, and avoid offence
To that Dark Power whose underlying crime
Heaves upward its perpetual turbulence.
But, if thine be the fate of all who break
The ground for truth's seed, or forerun their
    years
Till lost in distance, or with stout hearts make
A lane for freedom through the level spears,
Still take thou courage! God has spoken through
    thee,
Irrevocable, the mighty words, Be free!
The land shakes with them, and the slave's dull ear
Turns from the rice-swamp stealthily to hear.
Who would recall them now must first arrest
The winds that blow down from the free North-
    west,
Ruffling the Gulf; or like a scroll roll back
The Mississippi to its upper springs.
Such words fulfil their prophecy, and lack
But the full time to harden into things.

JOHN GREENLEAF WHITTIER.

HEROES.

THE winds that once the Argo bore
    Have died by Neptune's ruined shrines,
And her hull is the drift of the deep-sea floor,
    Though shaped of Pelion's tallest pines.

You may seek her crew on every isle
  Fair in the foam of Ægean seas,
But out of their rest no charm can wile
  Jason and Orpheus and Hercules.

And Priam's wail is heard no more
  By windy Ilion's sea-built walls;
Nor great Achilles, stained with gore,
  Shouts " O ye gods, 't is Hector falls ! "
On Ida's mount is the shining snow,
  But Jove has gone from its brow away;
And red on the plain the poppies grow
  Where the Greek and the Trojan fought that
    day.

Mother Earth, are the heroes dead?
  Do they thrill the soul of the years no more?
Are the gleaming snows and the poppies red
  All that is left of the brave of yore?
Are there none to fight as Theseus fought,
  Far in the young world's misty dawn?
Or teach as gray-haired Nestor taught?
  Mother Earth, are the heroes gone?

Gone? In a grander form they rise.
  Dead? We may clasp their hands in ours,
And catch the light of their clearer eyes,
  And wreathe their brows with immortal flowers.
Wherever a noble deed is done,
  'T is the pulse of a hero's heart is stirred;
Wherever Right has a triumph won,
  There are the heroes' voices heard.

Their armor rings on a fairer field
Than the Greek and the Trojan fiercely trod;
For Freedom's sword is the blade they wield,
And the gleam above is the smile of God.
So, in his isle of calm delight,
Jason may sleep the years away;
For the heroes live, and the sky is bright,
And the world is a braver world to-day.

EDNA DEAN PROCTOR.

LAUS DEO!

[On hearing the bells ring on the passage of the Constitutional Amendment abolishing slavery.]

It is done!
Clang of bell and roar of gun
Send the tidings up and down.
How the belfries rock and reel!
How the great guns, peal on peal,
Fling the joy from town to town!

Ring, O bells!
Every stroke exulting tells
Of the burial hour of crime.
Loud and long, that all may hear,
Ring for every listening ear
Of Eternity and Time!

Let us kneel:
God's own voice is in that peal,
And this spot is holy ground.
Lord, forgive us! What are we,
That our eyes this glory see,
That our ears have heard the sound!

For the Lord
On the whirlwind is abroad;
In the earthquake he has spoken;
He has smitten with his thunder
The iron walls asunder,
And the gates of brass are broken!

Loud and long
Lift the old exulting song;
Sing with Miriam by the sea:
He has cast the mighty down;
Horse and rider sink and drown;
He has triumphed gloriously!

Did we dare,
In our agony of prayer,
Ask for more than He has done?
When was ever his right hand
Over any time or land
Stretched as now beneath the sun?

How they pale,
Ancient myth and song and tale,
In this wonder of our days,
When the cruel rod of war
Blossoms white with righteous law,
And the wrath of man is praise!

Blotted out!
All within and all about
Shall a fresher life begin;
Freer breathe the universe
As it rolls its heavy curse
On the dead and buried sin.

It is done!
In the circuit of the sun
Shall the sound thereof go forth.
It shall bid the sad rejoice,
It shall give the dumb a voice,
It shall belt with joy the earth!

Ring and swing,
Bells of joy! On morning's wing
Send the song of praise abroad!
With a sound of broken chains,
Tell the nations that He reigns,
Who alone is Lord and God!

JOHN GREENLEAF WHITTIER.

A HOLY NATION.

LET Liberty run onward with the years,
And circle with the seasons; let her break
The tyrant's harshness, the oppressor's spears;
Bring ripened recompenses that shall make
Supreme amends for sorrow's long arrears;
Drop holy benison on hearts that ache;
Put clearer radiance into human eyes,
And set the glad earth singing to the skies.

Clean natures coin pure statutes. Let us cleanse
The hearts that beat within us; let us mow
Clear to the roots our falseness and pretence,
Tread down our rank ambitions, overthrow
Our braggart moods of puffed self-consequence,
Plough up our hideous thistles which do grow
Faster than maize in May time, and strike dead
The base infections our low greeds have bred.

RICHARD REALF.

III.

WAR.

BATTLE OF THE ANGELS.

FROM " PARADISE LOST," BOOK VI.

THE ARRAY.

Now went forth the morn,
Such as in highest heaven, arrayed in gold
Empyreal; from before her vanished night,
Shot through with orient beams; when all the
    plain
Covered with thick embattled squadrons bright,
Chariots, and flaming arms, and fiery steeds,
Reflecting blaze on blaze, first met his view.

. . . . .

The apostate in his sun-bright chariot sat,
Idol of majesty divine, enclosed
With flaming cherubim, and golden shields;
Then lighted from his gorgeous throne, for now
'Twixt host and host but narrow space was left,
A dreadful interval, and front to front
Presented stood in terrible array
Of hideous length : before the cloudy van,
On the rough edge of battle ere it joined,

Satan, with vast and haughty strides advanced,
Came towering, armed in adamant and gold.

THE CONFLICT.

Michael bid sound
The archangel trumpet; through the vast of
    heaven
It sounded, and the faithful armies rung
Hosanna to the Highest: nor stood at gaze
The adverse legions, nor less hideous joined
The horrid shock. Now storming fury rose,
And clamor, such as heard in heaven till now
Was never; arms on armor clashing brayed
Horrible discord, and the madding wheels
Of brazen chariots raged; dire was the noise
Of conflict; overhead the dismal hiss
Of fiery darts in flaming volleys flew,
And flying vaulted either host with fire.
So under fiery cope together rushed
Both battles main, with ruinous assault
And inextinguishable rage. All heaven
Resounded; and had earth been then, all earth
Had to her centre shook.

     ·   ·   ·   ·   ·

Deeds of eternal fame
Were done, but infinite: for wide was spread
That war, and various: sometimes on firm ground
A standing fight, then, soaring on main wing,
Tormented all the air; all air seemed then
Conflicting fire.

     ·   ·   ·   ·   ·

Forthwith (behold the excellence, the power
Which God hath in his mighty angels placed!)
Their arms away threw, and to the hills
(For earth hath this variety from heaven,
Of pleasures situate in hill and dale),
Light as the lightning glimpse they ran, they flew,
From their foundations loosening to and fro,
They plucked the seated hills, with all their load,
Rocks, waters, woods, and by the shaggy tops
Uplifting bore them in their hands: amaze,
Be sure, and terror, seized the rebel host,
When coming towards them so dread they saw
The bottom of the mountains upward turned,
.   .   .   .   and on their heads
Main promontories flung, which in the air
Came shadowing, and oppressed whole legions
    armed;
Their armor helped their harm, crushed in and
    bruised
Into their substance pent, which wrought them
    pain
Implacable, and many a dolorous groan;
Long struggling underneath, ere they could wind
Out of such prison, though spirits of purest light,
Purest at first, now gross by sinning grown.
The rest, in imitation, to like arms
Betook them, and the neighboring hills uptore:
So hills amid the air encountered hills,
Hurled to and fro with jaculation dire,
That underground they fought in dismal shade;
Infernal noise! war seemed a civil game
To this uproar; horrid confusion heaped
Upon confusion rose.

THE VICTOR.

So spake the Son, and into terror changed
His countenance too severe to be beheld,
And full of wrath bent on his enemies.
At once the four spread out their starry wings
With dreadful shade contiguous, and the orbs
Of his fierce chariot rolled, as with the sound
Of torrent floods, or of a numerous host.
He on his impious foes right onward drove,
Gloomy as night: under his burning wheels
The steadfast empyrean shook throughout.
All but the throne itself of God. Full soon
Among them he arrived; in his right hand
Grasping ten thousand thunders, which he sent
Before him, such as in their souls infixèd
Plagues: they, astonished, all resistance lost,
All courage; down their idle weapons dropt;
O'er shields, and helms, and helmèd heads he rode
Of thrones and mighty seraphim prostràte,
That wished the mountains now might be again
Thrown on them, as a shelter from his ire.
Nor less on either side tempestuous fell
His arrows, from the fourfold-visaged Four
Distinct with eyes, and from the living wheels
Distinct alike with multitude of eyes;
One spirit in them ruled; and every eye
Glared lightning, and shot forth pernicious fire
Among the accursed, that withered all their
    strength,
And of their wonted vigor left them drained,
Exhausted, spiritless, afflicted, fallen.
Yet half his strength he put not forth, but
    checked

His thunder in mid volley; for he meant
Not to destroy, but root them out of heaven:
The overthrown he raised, and as a herd
Of goats or timorous flock together thronged,
Drove them before him thunderstruck, pursued
With terrors and with furies, to the bounds
And crystal wall of heaven; which, opening wide,
Rolled inward, and a spacious gap disclosed
Into the wasteful deep: the monstrous sight
Struck them with horror backward, but far worse
Urged them behind: headlong themselves they
        threw
Down from the verge of heaven; eternal wrath
Burnt after them to the bottomless pit.

MILTON.

THE DESTRUCTION OF SENNACHERIB.

FROM " HEBREW MELODIES."

THE Assyrian came down like the wolf on the
        fold,
And his cohorts were gleaming in purple and
        gold;
And the sheen of their spears was like stars on
        the sea,
When the blue wave rolls nightly on deep Galilee.

Like the leaves of the forest when summer is
        green,
That host with their banners at sunset were seen:
Like the leaves of the forest when autumn hath
        blown,
That host on the morrow lay withered and strown.

For the Angel of Death spread his wings on the
 blast,
And breathed in the face of the foe as he passed;
And the eyes of the sleepers waxed deadly and
 chill,
And their hearts but once heaved, and forever
 grew still!

And there lay the steed with his nostril all
 wide,
But through it there rolled not the breath of his
 pride:
And the foam of his gasping lay white on the
 turf,
And cold as the spray of the rock-beating surf.

And there lay the rider distorted and pale,
With the dew on his brow, and the rust on his
 mail;
And the tents were all silent, the banners alone,
The lances unlifted, the trumpet unblown.

And the widows of Ashur are loud in their wail,
And the idols are broke in the temple of Baal;
And the might of the Gentile, unsmote by the
 sword,
Hath melted like snow in the glance of the Lord!

       LORD BYRON.

THE SCHOOL OF WAR.

FROM "TAMBURLAINE."

TAMBURLAINE.—But now, my boys, leave off and
    list to me,
That mean to teach you rudiments of war:
I 'll have you learn to sleep upon the ground,
March in your armor through watery fens,
Sustain the scorching heat and freezing cold,
Hunger and thirst, right adjuncts of the war,
And after this to scale a castle wall,
Besiege a fort, to undermine a town,
And make whole cities caper in the air.
Then next the way to fortify your men:
In champion grounds, what figure serves you best,
For which the quinque-angle form is meet,
Because the corners there may fall more flat
Whereas the fort may fittest be assailed,
And sharpest where the assault is desperate.
The ditches must be deep; the counterscarps
Narrow and steep; the walls made high and broad;
The bulwarks and the rampires large and strong,
With cavalieros and thick counterforts,
And room within to lodge six thousand men.
It must have privy ditches, countermines,
And secret issuings to defend the ditch;
It must have high argins and covered ways,
To keep the bulwark fronts from battery,
And parapets to hide the musketers;
Casemates to place the great artillery;
And store of ordnance, that from every flank
May scour the outward curtains of the fort,

Dismount the cannon of the adverse part,
Murder the foe, and save the walls from breach.
When this is learned for service on the land,
By plain and easy demonstration
I 'll teach you how to make the water mount,
That you may dry-foot march through lakes and
    pools,
Deep rivers, havens, creeks, and little seas,
And make a fortress in the raging waves,
Fenced with the concave of monstrous rock,
Invincible by nature of the place.
When this is done then are ye soldiers,
And worthy sons of Tamburlaine the Great.
    CALYPHAS.—My lord, but this is dangerous to
    be done:
We may be slain or wounded ere we learn.
    TAMBURLAINE.—Villain! Art thou the son of
    Tamburlaine,
And fear'st to die, or with a curtle-axe
To hew thy flesh, and make a gaping wound?
Hast thou beheld a peal of ordnance strike
A ring of pikes, mingled with shot and horse,
Whose shattered limbs, being tossed as high as
    Heaven,
Hang in the air as thick as sunny motes,
And canst thou, coward, stand in fear of death?
Hast thou not seen my horsemen charge the foe,
Shot through the arms, cut overthwart the hands,
Dyeing their lances with their streaming blood,
And yet at night carouse within my tent,
Filling their empty veins with airy wine,
That, being concocted, turns to crimson blood,—
And wilt thou shun the field for fear of wounds?

View me, thy father, that hath conquered kings,
And with his horse marched round about the earth
Quite void of scars and clear from any wound,
That by the wars lost not a drop of blood,—
And see him lance his flesh to teach you all.

(*He cuts his arm.*)

A wound is nothing, be it ne'er so deep;
Blood is the god of war's rich livery.
Now look I like a soldier, and this wound
As great a grace and majesty to me,
As if a chain of gold, enamellèd,
Enchased with diamonds, sapphires, rubies,
And fairest pearl of wealthy India,
Were mounted here under a canopy,
And I sate down clothed with a massy robe,
That late adorned the Afric potentate,
Whom I brought bound unto Damascus' walls.
Come, boys, and with your fingers search my
      wound,
And in my blood wash all your hands at once,
While I sit smiling to behold the sight.
Now, my boys, what think ye of a wound?

    CALYPHAS.—I know not what I should think of
    it; methinks it is a pitiful sight.

    CELEBINUS.—'T is nothing: give me a wound,
    father.

    AMYRAS.—And me another, my lord.

    TAMBURLAINE.—Come, sirrah, give me your
    arm.

    CELEBINUS.—Here, father, cut it bravely, as
    as you did your own.

    TAMBURLAINE.—It shall suffice thou darest
    abide a wound:

My boy, thou shalt not lose a drop of blood
Before we meet the army of the Turk;
But then run desperate through the thickest
    throngs,
Dreadless of blows, of bloody wounds, and death;
And let the burning of Larissa-walls,
My speech of war, and this my wound you see,
Teach you, my boys, to bear courageous minds,
Fit for the followers of great Tamburlaine!

CHRISTOPHER MARLOWE.

CATILINE TO THE ROMAN ARMY.

FROM " CATILINE," ACT V. SC. 2.

SOUND all to arms! (*A flourish of trumpets.*)
Call in the captains,—(*To an officer.*)
        I would speak with them!

      (*The officer goes.*)

Now, Hope! away,—and welcome gallant Death!
Welcome the clanging shield, the trumpet's yell,—
Welcome the fever of the mounting blood,
That makes wounds light, and battle's crimson
    toil
Seem but a sport,—and welcome the cold bed,
Where soldiers with their upturned faces lie,—
And welcome wolf's and vulture's hungry throats,
That make their sepulchres! We fight to-night.

      (*The soldiery enter.*)

Centurions! all is ruined! I disdain
To hide the truth from you. The die is thrown!
And now, let each that wishes for long life

Put up his sword, and kneel for peace to Rome.
Ye all are free to go. What! no man stirs!
Not one! a soldier's spirit in you all?
Give me your hands!   (This moisture in my eyes
Is womanish,—'t will pass.)   My noble hearts!
Well have you chosen to die!   For, in my mind,
The grave is better than o'erburdened life;
Better the quick release of glorious wounds,
Than the eternal taunts of galling tongues;
Better the spear-head quivering in the heart,
Than daily struggle against fortune's curse;
Better, in manhood's muscle and high blood,
To leap the gulf, than totter to its edge
In poverty, dull pain, and base decay.
Once more, I say,—are ye resolved?
            (*The soldiers shout,* "All! All!")
Then, each man to his tent, and take the arms
That he would love to die in,—for, *this hour*,
We storm the Consul's camp.   A last farewell!

            (*He takes their hands.*)

When next we meet,—we 'll have no time to look,
How parting clouds a soldier's countenance.
Few as we are, we 'll rouse them with a peal
That shall shake Rome!
Now to your cohorts' heads;—the word 's—Re-
    venge!

                        GEORGE CROLY.

CARACTACUS.

Before proud Rome's imperial throne
    In mind's unconquered mood,
As if the triumph were his own,
    The dauntless captive stood.
None, to have seen his free-born air,
Had fancied him a captive there.

Though, through the crowded streets of Rome,
    With slow and stately tread,
Far from his own loved island home,
    That day in triumph led,—
Unbound his head, unbent his knee,
Undimmed his eye, his aspect free.

A free and fearless glance he cast
    On temple, arch, and tower,
By which the long procession passed
    Of Rome's victorious power;
And somewhat of a scornful smile
Upcurled his haughty lip the while.

And now he stood, with brow serene,
    Where slaves might prostrate fall,
Bearing a Briton's manly mien
    In Cæsar's palace hall;
Claiming, with kindled brow and cheek,
The liberty e'en there to speak.

Nor could Rome's haughty lord withstand
    The claim that look preferred,

But motioned with uplifted hand
  The suppliant should be heard,—
If he indeed a suppliant were
  Whose glance demanded audience there.

Deep stillness fell on all the crowd,
  From Claudius on his throne
Down to the meanest slave that bowed
  At his imperial throne;
Silent his fellow-captive's grief
As fearless spoke the Island Chief:

" Think not, thou eagle Lord of Rome,
  And master of the world,
Though victory's banner o'er thy dome
  In triumph now is furled,
I would address thee as thy slave,
But as the bold should greet the brave!

" I might, perchance, could I have deigned
  To hold a vassal's throne,
E'en now in Britain's isle have reigned
  A king in name alone,
Yet holding, as thy meek ally,
A monarch's mimic pageantry.

" Then through Rome's crowded streets to-day
  I might have rode with thee,
Not in a captive's base array,
  But fetterless and free,—
If freedom he could hope to find,
Whose bondage is of heart and mind.

" But canst thou marvel that, freeborn,
  With heart and soul unquelled,
Throne, crown, and sceptre I should scorn,
  By thy permission held?
Or that I should retain my right
Till wrested by a conqueror's might?

" Rome, with her palaces and towers,
  By us unwished, unreft,
Her homely huts and woodland bowers
  To Britain might have left;
Worthless to you their wealth must be,
But dear to us, for they were free!

" I might have bowed before, but where
  Had been thy triumph now?
To my resolve no yoke to bear
  Thou ow'st thy laurelled brow;
Inglorious victory had been thine,
And more inglorious bondage mine.

" Now I have spoken, do thy will;
  Be life or death my lot,
Since Britain's throne no more I fill,
  To me it matters not.
My fame is clear; but on my fate
Thy glory or thy shame must wait."

He ceased; from all around upsprung
  A murmur of applause,
For well had truth and freedom's tongue
  Maintained their holy cause.
The conqueror was the captive then;
He bade the slave be free again.

                              BERNARD BARTON.

SEMPRONIUS' SPEECH FOR WAR.

FROM "CATO," ACT II. SC. 1.

MY voice is still for war.
Gods! can a Roman senate long debate
Which of the two to choose, slavery or death?
No; let us rise at once, gird on our swords,
And at the head of our remaining troops
Attack the foe, break through the thick array
Of his thronged legions, and charge home upon
  him.
Perhaps some arm, more lucky than the rest,
May reach his heart, and free the world from
  bondage.
Rise! Fathers, rise! 't is Rome demands your help:
Rise, and revenge her slaughtered citizens,
Or share their fate! The corpse of half her
  senate
Manures the fields of Thessaly, while we
Sit here deliberating, in cold debate,
If we should sacrifice our lives to honor,
Or wear them out in servitude and chains.
Rouse up, for shame! our brothers of Pharsalia
Point at their wounds, and cry aloud,—" To
  battle!"
Great Pompey's shade complains that we are slow,
And Scipio's ghost walks unrevenged amongst us.

JOSEPH ADDISON.

THE DEATH OF LEONIDAS.

IT was the wild midnight,—
  A storm was on the sky;
The lightning gave its light,
  And the thunder echoed by.

The torrent swept the glen,
  The ocean lashed the shore;
Then rose the Spartan men,
  To make their bed in gore!

Swift from the deluge ground
  Three hundred took the shield;
Then, silent, gathered round
  The leader of the field!

He spake no warrior word,
  He bade no trumpet blow,
But the signal thunder roared,
  And they rushed upon the foe.

The fiery element
  Showed, with one mighty gleam,
Rampart, and flag, and tent,
  Like the spectres of a dream.

All up the mountain's side,
  All down the woody vale,
All by the rolling tide
  Waved the Persian banners pale.

And foremost from the pass,
   Among the slumbering band,
Sprang King Leonidas,
   Like the lightning's living brand.

Then double darkness fell,
   And the forest ceased its moan;
But there came a clash of steel,
   And a distant dying groan.

Anon, a trumpet blew,
   And a fiery sheet burst high,
That o'er the midnight threw
   A blood-red canopy.

A host glared on the hill;
   A host glared by the bay;
But the Greeks rushed onward still,
   Like leopards in their play.

The air was all a yell,
   And the earth was all a flame,
Where the Spartan's bloody steel
   On the silken turbans came;

And still the Greek rushed on
   Where the fiery torrent rolled,
Till like a rising sun
   Shone Xerxes' tent of gold.

They found a royal feast,
   His midnight banquet, there;

And the treasures of the East
Lay beneath the Doric spear.

Then sat to the repast
The bravest of the brave!
That feast must be their last,
That spot must be their grave.

They pledged old Sparta's name
In cups of Syrian wine,
And the warrior's deathless fame
Was sung in strains divine.

They took the rose-wreathed lyres
From eunuch and from slave,
And taught the languid wires,
The sounds that Freedom gave.

But now the morning star
Crowned Œta's twilight brow;
And the Persian horn of war
From the hills began to blow.

Up rose the glorious rank,
To Greece one cup poured high,
Then hand in hand they drank,
" To immortality! "

Fear on King Xerxes fell,
When, like spirits from the tomb,
With shout and trumpet knell,
He saw the warriors come.

But down swept all his power,
  With chariot and with charge;
Down poured the arrows' shower,
  Till sank the Dorian's targe.

They gathered round the tent,
  With all their strength unstrung;
To Greece one look they sent,
  Then on high their torches flung.

The king sat on the throne,
  His captains by his side,
While the flame rushed roaring on,
  And their Pæan loud replied.

Thus fought the Greek of old!
  Thus will he fight again!
Shall not the self-same mould
  Bring forth the self-same men?

GEORGE CROLY.

SONG OF THE GREEKS.

[1821.]

AGAIN to the battle, Achaians!
  Our hearts bid the tyrants defiance;
Our land,—the first garden of Liberty's-tree,—
Has been, and shall yet be, the land of the free;
  For the cross of our faith is replanted,
  The pale dying crescent is daunted,
And we march that the footprints of Mahomet's
    slaves

May be washed out in blood from our fore-
    fathers' graves.
  Their spirits are hovering o'er us,
  And the sword shall to glory restore us.

    Ah! what though no succor advances,
    Nor Christendom's chivalrous lances
Are stretched in our aid?—Be the combat our
    own!
And we 'll perish or conquer more proudly alone;
  For we 've sworn by our country's assaulters,
  By the virgins they 've dragged from our altars,
By our massacred patriots, our children in chains,
By our heroes of old, and their blood in our veins,
    That, living, we will be victorious,
    Or that, dying, our deaths shall be glorious.

    A breath of submission we breathe not:
    The sword that we 've drawn we will sheathe
    not:
Its scabbard is left where our martyrs are laid,
And the vengeance of ages has whetted its blade.
    Earth may hide, waves engulf, fire consume us;
    But they shall not to slavery doom us:
If they rule, it shall be o'er our ashes and
    graves:—
But we 've smote them already with fire on the
    waves,
    And new triumphs on land are before us;—
    To the charge!—Heaven's banner is o'er us.

    This day—shall ye blush for its story;
    Or brighten your lives with its glory?—

Our women—oh, say, shall they shriek in despair,
Or embrace us from conquest, with wreaths in
   their hair?
  Accursed may his memory blacken,
  If a coward there be that would slacken
Till we 've trampled the turban, and shown our-
   selves worth
Being sprung from and named for, the godlike
  of earth.
  Strike home!—and the world shall revere us
  As heroes descended from heroes.

  Old Greece lightens up with emotion!
  Her inlands, her isles of the ocean,
Fanes rebuilt, and fair towns, shall with jubilee
   ring,
And the Nine shall new hallow their Helicon's
   spring.
  Our hearts shall be kindled in gladness,
  That were cold, and extinguished in sadness;
Whilst our maidens shall dance with their white
   waving arms,
Singing joy to the brave that delivered their
   charms,—
  When the blood of yon Mussulman cravens
  Shall have crimsoned the beaks of our ravens!
              THOMAS CAMPBELL.

MARCO BOZZARIS.

[AT LASPI—ANCIENT PLATÆA—AUGUST 20, 1823.]

AT midnight, in his guarded tent,
　The Turk was dreaming of the hour
When Greece, her knee in suppliance bent,
　Should tremble at his power.
In dreams, through camp and court, he bore
The trophies of a conqueror;
　In dreams his song of triumph heard;
Then wore his monarch's signet-ring,
Then pressed that monarch 's throne—a king;
As wild his thoughts, and gay of wing,
　As Eden's garden bird.

At midnight, in the forest shades,
　Bozzaris ranged his Suliote band,—
True as the steel of their tried blades,
　Heroes in heart and hand.
There had the Persian's thousands stood,
There had the glad earth drunk their blood,
　On old Platæa's day;
And now there breathed that haunted air
The sons of sires who conquered there,
With arm to strike, and soul to dare,
　As quick, as far, as they.

An hour passed on, the Turk awoke:
　That bright dream was his last;
He woke—to hear his sentries shriek,
　"To arms! they come! the Greek! the
　Greek!"

He woke—to die midst flame, and smoke,
And shout, and groan, and sabre-stroke,
  And death-shots falling thick and fast
As lightnings from the mountain-cloud;
And heard, with voice as trumpet loud,
  Bozzaris cheer his band:
" Strike—till the last armed foe expires;
Strike—for your altars and your fires;
Strike—for the green graves of your sires,
  God, and your native land! "

They fought—like brave men, long and well;
  They piled that ground with Moslem slain:
They conquered—but Bozzaris fell,
  Bleeding at every vein.
His few surviving comrades saw
His smile when rang their proud hurrah,
  And the red field was won;
Then saw in death his eyelids close
Calmly, as to a night 's repose,
  Like flowers at set of sun.

Come to the bridal chamber, Death,
  Come to the mother, when she feels,
For the first time, her first-born's breath;
  Come when the blessèd seals
That close the pestilence are broke,
And crowded cities wail its stroke;
Come in consumption's ghastly form,
The earthquake shock, the ocean storm;
Come when the heart beats high and warm,
  With banquet song and dance and wine,—
And thou art terrible; the tear,

The groan, the knell, the pall, the bier,
And all we know, or dream, or fear
   Of agony, are thine.

But to the hero, when his sword
   Has won the battle for the free,
Thy voice sounds like a prophet's word,
And in its hollow tones are heard
   The thanks of millions yet to be.
Come when his task of fame is wrought;
Come with her laurel-leaf, blood-bought;
   Come in her crowning hour,—and then
Thy sunken eye's unearthly light
To him is welcome as the sight
   Of sky and stars to prisoned men;
Thy grasp is welcome as the hand
Of brother in a foreign land;
Thy summons welcome as the cry
That told the Indian isles were nigh
   To the world-seeking Genoese,
When the land-wind, from woods of palm,
And orange-groves, and fields of balm,
   Blew o'er the Haytian seas.

Bozzaris! with the storied brave
   Greece nurtured in her glory's time,
Rest thee; there is no prouder grave,
   Even in her own proud clime.
She wore no funeral weeds for thee,
   Nor bade the dark hearse wave its plume,
Like torn branch from death's leafless tree,
In sorrow's pomp and pageantry,
   The heartless luxury of the tomb.

But she remembers thee as one
Long loved, and for a season gone.
For thee her poet's lyre is wreathed,
Her marble wrought, her music breathed;
For thee she rings the birthday bells;
Of thee her babes' first lisping tells;
For thine her evening prayer is said
At palace couch and cottage bed.
Her soldier, closing with the foe,
Gives for thy sake a deadlier blow;
His plighted maiden, when she fears
For him, the joy of her young years,
Thinks of thy fate, and checks her tears.
    And she, the mother of thy boys,
Though in her eye and faded cheek
Is read the grief she will not speak,
    The memory of her buried joys,—
And even she who gave thee birth,—
Will, by her pilgrim-circled hearth,
    Talk of thy doom without a sigh;
For thou art freedom's now, and fame's,—
One of the few, the immortal names
    That were not born to die.

FITZ-GREENE HALLECK.

HARMOSAN.

Now the third and fatal conflict for the Persian
    throne was done,
And the Moslem's fiery valor had the crowning
    victory won.

Harmosan, the last and boldest the invader to
defy,
Captive, overborn by numbers, they were bringing
forth to die.

Then exclaimed that noble captive: " Lo, I perish
in my thirst;
Give me but one drink of water, and let then arrive the worst!"

In his hand he took the goblet: but awhile the
draught forbore,
Seeming doubtfully the purpose of the foeman to
explore.

Well might then have paused the bravest—for,
around him, angry foes
With a hedge of naked weapons did the lonely
man enclose.

" But what fear'st thou?" cried the caliph; " is it,
friend, a secret blow?
Fear it not! our gallant Moslems no such treacherous dealing know.

" Thou may'st quench thy thirst securely, for thou
shalt not die before
Thou hast drunk that cup of water—this reprieve
is thine—no more!"

Quick the satrap dashed the goblet down to earth
with ready hand,
And the liquid sank forever, lost amid the burning sand.

"Thou hast said that mine my life is, till the
water of that cup
I have drained; then bid thy servants that spilled
water gather up!"

For a moment stood the caliph as by doubtful pas-
sions stirred—
Then exclaimed: "For ever sacred must remain a
monarch's word.
Bring another cup, and straightway to the noble
Persian give:
Drink, I said before, and perish—now I bid thee
drink and live!"

RICHARD CHENEVIX TRENCH.

BATTLE SCENE.

FROM "THE CID."

THEN cried my Cid—"In charity, as to the
rescue—ho!"
With bucklers braced before their breasts, with
lances pointing low,
With stooping crests and heads bent down above
the saddle-bow,
All firm of hand and high of heart they roll upon
the foe.
And he that in a good hour was born, his clarion
voice rings out,
And clear above the clang of arms is heard his
battle shout:
"Among them, gentlemen! Strike home for the
love of charity!"

The champion of Bivar is here—Ruy Diaz—I am
    he!"
Then bearing where Bermuez still maintains un-
    equal fight,
Three hundred lances down they come, their pen-
    nons flickering white;
Down go three hundred Moors to earth, a man
    to every blow;
And when they wheel, three hundred more, as
    charging back they go.
It was a sight to see the lances rise and fall that
    day;
The shivered shields and riven mail, to see how
    thick they lay;
The pennons that went in snow-white came out a
    gory red;
The horses running riderless, the riders lying
    dead;
While Moors call on Mohammed, and "St.
    James!" the Christians cry,
And sixty score of Moors and more in narrow
    compass lie.

From the Spanish.
Translation of JOHN ORMSBY.

THE LORD OF BUTRAGO.

"Your horse is faint, my King, my Lord! your
    gallant horse is sick,—
His limbs are torn, his breast is gored, on his eye
    the film is thick;
Mount, mount on mine, O mount apace, I pray
    thee, mount and fly!

Or in my arms I 'll lift your Grace,—their trampling hoofs are nigh!

" My King, my King,! you 're wounded sore,—
the blood runs from your feet;
But only lay a hand before, and I 'll lift you to
your seat;
Mount, Juan, for they gather fast!—I hear their
coming cry,—
Mount, mount, and ride for jeopardy,—I 'll save
you though I die!

" Stand, noble steed! this hour of need,—be gentle as a lamb;
I 'll kiss the foam from off thy mouth,—thy master dear I am,—
Mount, Juan, mount; whate'er betide, away the
bridle fling,
And plunge the rowels in his side.—My horse
shall save my King!

" Nay, never speak; my sires, Lord King, received
their land from yours,
And joyfully their blood shall spring, so be it
thine secures;
If I should fly, and thou, my King, be found
among the dead,
How could I stand 'mong gentlemen, such scorn
on my gray head?

" Castile's proud dames shall never point the
finger of disdain,
And say there 's one that ran away when our
good lords were slain!

I leave Diego in your care,—you'll fill his
    father's place;
Strike, strike the spur, and never spare—God's
    blessing on your Grace!"

So spake the brave Montañez, Butrago's lord was
    he;
And turned him to the coming host in steadfast-
    ness and glee;
He flung himself among them, as they came down
    the hill,—
He died, God wot! but not before his sword had
    drunk its fill.

From the Spanish.
Translation of JOHN GIBSON LOCKHART.

HAKON'S DEFIANCE.

FROM "HAKON JARL."

[Olaf Trygvesön from Ireland is trying to introduce
Christianity, and reclaim his father's kingdom, in Norway, and has invaded the realm of Earl Hakon, a formi-
dable heathen usurper, who, after defeat in battle, unsuccessfully attempts to have King Olaf assassinated by
Thorer Klake, one of his adherents. But Olaf slays Klake,
and now visits Hakon, lying hid in a peasant's hut.]

Enter OLAF TRYGVESÖN, *muffled up in a gray cloak,*
    with a broad hat on his head.

HAKON [*without looking up*].—
My valiant Thorer Klake, hast come at last?
Hast been successful? Dost thou bring to me
What thou didst promise? Answer, Thorer
    Klake.

OLAF.—All things have happened as they
  should, my lord;
But pardon Thorer that he does not come
And bring himself King Olaf's head to thee—
'T was difficult for him. Tho:' knows he had
A sort of loathing that himself should bring it,
And so he sent me.
HAKON.—Well, 't is good; away,
And deeply bury it in the dark earth.
I will not look on it myself: my eye
Bears not such sights,—they reappear in dreams.
Bury the body with it. Tell thy lord
That he shall come at once.
  OLAF.—He is asleep.
  HAKON.—Asleep?
  OLAF.—A midday slumber; he lies stretched
Stiffly beneath a shadowy elder-tree.
HAKON.—Then wake him up. [*Aside.*] Asleep,
  Asleep, and after such
A deed—Ha! Thorer, I admire thee;
Thou hast rare courage. [*Aloud.*] Thrall, go
  wake him up.
  OLAF.—But wilt thou first not look at Olaf's
  head?
  HAKON.—No; I have said no.
  OLAF.—Thou dost think, my lord,
That perhaps it is a horrid frightful sight:
It is not so, my lord; for Olaf's head
Looks fresh and sound as any in the land.
  HAKON.—Away, I tell thee!
  OLAF.—I ne'er saw the like:
I always heard that Hakon was a hero,
Few like him in the North,—and does he fear

To see a lifeless and a corpseless head?
How wouldst thou tremble then, my lord, if thou
Shouldst see it on his body?
        HAKON [*turning round angrily*].—
Thrall, thou darest!
Where hast thou got it?
        OLAF [*takes his hat off, and throws off his
            cloak*].—
On my shoulders, Earl.
Forgive me that I bring it thee myself
In such a way: 't was easiest for me.
        HAKON.—What, Olaf! Ha! what treachery is
            here?
        OLAF.—Old gray-beard, spare thy rash, heroic
            wrath.
Attempt not to fight Olaf, but remember
That he has still his head upon his body,
And that thy impotent, gray-bearded strength
Was only fitting for the headless Olaf.   —
        HAKON [*rushes at him*].—
Ha, Hilfheim!
        OLAF [*strikes his sword, and says in a loud
            voice*].—
So, be quiet now, I say,
And sheathe thy sword again. My followers
Surround the house; my vessels are a match
For all of thine, and I myself have come
To win the country in an honest fight.
Thyself hast urged me with thy plots to do it.
Thou standest like a despicable thrall
In his own pitfall caught at last; but I
Will make no use of these advantages
Which fate has granted me. I am convinced

That I may boldly meet thee face to face.
Thy purpose, as thou seest, has wholly failed,
And in his own blood does thy Thorer swim.
Thou seest 't were easy for me to have seized
    thee;
To strike thee down were even easier still:
But I the Christian doctrine do confess,
And do such poor advantages despise.
So choose between two courses. Still be Earl
Of Hlade as thou wast, and do me homage,
Or else take flight; for when we meet again
'T will be the time for red and bleeding brows.
    HAKON [*proudly and quietly*].—
My choice is made. I choose the latter, Olaf.
Thou callest me a villain and a thrall;
That forces up a smile upon my lips.
Olaf, one hears indeed that thou art young;
It is by mockery and arrogance
That one can judge thy age. Now, look at me
Full in the eyes; consider well my brow:
Hast thou among the thralls e'er met such looks?
Dost think that cunning or that cowardice
Could e'er have carved these wrinkles on my brow?
I did entice thee hither. Ha! 't is true
I knew that thou didst wait but for a sign
To flutter after the enticing bait;
That in thy soul thou didst more highly prize
Thy kinship with an extinct race of kings
Than great Earl Hakon's world-renownèd deeds;
That thou didst watch the opportunity
To fall upon the old man in his rest.
Does it astonish thee that I should wish
Quickly to rid myself of such a foe?

That I deceived a dreamer who despised
The mighty gods,—does that astonish thee?
Does it astonish thee that I approved
My warrior's purpose, since a hostile fate
Attempted to dethrone, not only me,
But all Valhalla's gods?

OLAF.—Remember, Hakon,—
Remember, Hakon, that e'en thou thyself
Hast been a Christian; that thou wast baptized
By Bishop Popo, and that thou since then
Didst break thy oath. How many hast thou
　broken?

HAKON.—Accursed forever may that moment
　be
When by the cunning monk I was deceived,
And let myself be fooled by paltry tricks.
He held a red-hot iron in his hand,
After by magic he had covered it
With witches' ointment.

OLAF.—O thou blind old man!
Thy silver hair does make me pity thee.

HAKON.—Ha! spare thy pity; as thou seest
　me here,
Thou seest the last flash and the latest spark
Of ancient Northern force and hero's life;
And that, with all thy fever-stricken dreams,
Proud youth, thou shalt be powerless to quench.
I well do know it is the Christian custom
To pity, to convert, and to amend.
Our custom is to heartily despise you,
To ruminate upon your fall and death,
As foes to gods and to a hero's life.
That Hakon does, and therein does consist

His villainy. By Odin, and by Thor,
Thou shalt not quench old Norway's warlike
    flame
With all thy misty dreams of piety.
    OLAF.—'T is well: fate shall decide. We sepa-
    rate,
And woe to thee when next we meet again.
    HAKON.—Aye, woe to me if then I crush thee
    not.
    OLAF.—Heaven shall strike thee with its fiery
    might!
    HAKON.—No, with his hammer Thor the cross
    will smite!

From the Danish of ADAM GOTTLOB OEHLENSCHLÄGER.

Translation of SIR FRANK C. LASCELLES.

A DANISH BARROW

ON THE EAST DEVON COAST.

LIE still, old Dane, below thy heap!
    A sturdy-back and sturdy-limb,
    Whoe'er he was, I warrant him
Upon whose mound the single sheep
    Browses and tinkles in the sun,
    Within the narrow vale alone.

Lie still, old Dane! This restful scene
    Suits well thy centuries of sleep:
    The soft brown roots above thee creep,
The lotus flaunts his ruddy sheen,
    And,—vain memento of the spot,—
    The turquoise-eyed forget-me-not.

Lie still! Thy mother-land herself
   Would know thee not again : no more
   The Raven from the northern shore
Hails the bold crew to push for pelf,
   Through fire and blood and slaughtered kings
   'Neath the black terror of his wings.

And thou,—thy very name is lost!
   The peasant only knows that here
   Bold Alfred scooped thy flinty bier,
And prayed a foeman's prayer, and tost
   His auburn head, and said, " Oné more
   Of England's foes guards England's shore,"

And turned and passed to other feats,
   And left thee in thine iron robe,
   To circle with the circling globe,
While Time's corrosive dewdrop eats
   The giant warrior to a crust
   Of earth in earth, and rust in rust.

So lie : and let the children play
   And sit like flowers upon thy grave
   And crown with flowers,—that hardly have
A briefer blooming-tide than they ;—
   By hurrying years urged on to rest,
   As thou within the Mother's breast.

FRANCIS TURNER PALGRAVE.

HERMANN AND THUSNELDA.

HA! there comes he, with sweat, with blood of
　　　Romans,
And dust of the fight all stained! Oh, never
　　　　Saw I Hermann so lovely!
　　　　Never such fire in his eyes!

Come! I tremble for joy; hand me the Eagle
And the red dripping sword! come, breathe, and
　　　rest thee;
　　　　Rest thee here in my bosom;
　　　　Rest from the terrible fight!

Rest thee, while from thy brow I wipe the big
　　　drops,
And the blood from thy cheek!—that cheek, how
　　　glowing!
　　　　Hermann! Hermann! Thusnelda
　　　　Never so loved thee before!

No, not then, when thou first in old oak shadows,
With that manly brown arm didst wildly grasp
　　　me!
　　　　Spell-bound I read in thy look
　　　　That immortality then

Which thou now hast won. Tell to the forests,
Great Augustus, with trembling, amidst his gods
　　　now,
　　　　Drinks his nectar; for Hermann,
　　　　Hermann immortal is found!

" Wherefore curl'st thou my hair?   Lies not our
father
Cold and silent in death?   Oh, had Augustus
Only headed his army,—
He should lie bloodier there! "

Let me lift up thy hair; 't is sinking, Hermann:
Proudly thy locks should curl above the crown
now!
Sigmar is with the immortals!
Follow, and mourn him no more!

From the German of FRIEDRICH GOTTLIEB KLOPSTOCK.

THE BATTLE-SONG OF GUSTAVUS ADOLPHUS.

FEAR not, O little flock! the foe
Who madly seeks your overthrow,
Dread not his rage and power;
What though your courage sometimes faints?
His seeming triumph o'er God's saints
Lasts but a little hour.

Be of good cheer; your cause belongs
To him who can avenge your wrongs,
Leave it to him, our Lord.
Though hidden now from all our eyes,
He sees the Gideon who shall rise
To save us, and his word.

As true as God's own word is true,
Not earth or hell with all their crew
Against us shall prevail.

A jest and by-word are they grown;
God is with us, we are his own,
   Our victory cannot fail.

Amen, Lord Jesus; grant our prayer!
Great Captain, now thine arm make bare;
   Fight for us once again!
So shall the saints and martyrs raise
A mighty chorus to thy praise,
   World without end! Amen.

From the German of MICHAEL ALTENBURG.

SWORD SONG.

SWORD, on my left side gleaming,
What means thy bright eye's beaming?
   It makes my spirit dance
   To see thy friendly glance.
     Hurrah!

" A valiant rider bears me;
A free-born German wears me:
   That makes my eye so bright;
   That is the sword's delight."
     Hurrah!

Yes, good sword, I *am* free,
And love thee heartily,
   And clasp thee to my side,
   E'en as the plighted bride.
     Hurrah!

" And I to thee, by Heaven,
My light steel life have given;

When shall the knot be tied?
When wilt thou take thy bride? "
    Hurrah!

The trumpet's solemn warning
Shall hail the bridal morning,
When cannon-thunders wake,
Then my true-love I take.
    Hurrah!

" O blessèd, blessèd meeting!
My heart is wildly beating:
Come, bridegroom, come for me;
My garland waiteth thee."
    Hurrah!

Why in the scabbard rattle,
So wild, so fierce for battle?
What means this restless glow?
My sword, why clatter so?
    Hurrah!

" Well may thy prisoner rattle;
My spirit yearns for battle.
Rider, 't is war's wild glow
That makes me tremble so."
    Hurrah!

Stay in thy chamber near,
My love; what wilt thou here?
Still in thy chamber bide;
Soon, soon I take my bride.
    Hurrah!

" Let me not longer wait :
Love's garden blooms in state,
With roses bloody-red,
And many a bright death-bed."
     Hurrah!

Now, then, come forth, my bride!
Come forth, thou rider's pride!
Come out, my good sword, come!
Forth to thy father's home!
     Hurrah!

" O, in the field to prance
The glorious wedding dance!
How, in the sun's bright beams,
Bride-like the clear steel gleams! "
     Hurrah!

Then forward, valiant fighters!
And forward, German riders!
And when the heart grows cold,
Let each his love infold.
     Hurrah!

Once on the left it hung,
And stolen glances flung;
Now clearly on your right
Doth God each fond bride plight.
     Hurrah!

Then let your hot lips feel
That virgin cheek of steel;

One kiss,—and woe betide
Him who forsakes the bride.
    Hurrah!

Now let the loved one sing;
Now let the clear blade ring,
Till the bright sparks shall fly,
Heralds of victory!
    Hurrah!

For, hark! the trumpet's warning
Proclaims the marriage morning;
It dawns in festal pride;
Hurrah, thou Iron Bride!
    Hurrah!

From the German of KARL THEODOR KÖRNER.
Translation of CHARLES TIMOTHY BROOKS.

THE TROOPER'S DEATH.

THE weary night is o'er at last!
We ride so still, we ride so fast!
    We ride where Death is lying.
The morning wind doth coldly pass,
Landlord! we 'll take another glass,
    Ere dying.

Thou, springing grass, that art so green,
Shall soon be rosy red, I ween,
    My blood the hue supplying!
I drink the first glass, sword in hand,
To him who for the Fatherland
    Lies dying!

Now quickly comes the second draught,
And that shall be to freedom quaffed
While freedom's foes are flying!
The rest, O land, our hope and faith!
We'd drink to thee with latest breath,
Though dying!

My darling!—ah, the glass is out!
The bullets ring, the riders shout—
No time for wine or sighing!
There! bring my love the shattered glass—
Charge! On the foe! no joys surpass
Such dying!

From the German of GEORG HERWEGH.
Translation of ROSSITER W. RAYMOND.

BINGEN ON THE RHINE.

A SOLDIER of the Legion lay dying in Algiers,
There was lack of woman's nursing, there was
dearth of woman's tears;
But a comrade stood beside him, while his life-
blood ebbed away,
And bent, with pitying glances, to hear what he
might say.
The dying soldier faltered, and he took that com-
rade's hand,
And he said, "I nevermore shall see my own,
my native land;
Take a message, and a token, to some distant
friends of mine,
For I was born at Bingen,—at Bingen on the
Rhine.

"Tell my brothers and companions, when they
    meet and crowd around,
To hear my mournful story, in that pleasant
    vineyard ground,
That we fought the battle bravely, and when the
    day was done,
Full many a corse lay ghastly pale beneath the
    setting sun;
And, mid the dead and dying, were some grown
    old in wars,—
The death-wound on their gallant breasts, the
    last of many scars;
And some were young, and suddenly beheld life's
    morn decline,—
And one had come from Bingen,—fair Bingen on
    the Rhine.

"Tell my mother that her other son shall com-
    fort her old age;
For I was still a truant bird, that thought his
    home a cage.
For my father was a soldier, and even as a child
My heart leaped forth to hear him tell of strug-
    gles fierce and wild;
And when he died, and left us to divide his scanty
    hoard,
I let them take whate'er they would,—but kept
    my father's sword;
And with boyish love I hung it where the bright
    light used to shine,
On the cottage wall at Bingen,—calm Bingen on
    the Rhine.

" Tell my sister not to weep for me, and sob with
  drooping head,
When the troops come marching home again
  with glad and gallant tread,
But to look upon them proudly, with a calm and
  steadfast eye,
For her brother was a soldier too, and not afraid
  to die;
And if a comrade seek her love, I ask her in my
  name
To listen to him kindly, without regret or shame,
And to hang the old sword in its place (my fath-
  er's sword and mine)
For the honor of old Bingen,—dear Bingen on the
  Rhine.

" There's another,—not a sister; in the happy
  days gone by
You'd have known her by the merriment that
  sparkled in her eye;
Too innocent for coquetry,—too fond for idle
  scorning,—
O friend! I fear the lightest heart makes sometimes heaviest mourning!
Tell her the last night of my life (for, ere the
  moon be risen,
My body will be out of pain, my soul be out of
  prison),—
I dreamed I stood with *her,* and saw the yellow
  sunlight shine
On the vine-clad hills of Bingen,—fair Bingen on
  the Rhine.

" I saw the blue Rhine sweep along,—I heard,
or seemed to hear,
The German songs we used to sing, in chorus
sweet and clear;
And down the pleasant river, and up the slant-
ing hill,
The echoing chorus sounding, through the evening
calm and still;
And her glad blue eyes were on me, as we passed,
with friendly talk,
Down many a path beloved of yore, and well-
remembered walk!
And her little hand lay lightly, confidingly in
mine,—
But we 'll meet no more at Bingen,—loved Bingen
on the Rhine."

His trembling voice grew faint and hoarse,—his
grasp was childish weak,—
His eyes put on a dying look,—he sighed and
ceased to speak;
His comrade bent to lift him, but the spark of
life had fled,—
The soldier of the Legion in a foreign land is
dead!
And the soft moon rose up slowly, and calmly
she looked down
On the red sand of the battle-field, with bloody
corses strewn;
Yes, calmly on that dreadful scene her pale light
seemed to shine,
As it shone on distant Bingen,—fair Bingen on
the Rhine.

CAROLINE ELIZABETH SARAH NORTON.

HOHENLINDEN.

[1800.]

On Linden, when the sun was low,
All bloodless lay the untrodden snow,
And dark as winter was the flow
Of Iser, rolling rapidly.

But Linden saw another sight
When the drum beat, at dead of night,
Commanding fires of death to light
The darkness of her scenery.

By torch and trumpet fast arrayed,
Each horseman drew his battle-blade,
And furious every charger neighed,
To join the dreadful revelry.

Then shook the hills with thunder riven,
Then rushed the steeds to battle driven,
And louder than the bolts of heaven
Far flashed the red artillery.

But redder yet that light shall glow
On Linden's hills of stainèd snow,
And bloodier yet the torrent flow
Of Iser, rolling rapidly.

'T is morn, but scarce yon level sun
Can pierce the war-clouds, rolling dun,
Where furious Frank and fiery Hun
Shout in their sulphurous canopy.

The combat deepens. On, ye brave,
Who rush to glory, or the grave!
Wave, Munich! all thy banners wave,
And charge with all thy chivalry!

Few, few shall part where many meet!
The snow shall be their winding-sheet,
And every turf beneath their feet
Shall be a soldier's sepulchre.

THOMAS CAMPBELL.

IVRY.

[1590.]

Now glory to the Lord of hosts, from whom all
glories are!
And glory to our sovereign liege, King Henry of
Navarre!
Now let there be the merry sound of music and
the dance,
Through thy corn-fields green, and sunny vines, O
pleasant land of France!
And thou, Rochelle, our own Rochelle, proud city
of the waters,
Again let raptures light the eyes of all thy mourn-
ing daughters;
As thou wert constant in our ills, be joyous in
our joys;
For cold and stiff and still are they who wrought
thy walls annoy.
Hurrah! hurrah! a single field hath turned the
chance of war!
Hurrah! hurrah! for Ivry, and Henry of Navarre.

Oh! how our hearts were beating, when, at the
dawn of day,
We saw the army of the League drawn out in long
array;
With all its priest-led citizens, and all its rebel
peers,
And Appenzel's stout infantry, and Egmont's
Flemish spears.
There rode the brood of false Lorraine, the curses
of our land;
And dark Mayenne was in the midst, a truncheon
in his hand;
An as we looked on them, we thought of Seine's
empurpled flood,
And good Coligni's hoary hair all dabbled with
his blood;
And we cried unto the living God, who rules the
fate of war,
To fight for His own holy name, and Henry of
Navarre.

The king has come to marshal us, in all his armor
drest;
And he has bound a snow-white plume upon his
gallant crest.
He looked upon his people, and a tear was in his
eye;
He looked upon the traitors, and his glance was
stern and high.
Right graciously he smiled on us, as rolled from
wing to wing,
Down all our line, a deafening shout: God save
our lord the king!

" And if my standard-bearer fall, as fall full well
      he may—
For never saw I promise yet of such a bloody
      fray—
Press where you see my white plume shine amidst
      the ranks of war,
And be your oriflamme to-day the helmet of Na-
      varre."

Hurrah! the foes are moving. Hark to the min-
      gled din,
Of fife, and steed, and trump, and drum, and roar-
      ing culverin.
The fiery duke is pricking fast across Saint An-
      dré's plain,
With all the hireling chivalry of Guelders and
      Almayne.
Now by the lips of those ye love, fair gentlemen
      of France,
Charge for the golden lilies—upon them with the
      lance!
A thousand spurs are striking deep, a thousand
      spears in rest,
A thousand knights are pressing close behind the
      snow-white crest;
And in they burst, and on they rushed, while, like
      a guiding star,
Amidst the thickest carnage blazed the helmet of
      Navarre.

Now, God be praised, the day is ours: Mayenne
      hath turned his rein;
D'Aumale hath cried for quarter; the Flemish
      count is slain;

Their ranks are breaking like thin clouds before a
    Biscay gale;
The field is heaped with bleeding steeds, and flags,
    and cloven mail.
And then we thought on vengeance, and, all along
    our van,
Remember Saint Bartholomew! was passed from
    man to man.
But out spake gentle Henry—" No Frenchmen is
    my foe:
Down, down, with every foreigner, but let your
    brethren go."
Oh! was there ever such a knight, in friendship or
    in war,
As our sovereign lord, King Henry, the soldier of
    Navarre?

Right well fought all the Frenchmen who fought
    for France to-day;
And many a lordly banner God gave them for a
    prey.
But we of the religion have borne us best in
    fight;
And the good lord of Rosny hath ta'en the cornet
    white—
Our own true Maximilian the cornet white hath
    ta'en,
The cornet white with crosses black, the flag of
    false Lorraine.
Up with it high; unfurl it wide—that all the host
    may know
How God hath humbled the proud house which
    wrought His Church such woe.

Then on the ground, while trumpets sound their
    loudest point of war,
Fling the red shreds, a footcloth meet for Henry
    of Navarre.

Ho! maidens of Vienna; ho! matrons of Lucerne—
Weep, weep, and rend your hair for those who
    never shall return.
Ho! Philip, send, for charity, thy Mexican pis-
    toles,
That Antwerp monks may sing a mass for thy
    poor spearmen's souls.
Ho! gallant nobles of the League, look that your
    arms be bright;
Ho! burghers of St. Genevieve, keep watch and
    ward to-night;
For our God hath crushed the tyrant, our God
    hath raised the slave,
And mocked the counsel of the wise, and the valor
    of the brave.
Then glory to His holy name, from whom all
    glories are;
And glory to our sovereign lord, King Henry of
    Navarre!

LORD MACAULAY.

INCIDENT OF THE FRENCH CAMP.

You know we French stormed Ratisbon:
    A mile or so away,
On a little mound, Napoleon
    Stood on our storming-day;

With neck out-thrust, you fancy how,
  Legs wide, arms locked behind,
As if to balance the prone brow,
  Oppressive with its mind.

Just as perhaps he mused, " My plans
  That soar, to earth may fall,
Let once my army-leader Lannes
  Waver at yonder wall,"
Out 'twixt the battery-smokes there flew
  A rider, bound on bound
Full-galloping; nor bridle drew
  Until he reached the mound.

Then off there flung in smiling joy,
  And held himself erect
By just his horse's mane, a boy:
  You hardly could suspect
(So tight he kept his lips compressed,
  Scarce any blood came through),
You looked twice ere you saw his breast
  Was all but shot in two.

" Well," cried he, " Emperor, by God's grace
  We 've got you Ratisbon!
The marshal 's in the market-place,
  And you 'll be there anon
To see your flag-bird flap his vans
  Where I, to heart's desire,
Perched him! " The chief 's eye flashed; his plans
  Soared up again like fire.

The chief's eye flashed; but presently
  Softened itself, as sheathes

A film the mother-eagle's eye
  When her bruised eaglet breathes:
"You 're wounded!" "Nay," his soldier's pride
  Touched to the quick, he said:
"I 'm killed, sire!" And, his chief beside,
  Smiling, the boy fell dead.

                              ROBERT BROWNING.

THE BRONZE STATUE OF NAPOLEON.

THE work is done! the spent flame burns no more,
  The furnace fires smoke and die,
The iron flood boils over. Ope the door,
  And let the haughty one pass by!
Roar, mighty river, rush upon your course,
  A bound,—and, from your dwelling past,
Dash forward, like a torrent from its source,
  A flame from the volcano cast!
To gulp your lava-waves earth's jaws extend,
  Your fury in one mass fling forth,—
In your steel mould, O Bronze, a slave descend,
  An emperor return to earth!
Again NAPOLEON,—'t is his form appears!
  Hard soldier in unending quarrel,
Who cost so much of insult, blood, and tears,
  For only a few boughs of laurel!

For mourning France it was a day of grief,
  When, down from its high station flung,
His mighty statue, like some shameful thief,
  In coils of a vile rope was hung;

When we beheld at the grand column's base,
  And o'er a shrieking cable bowed,
The stranger's strength that mighty bronze dis-
    place
  To hurrahs of a foreign crowd;
When, forced by thousand arms, head-foremost
    thrown,
  The proud mass cast in monarch mould
Made sudden fall, and on the hard, cold stone
  Its iron carcass sternly rolled.
The Hun, the stupid Hun, with soiled, rank skin,
  Ignoble fury in his glance,
The emperor's form the kennel's filth within
  Drew after him, in face of France!
On those within whose bosoms hearts hold reign,
  That hour like remorse must weigh
On each French brow,—'t is the eternal stain,
  Which only death can wash away!
I saw, where palace-walls gave shade and ease,
  The wagons of the foreign force;
I saw them strip the bark which clothed our trees,
  To cast it to their hungry horse.
I saw the Northman, with his savage lip,
  Bruising our flesh till black with gore,
Our bread devour,—on our nostrils sip
  The air which was our own before!

In the abasement and the pain,—the weight
  Of outrages no words make known,—
I charged one only being with my hate:
  Be thou accursed, Napoleon!
O lank-haired Corsican, your France was fair,
  In the full sun of Messidor!

She was a tameless and a rebel mare,
  Nor steel bit nor gold rein she bore;
Wild steed with rustic flank;—yet, while she
    trod,—
  Reeking with blood of royalty,
But proud with strong foot striking the old sod,
  At last, and for the first time, free,—
Never a hand, her virgin form passed o'er,
  Left blemish nor affront essayed;
And never her broad sides the saddle bore,
  Nor harness by the stranger made.
A noble vagrant,—with coat smooth and bright,
  And nostril red, and action proud,—
As high she reared, she did the world affright
  With neighings which rang long and loud.
You came; her mighty loins, her paces scanned,
  Pliant and eager for the track;
Hot Centaur, twisting in her mane your hand,
  You sprang all booted to her back.
Then, as she loved the war's exciting sound,
  The smell of powder and the drum,
You gave her Earth for exercising ground,
  Bade Battles as her pastimes come!
Then, no repose for her,—no nights, no sleep!
  The air and toil for evermore!
And human forms like unto sand crushed deep,
  And blood which rose her chest before!
Through fifteen years her hard hoofs' rapid
    course
  So ground the generations,
And she passed smoking in her speed and force
  Over the breast of nations;

Till,—tired in ne'er earned goal to place vain
     trust,
   To tread a path ne'er left behind,
To knead the universe and like a dust
   To uplift scattered human kind,—
Feebly and worn, and gasping as she trode,
   Stumbling each step of her career,
She craved for rest the Corsican who rode.
   But, torturer! you would not hear;
You pressed her harder with your nervous thigh,
   You tightened more the goading bit,
Choked in her foaming mouth her frantic cry,
   And brake her teeth in fury-fit.
She rose,—but the strife came. From farther fall
   Saved not the curb she could not know,—
She went down, pillowed on the cannon-ball,
   And thou wert broken by the blow!

Now born again, from depths where thou wert
     hurled,
   A radiant eagle dost thou rise;
Winging thy flight again to rule the world,
   Thine image reascends the skies.
No longer now the robber of a crown,—
   The insolent usurper,—he,
With cushions of a throne, unpitying, down
   Who pressed the throat of Liberty,—
Old slave of the Alliance, sad and lone,
   Who died upon a sombre rock,
And France's image until death dragged on
   For chain, beneath the stranger's stroke,—
NAPOLEON stands, unsullied by a stain:
   Thanks to the flatterer's tuneful race,

The lying poets who ring praises vain,
  Has Cæsar 'mong the gods found place!
His image to the city-walls gives light;
  His name has made the city's hum,—
Still sounded ceaselessly, as through the fight
  It echoed farther than the drum.
From the high suburbs, where the people crowd,
  Doth Paris, an old pilgrim now,
Each day descend to greet the pillar proud,
  And humble there his monarch brow;—
The arms encumbered with a mortal wreath,
  With flowers for that bronze's pall,
(No mothers look on, as they pass beneath,—
  It grew beneath their tears so tall!)—
In working-vest, in drunkenness of soul,
  Unto the fife's and trumpet's tone,
Doth joyous Paris dance the Carmagnole
  Around the great Napoleon.

Thus, Gentle Monarchs, pass unnoted on!
  Mild Pastors of Mankind, away!
Sages, depart, as common brows have gone,
  Devoid of the immortal ray!
For vainly you make light the people's chain;
  And vainly, like a calm flock, come
On your own footsteps, without sweat or pain,
  The people,—treading towards their tomb.
Soon as your star doth to its setting glide,
  And its last lustre shall be given
By your quenched name,—upon the popular tide
  Scarce a faint furrow shall be riven.
Pass, pass ye on! For you no statue high!
  Your names shall vanish from the horde:

Their memory is for those who lead to die
  Beneath the cannon and the sword;
Their love, for him who on the humid field
  By thousands lays to rot their bones;
For him, who bids them pyramids to build,—
  And bear upon their backs the stones!

From the French of AUGUSTE BARBIER.

ON THE WARRES IN IRELAND.

FROM " EPIGRAMS," BOOK IV. EPIGRAM 6.

I PRAISED the speech, but cannot now abide it,
That warre is sweet to those that have not try'd
    it;
For I have proved it now and plainly see 't,
It is so sweet, it maketh all things sweet.
At home Canaric wines and Greek grow lothsome;
Here milk is nectar, water tasteth toothsome.
There without baked, rost, boyl'd, it is no cheere;
Bisket we like, and Bonny Clabo here.
There we complain of one wan roasted chick;
Here meat worse cookt ne're makes us sick.
At home in silken sparrers, beds of Down,
We scant can rest, but still tosse up and down;
Here we can sleep, a saddle to our pillow,
A hedge the Curtaine, Canopy a Willow.
There if a child but cry, O what a spite!
Here we can brook three larums in one night.
There homely rooms must be perfumed with
    Roses;
Here match and powder ne're offend our noses.

There from a storm of rain we run like Pullets;
Here we stand fast against a shower of bullets.
Lo, then how greatly their opinions erre,
That think there is no great delight in warre;
  But yet for this, sweet warre, Ile be thy debtor,
  I shall forever love my home the better.

SIR JOHN HARRINGTON.

ALFRED THE HARPER.

DARK fell the night, the watch was set,
The host was idly spread,
The Danes around their watchfires met,
Caroused, and fiercely fed.

The chiefs beneath a tent of leaves
And Guthrum, king of all,
Devoured the flesh of England's beeves,
And laughed at England's fall.
Each warrior proud, each Danish earl,
In mail of wolf-skin clad,
Their bracelets white with plundered pearl,
Their eyes with triumph mad.

From Humber-land to Severn-land,
And on to Tamar stream,
Where Thames makes green the towery strand,
Where Medway's waters gleam,—
With hands of steel and mouths of flame
They raged the kingdom through;
And where the Norseman sickle came,
No crop but hunger grew.

They loaded many an English horse
With wealth of cities fair;
They dragged from many a father's corse
The daughter by her hair.
And English slaves, and gems and gold,
Were gathered round the feast;
Till midnight in their woodland hold,
O, never that riot ceased.

In stalked a warrior tall and rude
Before the strong sea-kings;
" Ye Lords and Earls of Odin's brood,
Without a harper sings.
He seems a simple man and poor,
But well he sounds the lay;
And well, ye Norseman chiefs, be sure,
Will ye the song repay."

In trod the bard with keen cold look,
And glanced along the board,
That with the shout and war-cry shook
Of many a Danish lord.
But thirty brows, inflamed and stern,
Soon bent on him their gaze,
While calm he gazed, as if to learn
Who chief deserved his praise.

Loud Guthrum spake,—" Nay, gaze not thus,
Thou Harper weak and poor!
By Thor! who bandy looks with us
Must worse than looks endure.
Sing high the praise of Denmark's host,
High praise each dauntless Earl;

The brave who stun this English coast
With war's unceasing whirl."

The Harper slowly bent his head,
And touched aloud the string;
Then raised his face, and boldly said,
" Hear thou my lay, O King!
High praise from every mouth of man
To all who boldly strive,
Who fall where first the fight began,
And ne'er go back alive.

" Fill high your cups, and swell the shout,
At famous Regnar's name!
Who sank his host in bloody rout,
When he to Humber came.
His men were chased, his sons were slain,
And he was left alone.
They bound him in an iron chain
Upon a dungeon stone.

" With iron links they bound him fast;
With snakes they filled the hole,
That made his flesh their long repast,
And bit into his soul.

" Great chiefs, why sink in gloom your eyes?
Why champ your teeth in pain?
Still lives the song though Regnar dies!
Fill high your cups again!
Ye too, perchance, O Norseman lords!
Who fought and swayed so long,

Shall soon but live in minstrel words,
And owe your names to song.

" This land has graves by thousands more
Than that where Regnar lies.
When conquests fade, and rule is o'er,
The sod must close your eyes.
How soon, who knows? Not chief, nor bard;
And yet to me 't is given,
To see your foreheads deeply scarred,
And guess the doom of Heaven.

" I may not read or when or how,
But, Earls and Kings, be sure
I see a blade o'er every brow,
Where pride now sits secure.
Fill high the cups, raise loud the strain!
When chief and monarch fall,
Their names in song shall breathe again,
And thrill the feastful hall."

Grim sat the chiefs; one heaved a groan,
And one grew pale with dread,
His iron mace was grasped by one,
By one his wine was shed.
And Guthrum cried, " Nay, bard, no more
We hear thy boding lay;
Make drunk the song with spoil and gore!
Light up the joyous fray!"
" Quick throbs my brain,"—so burst the song,—
" To hear the strife once more.
The mace, the axe, they rest too long;
Earth cries, My thirst is sore.
16

More blithely twang the strings of bows
Than strings of harps in glee;
Red wounds are lovelier than the rose
Or rosy lips to me.

" O, fairer than a field of flowers,
When flowers in England grew,
Would be the battle's marshalled powers,
The plain of carnage new.
With all its death before my soul
The vision rises fair;
Raise loud the song, and drain the bowl!
I would that I were there!"

Loud rang the harp, the minstrel's eye
Rolled fiercely round the throng;
It seemed two crashing hosts were nigh,
Whose shock aroused the song.
A golden cup King Guthrum gave
To him who strongly played;
And said, " I won it from the slave
Who once o'er England swayed."

King Guthrum cried, " 'T was Alfred's own;
Thy song befits the brave:
The King who cannot guard his throne
Nor wine nor song shall have."
The minstrel took the goblet bright,
And said, " I drink the wine
To him who owns by justest right
The cup thou bid'st be mine.
To him, your Lord, O shout ye all!
His meed be deathless praise!

The King who dares not nobly fall,
Dies basely all his days."

" The praise thou speakest," Guthrum said,
" With sweetness fills mine ear;
For Alfred swift before me fled,
And left me monarch here.
The royal coward never dared
Beneath mine eye to stand.
O, would that now this feast he shared,
And saw me rule his land!"

Then stern the minstrel rose, and spake,
And gazed upon the King,—
" Not now the golden cup I take,
Nor more to thee I sing.
Another day, a happier hour,
Shall bring me here again:
The cup shall stay in Guthrum's power,
Till I demand it then."

The Harper turned and left the shed,
Nor bent to Guthrum's crown;
And one who marked his visage said
It wore a ghastly frown.
The Danes ne'er saw that Harper more,
For soon as morning rose,
Upon their camp King Alfred bore,
And slew ten thousand foes.

JOHN STERLING.

CHEVY-CHACE.

[A modernized form of the old ballad of the "Hunting
o' the Cheviot." Some circumstances of the battle of Otter-
bourne (A. D. 1388) are woven into the ballad, and the
affairs of the two events are confounded. The ballad
preserved in the "Percy Reliques" is probably as old as
1574. The one following is not later than the time of
Charles II.]

GOD prosper long our noble king,
　　Our lives and safeties all;
A woful hunting once there did
　　In Chevy-Chace befall.

To drive the deer with hound and horn
　　Earl Piercy took his way;
The child may rue that is unborn
　　The hunting of that day.

The stout Earl of Northumberland
　　A vow to God did make,
His pleasure in the Scottish woods
　　Three summer days to take,—

The chiefest harts in Chevy-Chace
　　To kill and bear away.
These tidings to Earl Douglas came,
　　In Scotland where he lay;

Who sent Earl Piercy present word
　　He would prevent his sport.
The English earl, not fearing that,
　　Did to the woods resort,

With fifteen hundred bowmen bold,
  All chosen men of might,
Who knew full well in time of need
  To aim their shafts aright.

The gallant greyhounds swiftly ran
  To chase the fallow deer;
On Monday they began to hunt,
  When daylight did appear;

And long before high noon they had
  A hundred fat bucks slain;
Then, having dined, the drovers went
  To rouse the deer again.

The bowmen mustered on the hills,
  Well able to endure;
And all their rear, with special care,
  That day was guarded sure.

The hounds ran swiftly through the woods
  The nimble deer to take,
That with their cries the hills and dales
  An echo shrill did make.

Lord Piercy to the quarry went,
  To view the slaughtered deer;
Quoth he, " Earl Douglas promisèd
  This day to meet me here;

" But if I thought he would not come,
  No longer would I stay; "
With that a brave young gentleman
  Thus to the earl did say:—

" Lo, yonder doth Earl Douglas come,—
His men in armor bright;
Full twenty hundred Scottish spears
All marching in our sight;

" All men of pleasant Tividale,
Fast by the river Tweed ; "
" Then cease your sports," Earl Piercy said,
" And take your bows with speed;

" And now with me, my countrymen,
Your courage forth advance;
For never was there champion yet,
In Scotland or in France,

" That ever did on horseback come,
But if my hap it were,
I durst encounter man for man,
With him to break a spear."

Earl Douglas on his milk-white steed,
Most like a baron bold,
Rode foremost of his company,
Whose armor shone like gold.

" Show me," said he, " whose men you be,
That hunt so boldly here,
That, without my consent, do chase
And kill my fallow-deer."

The first man that did answer make,
Was noble Piercy, he—

Who said, " We list not to declare,
    Nor show whose men we be :

" Yet will we spend our dearest blood
    Thy chiefest harts to slay."
Then Douglas swore a solemn oath,
    And thus in rage did say :—

" Ere thus I will out-bravèd be,
    One of us two shall die;
I know thee well, an earl thou art,—
    Lord Piercy, so am I.

" But trust me, Piercy, pity it were,
    And great offence, to kill
Any of these our guiltless men,
    For they have done no ill.

" Let you and me the battle try,
    And set our men aside."
" Accursed be he," Earl Piercy said,
    " By whom this is denied."

Then stepped a gallant squire forth,
    Witherington was his name,
Who said, " I would not have it told
    To Henry, our king, for shame,

" That e'er my captain fought on foot,
    And I stood looking on.
You two be earls," said Witherington,
    " And I a squire alone;

" I 'll do the best that do I may,
　　While I have power to stand;
While I have power to wield my sword
　　I 'll fight with heart and hand."

Our English archers bent their bows,—
　　Their hearts were good and true;
At the first flight of arrows sent,
　　Full fourscore Scots they slew.

Yet stays Earl Douglas on the bent,
　　As chieftain stout and good;
As valiant captain, all unmoved,
　　The shock he firmly stood.

His host he parted had in three,
　　As leader ware and tried;
And soon his spearmen on their foes
　　Bore down on every side.

Throughout the English archery
　　They dealt full many a wound;
But still our valiant Englishmen
　　All firmly kept their ground.

And throwing straight their bows away,
　　They grasped their swords so bright;
And now sharp blows, a heavy shower,
　　On shields and helmets light.

They closed full fast on every side,—
　　No slackness there was found;

And many a gallant gentleman
  Lay gasping on the ground.

In truth, it was a grief to see
  How each one chose his spear,
And how the blood out of their breasts
  Did gush like water clear.

At last these two stout earls did meet;
  Like captains of great might,
Like lions wode, they laid on lode,
  And made a cruel fight.

They fought until they both did sweat,
  With swords of tempered steel,
Until the blood, like drops of rain,
  They trickling down did feel.

"Yield thee, Lord Piercy," Douglas said,
  "In faith I will thee bring
Where thou shalt high advancèd be
  By James, our Scottish king.

"Thy ransom I will freely give,
  And this report of thee,—
Thou art the most courageous knight
  That ever I did see."

"No, Douglas," saith Earl Piercy then,
  "Thy proffer I do scorn;
I will not yield to any Scot
  That ever yet was born."

With that there came an arrow keen
  Out of an English bow,
Which struck Earl Douglas to the heart,—
  A deep and deadly blow;

Who never spake more words than these:
  " Fight on, my merry men all;
For why, my life is at an end;
  Lord Piercy sees my fall."

Then leaving life, Earl Piercy took
  The dead man by the hand;
And said, " Earl Douglas, for thy life
  Would I had lost my land.

" In truth, my very heart doth bleed
  With sorrow for thy sake;
For sure a more redoubted knight
  Mischance did never take."

A knight amongst the Scots there was
  Who saw Earl Douglas die,
Who straight in wrath did vow avenge
  Upon the Earl Piercy.

Sir Hugh Mountgomery was he called,
  Who, with a spear full bright,
Well mounted on a gallant steed,
  Ran fiercely through the fight;

And past the English archers all,
  Without a dread or fear;

And through Earl Piercy's body then
  He thrust his hateful spear.

With such vehement force and might
  He did his body gore,
The staff ran through the other side
  A large cloth-yard and more.

So thus did both these nobles die,
  Whose courage none could stain.
An English archer then perceived
  The noble earl was slain.

He had a bow bent in his hand,
  Made of a trusty tree;
An arrow of a cloth-yard long
  To the hard head haled he.

Against Sir Hugh Mountgomery
  So right the shaft he set,
The gray goose wing that was thereon
  In his heart's blood was wet.

This fight did last from break of day
  Till setting of the sun;
For when they rung the evening-bell
  The battle scarce was done.

With stout Earl Piercy there were slain
  Sir John of Egerton,
Sir Robert Ratcliff, and Sir John,
  Sir James, that bold baron.

And with Sir George and stout Sir James,
    Both knights of good account,
Good Sir Ralph Raby there was slain,
    Whose prowess did surmount.

For Witherington my heart is woe
    That ever he slain should be,
For when his legs were hewn in two,
    He knelt and fought on his knee.

And with Earl Douglas there was slain
    Sir Hugh Mountgomery,
Sir Charles Murray, that from the field
    One foot would never flee;

Sir Charles Murray of Ratcliff, too,—
    His sister's son was he;
Sir David Lamb, so well esteemed,
    But saved he could not be.

And the Lord Maxwell in like case
    Did with Earl Douglas die:
Of twenty hundred Scottish spears,
    Scarce fifty-five did fly.

Of fifteen hundred Englishmen,
    Went home but fifty-three;
The rest in Chevy-Chace were slain,
    Under the greenwood tree.

Next day did many widows come,
    Their husbands to bewail;

They washed their wounds in brinish tears,
But all would not prevail.

Their bodies, bathed in purple blood,
They bore with them away;
They kissed them dead a thousand times,
Ere they were clad in clay.

The news was brought to Edinburgh,
Where Scotland's king did reign,
That brave Earl Douglas suddenly
Was with an arrow slain:

" O heavy news," King James did say;
" Scotland can witness be
I have not any captain more
Of such account as he."

Like tidings to King Henry came
Within as short a space,
That Piercy of Northumberland
Was slain in Chevy-Chace:

" Now God be with him," said our King,
"' Since 't will no better be;
I trust I have within my realm
Five hundred as good as he:

" Yet shall not Scots or Scotland say
But I will vengeance take;
I 'll be revengèd on them all
For brave Earl Piercy's sake."

This vow full well the king performed
After at Humbledown;
In one day fifty knights were slain
With lords of high renown;

And of the rest, of small account,
Did many hundreds die:
Thus endeth the hunting of Chevy-Chace,
Made by the Earl Piercy.

God save the king, and bless this land,
With plenty, joy, and peace;
And grant, henceforth, that foul debate
'Twixt noblemen may cease.

ANONYMOUS.

SIR PATRICK SPENS.

[A confused echo of the Scotch expedition which should
have brought the Maid of Norway to Scotland, about 1285.]

THE king sits in Dunfermline town,
Drinking the blude-red wine,
" O whare will I get a skeely skipper,
To sail this new ship of mine!"

O up and spake an eldern knight,
Sat at the king's right knee,—
" Sir Patrick Spens is the best sailor,
That ever sailed the sea."

Our king has written a braid letter,
And sealed it with his hand,

And sent it to Sir Patrick Spens,
  Was walking on the strand.

" To Noroway, to Noroway,
  To Noroway o'er the faem;
The king's daughter of Noroway,
  'T is thou maun bring her hame."

The first word that Sir Patrick read,
  Sae loud loud laughèd he;
The neist word that Sir Patrick read,
  The tear blinded his e'e.

" O wha is this has done this deed,
  And tauld the king o' me,
To send us out, at this time of the year,
  To sail upon the sea?

" Be it wind, be it weet, be it hail, be it sleet,
  Our ship must sail the faem;
The king's daughter of Noroway,
  'T is we must fetch her hame."

They hoysed their sails on Monenday morn,
  Wi' a' the speed they may;
They hae landed in Noroway,
  Upon a Wodensday.

They hadna been a week, a week,
  In Noroway, but twae,
When that the lords o' Noroway
  Began aloud to say,—

" Ye Scottishmen spend a' our king's goud,
  And a' our queenis fee."
" Ye lie, ye lie, ye liars loud!
  Fu' loud I hear ye lie.

" For I brought as much white monie,
  As gane * my men and me,
And I brought a half-fou † o' gude red goud,
  Out o'er the sea wi' me.

" Make ready, make ready, my merrymen a'!
  Our gude ship sails the morn."
" Now, ever alake, my master dear,
  I fear a deadly storm!

" I saw the new moon, late yestreen,
  Wi' the auld moon in her arm;
And, if we gang to sea, master,
  I fear we 'll come to harm."

They hadna sailed a league, a league,
  A league but barely three,
When the lift grew dark, and the wind blew loud,
  And gurly grew the sea.

The ankers brak, and the topmasts lap,
  It was sic a deadly storm;
And the waves cam o'er the broken ship,
  Till a' her sides were torn.

" O where will I get a gude sailor,
  To take my helm in hand,

* Suffice.   † The eighth part of a peck.

Till I get up to the tall top-mast,
  To see if I can spy land?"

"O here am I, a sailor gude,
  To take the helm in hand,
Till you go up to the tall top-mast;
  But I fear you 'll ne'er spy land."

He hadna gane a step, a step,
  A step but barely ane,
When a bout flew out of our goodly ship,
  And the salt sea it came in.

"Gae, fetch a web o' silken claith,
  Another o' the twine,
And wap them into our ship's side,
  And let na the sea come in."

They fetched a web o' the silken claith,
  Another o' the twine,
And they wappèd them round that gude ship's
    side,
  But still the sea came in.

O laith, laith, were our gude Scots lords
  To weet their cork-heeled shoon!
But lang or a' the play was played,
  They wat their hats aboon.

And mony was the feather-bed,
  That flattered on the faem;
And mony was the gude lord's son,
  That never mair cam hame.
  17

The ladyes wrang their fingers white,
  The maidens tore their hair,
A' for the sake of their true loves;
  For them they 'll see na mair.

O lang, lang, may the ladyes sit,
  Wi' their fans into their hand,
Before they see Sir Patrick Spens
  Come sailing to the strand!

And lang, lang, may the maidens sit,
  Wi' their goud kaims in their hair,
A' waiting for their ain dear loves!
  For them they 'll see na mair.

O forty miles off Aberdeen,
  'T is fifty fathoms deep,
And there lies gude Sir Patrick Spens,
  Wi' the Scots lords at his feet.

ANONYMOUS BALLAD.

THE DOUGLAS TRAGEDY.

[This ballad exists in Denmark, and in other European
countries. The Scotch point out Blackhouse, on the wild
Douglas Burn, a tributary of the Yarrow, as the scene of
the tragedy.]

" RISE up, rise up, now, Lord Douglas," she says,
  " And put on your armor so bright;
Let it never be said, that a daughter of thine
  Was married to a lord under night.

" Rise up, rise up, my seven bold sons,
  And put on your armor so bright,

And take better care of your youngest sister,
  For your eldest 's awa the last night."

He 's mounted her on a milk-white steed,
  And himself on a dapple grey,
With a bugelet horn hung down by his side,
  And lightly they rade away.

Lord William lookit o'er his left shoulder,
  To see what he could see,
And there he spyed her seven brethren bold,
  Come riding over the lea.

" Light down, light down, Lady Marg'ret," he said,
  " And hold my steed in your hand,
Until that against your seven brothers bold,
  And your father, I mak a stand."

She held his steed in her milk-white hand,
  And never shed one tear,
Until that she saw her seven brethren fa',
  And her father hard fighting, who loved her so
    dear.

" O hold your hand, Lord William!" she said,
  " For your strokes they are wond'rous sair;
True lovers I can get many a ane,
  But a father I can never get mair."

O she 's ta'en out her handkerchief,
  It was o' the holland sae fine,
And aye she dighted her father's bloody wounds,
  That were redder than the wine.

"O chuse, O chuse, Lady Marg'ret," he said,
　"O whether will ye gang or bide?"
"I 'll gang, I 'll gang, Lord William," she said,
　"For ye have left me no other guide."

He 's lifted her on a milk-white steed,
　And himself on a dapple grey,
With a bugelet horn hung down by his side,
　And slowly they baith rade away.

O they rade on, and on they rade,
　And a' by the light of the moon,
Until they cam to yon wan water,
　And there they lighted down.

They lighted down to tak a drink
　Of the spring that ran sae clear;
And down the stream ran his gude heart's blood,
　And sair she gan to fear.

"Hold up, hold up, Lord William," she says,
　"For I fear that you are slain!"
"'T is naething but the shadow of my scarlet
　　cloak,
　That shines in the water sae plain."

O they rade on, and on they rade,
　And a' by the light of the moon,
Until they cam to his mother's ha' door,
　And there they lighted down.

"Get up, get up, lady mother," he says,
　"Get up, and let me in!—

Get up, get up, lady mother," he says,
" For this night my fair ladye I 've win.

" O mak my bed, lady mother," he says,
" O mak it braid and deep!
And lay Lady Marg'ret close at my back,
And the sounder I will sleep."

Lord William was dead lang ere midnight,
Lady Marg'ret lang ere day—
And all true lovers that go thegither,
May they have mair luck than they!

Lord William was buried in St. Mary's kirk,
Lady Margaret in Mary's quire;
Out o' the lady's grave grew a bonny red rose,
And out o' the knight's a brier.

And they twa met, and they twa plat,
And fain they wad be near;
And a' the warld might ken right weel,
They were twa lovers dear.

But bye and rade the Black Douglas,
And wow but he was rough!
For he pulled up the bonny brier,
And flang 't in St. Mary's loch.

ANONYMOUS BALLAD.

THE LAST HUNT.

Oh, it 's twenty gallant gentlemen
  Rode out to hunt the deer,
With mirth upon the silver horn
  And gleam upon the spear;
They galloped through the meadow-grass,
  They sought the forest's gloom,
And loudest rang Sir Morven's laugh,
  And lightest tost his plume.
    There 's no delight by day or night
    Like hunting in the morn;
    So busk ye, gallant gentlemen,
    And sound the silver horn!

They rode into the dark greenwood
  By ferny dell and glade,
And now and then upon their cloaks
  The yellow sunshine played;
They heard the timid forest-birds
  Break off amid their glee,
They saw the startled leveret,
  But not a stag did see.
    Wind, wind the horn, on summer morn!
    Though ne'er a buck appear,
    There 's health for horse and gentleman
    A-hunting of the deer!

They panted up Ben Lomond's side
  Where thick the leafage grew,
And when they bent the branches back
  The sunbeams darted through;

Sir Morven in his saddle turned,
  And to his comrades spake,
" Now quiet! we shall find a stag
  Beside the Brownies' Lake.
    Then sound not on the bugle-horn,
      Bend bush and do not break,
    Lest ye should start the timid hart
      A-drinking at the lake."

Now they have reached the Brownies' Lake,—
  A blue eye in the wood,—
And on its brink a moment's space
  All motionless they stood;
When, suddenly, the silence broke
  With fifty bowstrings' twang,
And hurtling through the drowsy air
  Full fifty arrows sang.
    Ah, better for those gentlemen,
      Than horn and slender spear,
    Were morion and buckler true,
      A-hunting of the deer.

Not one of that brave company
  Shall hunt the deer again;
Some fell beside the Brownies' Pool,
  Some dropt in dell or glen;
An arrow pierced Sir Morven's breast,
  His horse plunged in the lake,
And swimming to the farther bank
  He left a bloody wake.
    Ah, what avails the silver horn,
      And what the slender spear?
    There 's other quarry in the wood
      Beside the fallow deer!

O'er ridge and hollow sped the horse
  Besprent with blood and foam,
Nor slackened pace until at eve
  He brought his master home.
How tenderly the Lady Ruth
  The cruel dart withdrew!
" False Tirrell shot the bolt," she said,
  " That my Sir Morven slew! "
  Deep in the forest lurks the foe,
    While gayly shines the morn:
  Hang up the broken spear, and blow
  A dirge upon the horn.

      WILLIAM ROSCOE THAYER (*Paul Hermes*).

THE BALLAD OF AGINCOURT.

[1415.]

FAIR stood the wind for France,
When we our sails advance,
Nor now to prove our chance
  Longer will tarry;
But putting to the main,
At Kause, the mouth of Seine,
With all his martial train,
  Landed King Harry,

And taking many a fort,
Furnished in warlike sort,
Marchèd towards Agincourt
  In happy hour,—
Skirmishing day by day
With those that stopped his way,

Where the French general lay
    With all his power,

Which in his height of pride,
King Henry to deride,
His ransom to provide
    To the king sending;
Which he neglects the while,
As from a nation vile,
Yet, with an angry smile,
    Their fall portending.

And turning to his men,
Quoth our brave Henry then:
Though they to one be ten,
    Be not amazèd;
Yet have we well begun,
Battles so bravely won
Have ever to the sun
    By fame been raisèd.

And for myself, quoth he,
This my full rest shall be;
England ne'er mourn for me,
    Nor more esteem me,
Victor I will remain,
Or on this earth lie slain;
Never shall she sustain
    Loss to redeem me.

Poitiers and Cressy tell,
When most their pride did swell,
Under our swords they fell;
    No less our skill is

Than when our grandsire great,
Claiming the regal seat,
By many a warlike feat
    Lopped the French lilies.

The Duke of York so dread
The eager vaward led;
With the main Henry sped,
    Amongst his henchmen,
Excester had the rear,—
A braver man not there:
O Lord! how hot they were
    On the false Frenchmen!

They now to fight are gone;
Armor on armor shone;
Drum now to drum did groan,—
    To hear was wonder;
That with the cries they make
The very earth did shake;
Trumpet to trumpet spake,
    Thunder to thunder.

Well it thine age became,
O noble Erpingham!
Which did the signal aim
    To our hid forces;
When, from a meadow by,
Like a storm, suddenly,
The English archery
    Struck the French horses

With Spanish yew so strong,
Arrows a cloth-yard long,

That like to serpents stung,
  Piercing the weather;
None from his fellow starts,
But playing manly parts,
And, like true English hearts,
  Stuck close together.

When down their bows they threw,
And forth their bilboes drew,
And on the French they flew,
  Not one was tardy;
Arms were from shoulders sent;
Scalps to the teeth were rent;
Down the French peasants went;
  Our men were hardy.

This while our noble king,
His broadsword brandishing,
Down the French host did ding,
  As to o'erwhelm it;
And many a deep wound lent,
His arms with blood besprent,
And many a cruel dent
  Bruisèd his helmet.

Glo'ster, that duke so good,
Next of the royal blood,
For famous England stood
  With his brave brother,
Clarence, in steel so bright,
Though but a maiden knight,
Yet in that furious fight
  Scarce such another.

Warwick in blood did wade;
Oxford the foe invade,
And cruel slaughter made,
    Still as they ran up.
Suffolk his axe did ply;
Beaumont and Willoughby
Bare them right doughtily,
    Ferrers and Fanhope.

Upon Saint Crispin's day
Fought was this noble fray,
Which fame did not delay
    To England to carry;
O, when shall Englishmen
With such acts fill a pen,
Or England breed again
    Such a King Harry?

                    MICHAEL DRAYTON.

THE KING TO HIS SOLDIERS BEFORE HARFLEUR.

[1415.]

FROM " KING HENRY V.," ACT III. SC. 1.

ONCE more unto the breach, dear friends, once
    more;
Or close the wall up with our English dead!
In peace, there 's nothing so becomes a man,
As modest stillness, and humility:
But when the blast of war blows in our ears,
Then imitate the action of the tiger;
Stiffen the sinews, summon up the blood,

Disguise fair nature with hard-favored rage:
Then lend the eye a terrible aspèct;
Let it pry through the portage of the head,
Like the brass cannon; let the brow o'erwhelm it,
As fearfully as doth a gallèd rock
O'erhang and jutty his confounded base,
Swilled with the wild and wasteful ocean.
Now set the teeth, and stretch the nostril wide;
Hold hard the breath, and bend up every spirit
To his full height!—On, on, you noblest English,
Whose blood is fet from fathers of war-proof!
Fathers, that, like so many Alexanders,
Have, in these parts, from morn till even fought,
And sheathed their swords for lack of argument.
Dishonor not your mothers; now attest,
That those whom you called fathers, did beget
    you!
Be copy now to men of grosser blood,
And teach them how to war!—And you, good
    yeomen,
Whose limbs were made in England, show us here
The mettle of your pasture; let us swear
That you are worth your breeding: which I doubt
    not;
For there is none of you so mean and base,
That hath not noble lustre in your eyes.
I see you stand like greyhounds in the slips,
Straining upon the start. The game 's afoot;
Follow your spirit: and, upon this charge,
Cry—God for Harry! England! and Saint
    George!

                                SHAKESPEARE.

THE CAVALIER'S SONG.

A STEED! a steed of matchlesse speed,
  A sword of metal keene!
All else to noble heartes is drosse,
  All else on earth is meane.
The neighyinge of the war-horse prowde,
  The rowlinge of the drum,
The clangor of the trumpet lowde,
  Be soundes from heaven that come;
And oh! the thundering presse of knightes,
  Whenas their war-cryes swell,
May tole from heaven an angel bright,
  And rouse a fiend from hell.

Then mounte! then mounte, brave gallants all,
  And don your helmes amaine;
Deathe's couriers, fame and honor, call
  Us to the field againe.
No shrewish feares shall fill our eye
  When the sword-hilt 's in our hand—
Heart-whole we 'll part, and no whit sighe
  For the fayrest of the land;
Let piping swaine, and craven wight,
  Thus weepe and puling crye;
Our business is like men to fight,
  And hero-like to die!

WILLIAM MOTHERWELL.

GIVE A ROUSE.

KING CHARLES, and who 'll do him right now?
King Charles, and who 's ripe for fight now?
Give a rouse: here 's, in hell's despite now,
King Charles!

Who gave me the goods that went since?
Who raised me the house that sank once?
Who helped me to gold I spent since?
Who found me in wine you drank once?

(*Chorus*)

King Charles, and who 'll do him right now?
King Charles, and who 's ripe for fight now?
Give a rouse: here 's, in hell's despite now,
King Charles!

To whom used my boy George quaff else,
By the old fool's side that begot him?
For whom did he cheer and laugh else,
While Noll's damned troopers shot him?

(*Chorus*)

King Charles, and who 'll do him right now?
King Charles, and who 's ripe for fight now?
Give a rouse: here 's, in hell's despite now,
King Charles!

ROBERT BROWNING.

NASEBY.

[June, 1645.]

BY OBADIAH BIND-THEIR-KINGS-IN-CHAINS-AND-
THEIR-NOBLES-WITH-LINKS-OF-IRON ; SER-
GEANT IN IRETON'S REGIMENT.

O, WHEREFORE come ye forth, in triumph from the
　　north,
With your hands and your feet and your raiment
　　all red?
And wherefore doth your rout send forth a joyous
　　shout?
And whence be the grapes of the wine-press that
　　ye tread?

O, evil was the root, and bitter was the fruit,
And crimson was the juice of the vintage that we
　　trod:
For we trampled on the throng of the haughty and
　　the strong,
Who sate in the high places and slew the saints of
　　God.

It was about the noon of a glorious day of June,
That we saw their banners dance and their cui-
　　rasses shine,
And the man of blood was there, with his long
　　essenced hair,
And Astley, and Sir Marmaduke, and Rupert of
　　the Rhine.

Like a servant of the Lord, with his Bible and his
  sword,
The General rode along us to form us to the fight;
When a murmuring sound broke out, and swelled
  into a shout
Among the godless horsemen upon the tyrant's
  right.

And hark! like the roar of the billows on the shore,
The cry of battle rises along their charging line!
For God! for the cause!—for the Church! for the
  laws!
For Charles, king of England, and Rupert of the
  Rhine!

The furious German comes, with his clarions and
  his drums,
His bravoes of Alsatia, and pages of Whitehall;
They are bursting on our flanks. Grasp your
  pikes! Close your ranks!
For Rupert never comes but to conquer, or to fall.

They are here! They rush on! We are broken!
  We are gone!
Our left is borne before them like stubble on the
  blast.
O Lord, put forth thy might! O Lord, defend the
  right!
Stand back to back, in God's name! and fight it to
  the last!

Stout Skippon hath a wound; the centre hath
  given ground:
  18

Hark! hark! what means the trampling of horsemen on our rear?
Whose banner do I see, boys? 'T is he! thank God!
't is he, boys!
Bear up another minute! Brave Oliver is here.

Their heads all stooping low, their points all in
a row,
Like a whirlwind on the trees, like a deluge on
the dikes,
Our cuirassiers have burst on the ranks of the
Accurst,
And at a shock have scattered the forest of his
pikes.

Fast, fast the gallants ride, in some safe nook to
hide
Their coward heads, predestined to rot on Temple
Bar;
And he,—he turns, he flies:—shame on those cruel
eyes
That bore to look on torture, and dare not look on
war!

Ho! comrades, scour the plain; and, ere ye strip
the slain,
First give another stab to make your search secure;
Then shake from sleeves and pockets their broad-
pieces and lockets,
The tokens of the wanton, the plunder of the poor.

Fools! your doublets shone with gold, and your
hearts were gay and bold,

When you kissed your lily hands to your lemans
    to-day;
And to-morrow shall the fox, from her chambers
    in the rocks,
Lead forth her tawny cubs to howl above the prey.

Where be your tongues that late mocked at heaven
    and hell and fate?
And the fingers that once were so busy with your
    blades,
Your perfumed satin clothes, your catches and
    your oaths!
Your stage-plays and your sonnets, your diamonds
    and your spades?

Down! down! forever down, with the mitre and
    the crown!
With the Belial of the court, and the Mammon of
    the Pope!
There is woe in Oxford halls; there is wail in
    Durham's stalls;
The Jesuit smites his bosom; the bishop rends his
    cope.

And she of the seven hills shall mourn her chil-
    dren's ills,
And tremble when she thinks on the edge of
    England's sword;
And the kings of earth in fear shall shudder when
    they hear
What the hand of God hath wrought for the
    Houses and the Word!

THOMAS BABINGTON, LORD MACAULAY.

THE THREE SCARS.

This I got on the day that Goring
Fought through York, like a wild beast roaring—
The roofs were black, and the streets were full,
The doors built up with packs of wool;
But our pikes made way through a storm of shot,
Barrel to barrel till locks grew hot;
Frere fell dead, and Lucas was gone,
But the drum still beat and the flag went on.

This I caught from a swinging sabre,
All I had from a long night's labor;
When Chester * flamed, and the streets were red,
In splashing shower fell the molten lead,
The fire sprang up, and the old roof split,
The fire-ball burst in the middle of it;
With a clash and a clang the troopers they ran,
For the siege was over ere well began.

This I got from a pistol butt
(Lucky my head 's not a hazel nut) ;
The horse they raced, and scudded and swore;
There were Leicestershire gentlemen, seventy
    score;
Up came the " Lobsters," covered with steel—
Down we went with a stagger and reel;
Smash at the flag, I tore it to rag,
And carried it off in my foraging bag.

                    GEORGE WALTER THORNBURY.

* Siege of Chester, in the civil war, 1645.

FONTENOY.

[May 11, 1745.]

THRICE at the huts of Fontenoy the English column failed,
And twice the lines of Saint Antoine the Dutch in
vain assailed;
For town and slope were filled with fort and flanking battery,
And well they swept the English ranks and Dutch
auxiliary.
As vainly through De Barri's wood the British
soldiers burst,
The French artillery drove them back diminished
and dispersed.
The bloody Duke of Cumberland beheld with anxious eye,
And ordered up his last reserve, his latest chance
to try.
On Fontenoy, on Fontenoy, how fast his generals
ride!
And mustering came his chosen troops like clouds
at eventide.

Six thousand English veterans in stately column
tread;
Their cannon blaze in front and flank, Lord Hay
is at their head.
Steady they step adown the slopes, steady they
mount the hill,
Steady they load, steady they fire, moving right
onward still,

Betwixt the wood and Fontenoy, as through a
    furnace-blast,
Through rampart, trench, and palisade, and bul-
    lets showering fast;
And on the open plain above they rose and kept
    their course,
With ready fire and grim resolve that mocked at
    hostile force.
Past Fontenoy, past Fontenoy, while thinner grow
    their ranks,
They break as breaks the Zuyder Zee through Hol-
    land's ocean-banks.

More idly than the summer flies, French tirailleurs
    rush round;
As stubble to the lava-tide, French squadrons
    strew the ground;
Bombshells and grape and round-shot tore, still on
    they marched and fired;
Fast. from each volley grenadier and voltigeur re-
    tired.
"Push on my household cavalry," King Louis
    madly cried.
To death they rush, but rude their shock, not un-
    avenged they died.
On through the camp the column trod—King
    Louis turned his rein.
"Not yet, my liege," Saxe interposed; "the Irish
    troops remain."
And Fontenoy, famed Fontenoy, had been a
    Waterloo,
Had not these exiles ready been, fresh, vehement,
    and true.

" Lord Clare," he said, "you have your wish ; there
    are your Saxon foes ! "
The Marshal almost smiles to see how furiously he
    goes.
How fierce the look these exiles wear, who 're wont
    to be so gay !
The treasured wrongs of fifty years are in their
    hearts to-day :
The treaty broken ere the ink wherewith 't was
    writ could dry ;
Their plundered homes, their ruined shrines, their
    women's parting cry ;
Their priesthood hunted down like wolves, their
    country overthrown—
Each looks as if revenge for all were staked on
    him alone.
On Fontenoy, on Fontenoy, nor ever yet else-
    where,
Rushed on to fight a nobler band than these proud
    exiles were.

O'Brien's voice is hoarse with joy, as, halting, he
    commands :
" Fix bayonets—charge ! " Like mountain-storm
    rush on those fiery bands.
Thin is the English column now, and faint their
    volleys grow,
Yet mustering all the strength they have, they
    make a gallant show.
They dress their ranks upon the hill, to face that
    battle-wind !
Their bayonets the breakers' foam, like rocks the
    men behind !

One volley crashes from their line, when through
   the surging smoke,
With empty guns clutched in their hands, the
   headlong Irish broke.
On Fontenoy, on Fontenoy, hark to that fierce
   huzza!
"Revenge! remember Limerick! dash down the
   Sacsanagh!"

Like lions leaping at a fold, when mad with hunger's pang,
Right up against the English line the Irish exiles
   sprang;
Bright was their steel, 't is bloody now, their guns
   are filled with gore;
Through scattered ranks and severed files and
   trampled flags they tore.
The English strove with desperate strength,
   paused, rallied, scattered, fled;
The green hillside is matted close with dying and
   with dead.
Across the plain and far away passed on that
   hideous wrack,
While cavalier and fantassin dash in upon their
   track.
On Fontenoy, on Fontenoy, like eagles in the sun,
With bloody plumes the Irish stand—the field is
   fought and won!

                    THOMAS OSBORNE DAVIS.

BATTLE OF THE BALTIC.

[April 2, 1801.]

OF Nelson and the north
  Sing the glorious day's renown,
When to battle fierce came forth
  All the might of Denmark's crown,
And her arms along the deep proudly shone;
  By each gun the lighted brand
  In a bold determined hand,
  And the prince of all the land
Led them on.

Like leviathans afloat
  Lay their bulwarks on the brine;
While the sign of battle flew
  On the lofty British line—
It was ten of April morn by the chime.
  As they drifted on their path
  There was silence deep as death;
  And the boldest held his breath
For a time.

But the might of England flushed
  To anticipate the scene;
And her van the fleeter rushed
  O'er the deadly space between.
" Hearts of oak!" our captain cried; when each
      gun
  From its adamantine lips
  Spread a death-shade round the ships,
  Like the hurricane eclipse
Of the sun.

Again! again! again!
  And the havoc did not slack,
Till a feeble cheer the Dane
  To our cheering sent us back;
Their shots along the deep slowly boom—
  Then ceased—and all is wail,
  As they strike the shattered sail,
  Or in conflagration pale,
Light the gloom.

Out spoke the victor then,
  As he hailed them o'er the wave:
" Ye are brothers! ye are men!
  And we conquer but to save;
So peace instead of death let us bring;
  But yield, proud foe, thy fleet,
  With the crews, at England's feet,
  And make submission meet
To our king."

Then Denmark blessed our chief,
  That he gave her wounds repose;
And the sounds of joy and grief
  From her people wildly rose,
As death withdrew his shades from the day.
  While the sun looked smiling bright
  O'er a wide and woful sight,
  Where the fires of funeral light
Died away.

Now joy, old England, raise!
  For the tidings of thy might,
By the festal cities' blaze,
  Whilst the wine-cup shines in light;

And yet, amidst that joy and uproar,
  Let us think of them that sleep
  Full many a fathom deep,
  By thy wild and stormy steep,
Elsinore!

Brave hearts! to Britain's pride
  Once so faithful and so true,
On the deck of fame that died,
  With the gallant good Riou—
Soft sigh the winds of heaven o'er their grave!
  While the billow mournful rolls,
  And the mermaid's song condoles,
  Singing glory to the souls
Of the brave!

               THOMAS CAMPBELL.

BURIAL OF SIR JOHN MOORE.

[Corunna, Spain, January 16, 1809.]

Not a drum was heard, not a funeral note,
  As his corse to the rampart we hurried;
Not a soldier discharged his farewell shot
  O'er the grave where our hero we buried.

We buried him darkly, at dead of night,
  The sods with our bayonets turning;
By the struggling moonbeams' misty light,
  And the lanthorn dimly burning.

No useless coffin enclosed his breast,
  Not in sheet or in shroud we wound him;

But he lay, like a warrior taking his rest,
  With his martial cloak around him.

Few and short were the prayers we said,
  And we spoke not a word of sorrow;
But we steadfastly gazed on the face that was
    dead,
  And we bitterly thought of the morrow.

We thought, as we hollowed his narrow bed,
  And smoothed down his lonely pillow,
That the foe and the stranger would tread o'er his
    head,
  And we far away on the billow!

Lightly they'll talk of the spirit that's gone,
  And o'er his cold ashes upbraid him,
But little he'll reck, if they let him sleep on
  In the grave where a Briton has laid him!

But half of our heavy task was done,
  When the clock struck the hour for retiring;
And we heard the distant and random gun
  That the foe was sullenly firing.

Slowly and sadly we laid him down,
  From the field of his fame fresh and gory;
We carved not a line, and we raised not a stone—
  But we left him alone with his glory.

               CHARLES WOLFE.

"PICCIOLA."

IT was a Sergeant old and gray,
    Well singed and bronzed from siege and pillage,
Went tramping in an army's wake
    Along the turnpike of the village.

For days and nights the winding host
    Had through the little place been marching,
And ever loud the rustics cheered,
    Till every throat was hoarse and parching.

The Squire and Farmer, maid and dame,
    All took the sight's electric stirring,
And hats were waved and staves were sung,
    And kerchiefs white were countless whirring.

They only saw a gallant show
    Of heroes stalwart under banners,
And, in the fierce heroic glow,
    'T was theirs to yield but wild hosannas.

The Sergeant heard the shrill hurrahs,
    Where he behind in step was keeping;
But glancing down beside the road
    He saw a little maid sit weeping.

"And how is this?" he gruffly said,
    A moment pausing to regard her;—
"Why weepest thou, my little chit?"
    And then she only cried the harder.

" And how is this, my little chit? "
 The sturdy trooper straight repeated,
" When all the village cheers us on,
 That you, in tears, apart are seated?

" We march two hundred thousand strong,
 And that 's a sight, my baby beauty,
To quicken silence into song
 And glorify the soldier's duty."

" It 's very, very grand, I know,"
 The little maid gave soft replying;
" And Father, Mother, Brother too,
 All say ' Hurrah ' while I am crying;

" But think—O Mr. Soldier, think,—
 How many little sisters' brothers
Are going all away to fight
 And may be *killed*, as well as others! "

" Why, bless thee, child," the Sergeant said,
 His brawny hand her curls caressing,
" 'T is left for little ones like thee
 To find that War 's not all a blessing."

And " Bless thee! " once again he cried;
 Then cleared his throat and looked indignant,
And marched away with wrinkled brow
 To stop the struggling tear benignant.

And still the ringing shouts went up
 From doorway, thatch, and fields of tillage;

The pall behind the standard seen
By one alone of all the village.

The oak and cedar bend and writhe
When roars the wind through gap and braken;
But 't is the tenderest reed of all
That trembles first when Earth is shaken.

ROBERT HENRY NEWELL.

WATERLOO.

[June 15, 1815.]

FROM "CHILDE HAROLD," CANTO III.

THERE was a sound of revelry by night,
And Belgium's capital had gathered then
Her beauty and her chivalry, and bright
The lamps shone o'er fair women and brave
 men;
A thousand hearts beat happily; and when
Music arose with its voluptuous swell,
Soft eyes looked love to eyes which spake again,
And all went merry as a marriage-bell;
But hush! hark! a deep sound strikes like a rising
 knell!

Did ye not hear it?—No; 't was but the wind,
Or the car rattling o'er the stony street;
On with the dance! let joy be unconfined!
No sleep till morn, when Youth and Pleasure
 meet
To chase the glowing Hours with flying feet,—
But, hark!—that heavy sound breaks in once
 more,

As if the clouds its echo would repeat;
And nearer, clearer, deadlier than before!
Arm! arm! it is—it is—the cannon's opening roar!

Within a windowed niche of that high hall
Sate Brunswick's fated chieftain; he did hear
That sound the first amidst the festival,
And caught its tone with Death's prophetic ear;
And when they smiled because he deemed it
  near,
His heart more truly knew that peal too well
Which stretchèd his father on a bloody bier,
And roused the vengeance blood alone could
  quell:
He rushed into the field, and, foremost fighting,
  fell.

Ah! then and there was hurrying to and fro,
And gathering tears, and tremblings of distress,
And cheeks all pale which but an hour ago
Blushed at the praise of their own loveliness;
And there were sudden partings, such as press
The life from out young hearts, and choking
  sighs
Which ne'er might be repeated: who would
  guess
If evermore should meet those mutual eyes
Since upon night so sweet such awful morn could
  rise!

And there was mounting in hot haste: the steed,
The mustering squadron, and the clattering car,
Went pouring forward with impetuous speed,

And swiftly forming in the ranks of war;
And the deep thunder peal on peal afar;
And near, the beat of the alarming drum
Roused up the soldier ere the morning star;
While thronged the citizens with terror dumb,
Or whispering with white lips,—" The foe! they
    come! they come!"

And wild and high the " Cameron's gathering "
    rose,
The war-note of Lochiel, which Albyn's hills
Have heard,—and heard, too, have her Saxon
    foes:
How in the noon of night that pibroch thrills
Savage and shrill! But with the breath which
    fills
Their mountain pipe, so fill the mountaineers
With the fierce native daring which instills
The stirring memory of a thousand years,
And Evan's, Donald's fame, rings in each clans-
    man's ears!

And Ardennes waves above them her green
    leaves,
Dewy with nature's tear-drops, as they pass,
Grieving, if aught inanimate e'er grieves,
 Over the unreturning brave,—alas!
Ere evening to be trodden like the grass
Which now beneath them, but above shall grow
In its next verdure, when this fiery mass
Of living valor, rolling on the foe,
And burning with high hope, shall moulder cold
    and low.

19

Last noon beheld them full of lusty life,
Last eve in Beauty's circle proudly gay,
The midnight brought the signal sound of strife,
The morn the marshalling in arms,—the day
Battle's magnificently stern array!
The thunder-clouds close o'er it, which when
    rent
The earth is covered thick with other clay,
Which her own clay shall cover, heaped and
    pent,
Rider and horse,—friend, foe,—in one red burial
    blent!

Their praise is hymned by loftier harps than
    mine;
Yet one I would select from that proud throng,
Partly because they blend me with his line,
And partly that I did his sire some wrong,
And partly that bright names will hallow song!
And his was of the bravest, and when showered
The death-bolts deadliest the thinned files along,
Even where the thickest of war's tempest low-
    ered,
They reached no nobler breast than thine, young,
    gallant Howard!

There have been tears and breaking hearts for
    thee,
And mine were nothing, had I such to give;
But when I stood beneath the fresh green tree,
Which living waves where thou didst cease to
    live,
And saw around me the wide field revive
With fruits and fertile promise, and the Spring

Come forth her work of gladness to contrive,
With all her reckless birds upon the wing,
I turned from all she brought to those she could
    not bring.

I turned to thee, to thousands, of whom each
And one as all a ghastly gap did make
In his own kind and kindred, whom to teach
Forgetfulness were mercy for their sake;
The Archangel's trump, not glory's, must awake
Those whom they thirst for; though the sound
    of Fame
May for a moment soothe, it cannot slake
The fever of vain longing, and the name
So honored but assumes a stronger, bitterer claim.

They mourn, but smile at length; and, smiling,
    mourn:
The tree will wither long before it fall;
The hull drives on, though mast and sail be torn;
The roof-tree sinks, but moulders on the hall
In massy hoariness; the ruined wall
Stands when its wind-worn battlements are
    gone;
The bars survive the captive they enthrall;
The day drags through though storms keep out
    the sun;
And thus the heart will break, yet brokenly live
    on;

Even as a broken mirror, which the glass
In every fragment multiplies, and makes
A thousand images of one that was

The same, and still the more, the more it breaks;
And thus the heart will do which not forsakes,
Living in shattered guise, and still, and cold,
And bloodless, with its sleepless sorrow aches,
Yet withers on till all without is old,
Showing no visible sign, for such things are un-
 told.

LORD BYRON.

BY THE ALMA RIVER.

[September 20, 1854.]

WILLIE, fold your little hands;
 Let it drop,—that " soldier " toy;
Look where father's picture stands,—
 Father, that here kissed his boy
Not a month since,—father kind,
Who this night may (never mind
Mother's sob, my Willie dear)
Cry out loud that He may hear
Who is God of battles,—cry,
" God keep father safe this day
 By the Alma River!"

Ask no more, child. Never heed
 Either Russ, or Frank, or Turk;
Right of nations, trampled creed,
 Chance-poised victory's bloody work;
Any flag i' the wind may roll
On thy heights, Sevastopol!
Willie, all to you and me
Is that spot, whate'er it be,

Where he stands—no other word—
Stands—God sure the child's prayers heard—
  Near the Alma River.

Willie, listen to the bells
  Ringing in the town to-day;
That 's for victory. No knell swells
  For the many swept away,—
Hundreds, thousands. Let us weep,
We, who need not,—just to keep
Reason clear in thought and brain
Till the morning comes again;
Till the third dread morning tell
Who they were that fought and—*fell*
  By the Alma River.

Come, we 'll lay us down, my child;
  Poor the bed is,—poor and hard;
But thy father, far exiled,
  Sleeps upon the open sward,
Dreaming of us two at home;
Or, beneath the starry dome,
Digs out trenches in the dark,
Where he buries—Willie, mark!—
Where *he buries* those who died
Fighting—fighting at his side—
  By the Alma River.

Willie, Willie, go to sleep;
  God will help us, O my boy!
He will make the dull hours creep
  Faster, and send news of joy;
When I need not shrink to meet

Those great placards in the street,
That for weeks will ghastly stare
In some eyes—child, say that prayer
Once again,—a different one,—
Say, " O God! Thy will be done
By the Alma River."

DINAH MARIA MULOCK CRAIK.

CHARGE OF THE LIGHT BRIGADE.

[October 25, 1854.]

HALF a league, half a league,
Half a league onward,
All in the valley of Death
Rode the six hundred.
" Forward, the Light Brigade!
Charge for the guns! " he said;
Into the valley of Death
Rode the six hundred.

" Forward, the Light Brigade! "
Was there a man dismayed?
Not though the soldier knew
Some one had blundered:
Theirs not to make reply,
Theirs not to reason why,
Theirs but to do and die:
Into the valley of Death
Rode the six hundred.

Cannon to right of them,
Cannon to left of them,

Cannon in front of them
  Volleyed and thundered;
Stormed at with shot and shell,
Boldly they rode and well;
Into the jaws of Death,
Into the mouth of Hell,
  Rode the six hundred.

Flashed all their sabres bare,
Flashed as they turned in air,
Sabring the gunners there,
Charging an army, while
  All the world wondered:
Plunged in the battery-smoke,
Right through the line they broke:
Cossack and Russian
Reeled from the sabre-stroke,
  Shattered and sundered.
Then they rode back, but not—
  Not the six hundred.

Cannon to right of them,
Cannon to left of them,
Cannon behind them
  Volleyed and thundered:
Stormed at with shot and shell,
While horse and hero fell,
They that had fought so well
Came through the jaws of Death
Back from the mouth of Hell,—
All that was left of them,
  Left of six hundred.

When can their glory fade?
O the wild charge they made!
All the world wondered.
Honor the charge they made!
Honor the Light Brigade,
Noble six hundred!

ALFRED, LORD TENNYSON.

THE RELIEF OF LUCKNOW.

[September 25, 1857.]

O, THAT last day in Lucknow fort!
We knew that it was the last;
That the enemy's lines crept surely on,
And the end was coming fast.

To yield to that foe meant worse than death;
And the men and we all worked on;
It was one day more of smoke and roar,
And then it would all be done.

There was one of us, a corporal's wife,
A fair, young, gentle thing,
Wasted with fever in the siege,
And her mind was wandering.

She lay on the ground, in her Scottish plaid,
And I took her head on my knee;
"When my father comes hame frae the pleugh,"
she said,
"Oh! then please wauken me."

She slept like a child on her father's floor,
  In the flecking of woodbine-shade,
When the house-dog sprawls by the open door,
  And the mother's wheel is stayed.

It was smoke and roar and powder-stench,
  And hopeless waiting for death;
And the soldier's wife, like a full-tired child,
  Seemed scarce to draw her breath.

I sank to sleep; and I had my dream
  Of an English village-lane,
And wall and garden;—but one wild scream
  Brought me back to the roar again.

There Jessie Brown stood listening
  Till a sudden gladness broke
All over her face; and she caught my hand
  And drew me near as she spoke:—

" The Hielanders! O, dinna ye hear
  The slogan far awa,
The McGregor's?—O, I ken it weel;
  It 's the grandest o' them a'!

" God bless thae bonny Hielanders!
  We 're saved! we 're saved! " she cried;
And fell on her knees; and thanks to God
  Flowed forth like a full flood-tide.

Along the battery-line her cry
  Had fallen among the men,

And they started back;—they were there to die;
  But was life so near them, then?

They listened for life; the rattling fire
  Far off, and the far-off roar,
Were all; and the colonel shook his head,
  And they turned to their guns once more.

But Jessie said, " The slogan 's done;
  But winna ye hear it noo,
The Campbells are comin'? It 's no' a dream;
  Our succors hae broken through! "

We heard the roar and the rattle afar,
  But the pipes we could not hear;
So the men plied their work of hopeless war
  And knew that the end was near.

It was not long ere it made its way,—
  A thrilling, ceaseless sound:
It was no noise from the strife afar,
  Or the sappers under ground.

It *was* the pipes of the Highlanders!
  And now they played *Auld Lang Syne;*
It came to our men like the voice of God,
  And they shouted along the line.

And they wept, and shook one another's hands,
  And the women sobbed in a crowd;
And every one knelt down where he stood,
  And we all thanked God aloud.

That happy day, when we welcomed them,
　　Our men put Jessie first;
And the general gave her his hand, and cheers
　　Like a storm from the soldiers burst.

And the pipers' ribbons and tartan streamed,
　　Marching round and round our line;
And our joyful cheers were broken with tears,
　　As the pipes played *Auld Lang Syne.*

ROBERT T. S. LOWELL.

DANNY DEEVER.

" WHAT are the bugles blowin' for? " said Files-
　　on-Parade.
" To turn you out, to turn you out," the Color-
　　Sergeant said.
" What makes you look so white, so white? " said
　　Files-on-Parade.
" I 'm dreadin' what I 've got to watch," the Color-
　　Sergeant said.
　　　For they 're hangin' Danny Deever, you can
　　　　hear the Dead March play,
　　　The regiment 's in 'ollow square—they 're
　　　　hangin' him to-day;
　　　They 've taken of his buttons off an' cut his
　　　　stripes away,
　　　An' they 're hangin' Danny Deever in the
　　　　mornin'.

" What makes the rear-rank breathe so 'ard? "
　　said Files-on-Parade.

" It 's bitter cold, it 's bitter cold," the Color-Ser-
geant said.
" What makes that front-rank man fall down? "
says Files-on-Parade.
" A touch o' sun, a touch o' sun," the Color-Ser-
geant said.
They are hangin' Danny Deever, they are
marchin' of 'im round,
They 'ave 'alted Danny Deever by 'is coffin
on the ground;
An' 'e 'll swing in 'arf a minute for a sneak-
in' shootin' hound—
O they 're hangin' Danny Deever in the
mornin'!

" 'Is cot was right-'and cot to mine," said Files-on-
Parade.
" 'E 's sleepin' out an' far to-night," the Color-
Sergeant said.
" I 've drunk 'is beer a score o' times," said Files-
on-Parade.
" 'E 's drinkin' bitter beer alone," the Color-Ser-
geant said.
They are hangin' Danny Deever, you must
mark 'im to 'is place,
For 'e shot a comrade sleepin'—you must
look 'im in the face;
Nine 'undred of 'is county an' the regiment's
disgrace,
While they 're hangin' Danny Deever in the
mornin'.

" What 's that so black agin the sun? " said Files-
on-Parade.

" It 's Danny fightin' 'ard for life," the Color-Ser-
    geant said.
" What 's that that whimpers over'ead? " said
    Files-on-Parade.
" It 's Danny's soul that 's passin' now," the Color-
    Sergeant said.
    For they 're done with Danny Deever, you
        can 'ear the quickstep play,
    The regiment 's in column, an' they 're
        marchin' us away;
    Ho! the young recruits are shakin', an'
        they 'll want their beer to-day,
    After hangin' Danny Deever in the mornin'.
                    RUDYARD KIPLING.

WHERE ARE THE MEN?

WHERE are the men who went forth in the
    morning,
    Hope brightly beaming in every face?
Fearing no danger,—the Saxon foe scorning,—
    Little thought they of defeat or disgrace!
Fallen is their chieftain—his glory departed—
    Fallen are the heroes who fought by his side!
Fatherless children now weep, broken-hearted,
    Mournfully wandering by Rhuddlan's dark tide!

Small was the band that escaped from the slaugh-
    ter,
    Flying for life as the tide 'gan to flow;
Hast thou no pity, thou dark rolling water?
    More cruel still than the merciless foe!

Death is behind them, and death is before them;
  Faster and faster rolls on the dark wave;
One wailing cry—and the sea closes o'er them;
  Silent and deep is their watery grave.

From the Welsh of TALIESSIN.
Translation of THOMAS OLIPHANT.

BRUCE AND THE SPIDER.

[About 1307.]

For Scotland's and for freedom's right
  The Bruce his part had played,
In five successive fields of fight
  Been conquered and dismayed;
Once more against the English host
His band he led, and once more lost
  The meed for which he fought;
And now from battle, faint and worn,
The homeless fugitive forlorn
  A hut's lone shelter sought.

And cheerless was that resting-place
  For him who claimed a throne:
His canopy, devoid of grace,
  The rude, rough beams alone;
The heather couch his only bed,—
Yet well I ween had slumber fled
  From couch of eider-down!
Through darksome night till dawn of day,
Absorbed in wakeful thoughts he lay
  Of Scotland and her crown.

The sun rose brightly, and its gleam
   Fell on that hapless bed,
And tinged with light each shapeless beam
   Which roofed the lowly shed;
When, looking up with wistful eye,
The Bruce beheld a spider try
   His filmy thread to fling
From beam to beam of that rude cot;
And well the insect's toilsome lot
   Taught Scotland's future king.

Six times his gossamery thread
   The wary spider threw;
In vain the filmy line was sped,
   For powerless or untrue
Each aim appeared, and back recoiled
The patient insect, six times foiled,
   And yet unconquered still;
And soon the Bruce, with eager eye,
Saw him prepare once more to try
   His courage, strength, and skill.

One effort more, his seventh and last—
   The hero hailed the sign!—
And on the wished-for beam hung fast
   That slender, silken line!
Slight as it was, his spirit caught
The more than omen, for his thought
   The lesson well could trace,
Which even " he who runs may read,"
That Perseverance gains its meed,
   And Patience wins the race.
                     BERNARD BARTON.

BANNOCKBURN.

[June 24, 1314.]

Scots, wha hae wi' Wallace bled,
Scots, wham Bruce has aften led;
Welcome to your gory bed,
    Or to victorie.

Now 's the day, and now 's the hour
See the front o' battle lour:
See approach proud Edward's power,—
    Chains and slaverie!

Wha will be a traitor knave?
Wha can fill a coward's grave?
Wha sae base as be a slave?
    Let him turn and flee!

Wha for Scotland's king and law
Freedom's sword will strongly draw,
Freeman stand, or freeman fa'?
    Let him follow me!

By Oppression's woes and pains!
By our sons in servile chains,
We will drain our dearest veins,
    But they shall be free!

Lay the proud usurpers low!
Tyrants fall in every foe!
Liberty 's in every blow!
    Let us do, or die!

ROBERT BURNS.

SONG OF CLAN-ALPINE.

FROM "THE LADY OF THE LAKE," CANTO II.

Loud a hundred clansmen raise
Their voices in their chieftain's praise.
Each boatman, bending to his oar,
With measured sweep the burthen bore,
In such wild cadence, as the breeze
Makes through December's leafless trees.
The chorus first could Allen know,
" Roderigh Vich Alpine, ho! ieroe!"
And near, and nearer, as they rowed,
Distinct the martial ditty flowed.

Hail to the Chief who in triumph advances!
Honored and blessed be the evergreen Pine!
Long may the tree, in his banner that glances,
Flourish, the shelter and grace of our line!
Heaven send it happy dew,
Earth lend it sap anew,
Gayly to bourgeon, and broadly to grow,
While every Highland glen
Sends our shouts back again,
" Roderigh Vich Alpine dhu, ho! ieroe!"

Ours is no sapling chance-sown by the fountain,
Blooming at Beltane, in winter to fade;
When the whirlwind has stripped every leaf on
the mountain,
The more shall Clan-Alpine exult in her shade.
Moored in the rifted rock,
Proof to the tempest's shock,
20

Firmer he roots him the ruder it blow;
  Menteith and Breadalbane, then,
  Echo his praise again,
"Roderigh Vich Alpine dhu, ho! ieroe!"

Proudly our pibroch has thrilled in Glen Fruin,
  And Bannachar's groans to our slogan re-
      plied;
Glen Luss and Ross-dhu, they are smoking in ruin,
  And the best of Loch-Lomond lie dead on her
      side.
    Widow and Saxon maid
    Long shall lament our raid,
  Think of Clan-Alpine with fear and with woe;
    Lennox and Leven-glen
    Shake when they hear again,
"Roderigh Vich Alpine dhu, ho! ieroe!"

Row, vassals, row, for the pride of the Highlands!
  Stretch to your oars for the evergreen Pine!
O that the rosebud that graces yon islands
  Were wreathed in a garland around him to
      twine!
    O that some seedling gem,
    Worthy such noble stem,
Honored and blessed in their shadow might grow!
    Loud should Clan-Alpine then
    Ring from the deepmost glen,
"Roderigh Vich Alpine dhu, ho! ieroe!"

                              SIR WALTER SCOTT.

BEAL' AN DHUINE.

[1411.]

FROM " THE LADY OF THE LAKE," CANTO VI.

THERE is no breeze upon the fern,
　No ripple on the lake,
Upon her eyrie nods the erne,
　The deer has sought the brake;
The small birds will not sing aloud,
　The springing trout lies still,
So darkly glooms yon thunder-cloud,
That swathes, as with a purple shroud,
　Benledi's distant hill.
Is it the thunder's solemn sound
　That mutters deep and dread,
Or echoes from the groaning ground
　The warrior's measured tread?
Is it the lightning's quivering glance
　That on the thicket streams,
Or do they flash on spear and lance
　The sun's retiring beams?
I see the dagger crest of Mar,
　I see the Moray's silver star
Wave o'er the cloud of Saxon war,
　That up the lake comes winding far!
To hero bound for battle strife,
　Or bard of martial lay,
'T were worth ten years of peaceful life,
　One glance at their array!

Their light-armed archers far and near
　Surveyed the tangled ground,

Their centre ranks, with pike and spear,
  A twilight forest frowned,
Their barbèd horsemen, in the rear,
  The stern battalia crowned.
No cymbal clashed, no clarion rang,
  Still were the pipe and drum;
Save heavy tread, and armor's clang,
  The sullen march was dumb.
There breathed no wind their crests to shake,
  Or wave their flags abroad;
Scarce the frail aspen seemed to quake,
  That shadowed o'er their road.
Their vaward scouts no tidings bring,
  Can rouse no lurking foe,
Nor spy a trace of living thing,
  Save when they stirred the roe;
The host moves like a deep sea wave,
Where rise no rocks its pride to brave,
  High swelling, dark, and slow.
The lake is passed, and now they gain
A narrow and a broken plain,
Before the Trosach's rugged jaws;
And here the horse and spearmen pause,
While, to explore the dangerous glen,
Dive through the pass the archer men.

At once there rose so wild a yell
Within that dark and narrow dell,
As all the fiends, from heaven that fell,
Had pealed the banner cry of hell!
Forth from the pass in tumult driven,
Like chaff before the winds of heaven,
  The archery appear:

For life! for life! their flight they ply—
And shriek, and shout, and battle-cry,
And plaids and bonnets waving high,
And broadswords flashing to the sky,
　Are maddening in the rear.
Onward they drive, in dreadful race,
　Pursuers and pursued;
Before that tide of flight and chase,
How shall it keep its rooted place,
　The spearmen's twilight wood?
—" Down, down," cried Mar, " your lances down!
　Bear back both friend and foe! "
Like reeds before the tempest's frown,
That serried grove of lances brown
　At once lay levelled low;
And closely shouldering side to side,
The bristling ranks the onset bide.—
—" We 'll quell the savage mountaineer,
　As their Tinchel * cows the game;
They come as fleet as forest deer,
　We 'll drive them back as tame."

Bearing before them, in their course,
The relics of the archer force,
Like wave with crest of sparkling foam,
Right onward did Clan-Alpine come.
Above the tide, each broadsword bright
Was brandishing like beam of light,
　Each targe was dark below;
And with the ocean's mighty swing,
When heaving to the tempest's wing,
　They hurled them on the foe.

* A circle of sportsmen, surrounding the deer.

I heard the lance's shivering crash,
As when the whirlwind rends the ash;
I heard the broadsword's deadly clang,
As if a hundred anvils rang!
But Moray wheeled his rearward flank—
Of horsemen on Clan-Alpine's flank—
  " My bannerman, advance!
I see," he cried, " their columns shake.
Now, gallants! for your ladies' sake,
  Upon them with the lance! "
The horsemen dashed among the rout,
  As deer break through the broom;
Their steeds are stout, their swords are out,
  They soon make lightsome room.
Clan-Alpine's best are backward borne—
  Where, where was Roderick then?
One blast upon his bugle-horn
  Were worth a thousand men!
And refluent through the pass of fear
  The battle's tide was poured;
Vanished the Saxon's struggling spear,
  Vanished the mountain sword.
As Bracklinn's chasm, so black and steep,
  Receives her roaring linn,
As the dark caverns of the deep
  Suck the wild whirlpool in,
So did the deep and darksome pass
Devour the battle's mingled mass;
None linger now upon the plain,
Save those who ne'er shall fight again.

                              SIR WALTER SCOTT.

PIBROCH OF DONUIL DHU.*

[1431.]

PIBROCH of Donuil Dhu,
  Pibroch of Donuil,
Wake thy wild voice anew,
  Summon Clan Conuil.
Come away, come away,
  Hark to the summons!
Come in your war array,
  Gentles and commons.

Come from deep glen, and
  From mountains so rocky;
The war-pipe and pennon
  Are at Inverlochy.
Come every hill-plaid, and
  True heart that wears one,
Come every steel blade, and
  Strong hand that bears one.

Leave untended the herd,
  The flock without shelter;
Leave the corpse uninterred,
  The bride at the altar;
Leave the deer, leave the steer,
  Leave nets and barges;
Come with your fighting gear,
  Broadswords and targes.

* Pipe-summons, or gathering-song, of Donald the Black.

Come as the winds come, when
　Forests are rended;
Come as the waves come, when
　Navies are stranded;
Faster come, faster come,
　Faster and faster,
Chief, vassal, page and groom,
　Tenant and master.

Fast they come, fast they come;
　See how they gather!
Wide waves the eagle plume
　Blended with heather.
Cast your plaids, draw your blades,
　Forward each man set!
Pibroch of Donuil Dhu,
　Knell for the onset!

SIR WALTER SCOTT.

FLODDEN FIELD.

[September, 1513.]

FROM " MARMION," CANTO VI.

A MOMENT then Lord Marmion stayed,
And breathed his steed, his men arrayed,
　Then forward moved his band,
Until, Lord Surrey's rear-guard won,
He halted by a cross of stone,
That, on a hillock standing lone,
　Did all the field command.

Hence might they see the full array
Of either host for deadly fray;

Their marshalled lines stretched east and west,
  And fronted north and south,
And distant salutation past
  From the loud cannon-mouth;
Not in the close successive rattle
That breathes the voice of modern battle,
  But slow and far between.—
The hillock gained, Lord Marmion stayed:
" Here, by this cross," he gently said,
  " You well may view the scene;
Here shalt thou tarry, lovely Clare:
O, think of Marmion in thy prayer!—
Thou wilt not?—well,—no less my care
Shall, watchful, for thy weal prepare.—
You, Blount and Eustace, are her guard,
  With ten picked archers of my train;
With England if the day go hard,
  To Berwick speed amain,—
But, if we conquer, cruel maid,
My spoils shall at your feet be laid,
  When here we meet again."
He waited not for answer there,
And would not mark the maid's despair,
  Nor heed the discontented look
From either squire: but spurred amain,
And, dashing through the battle-plain,
  His way to Surrey took.
          .   .   .   .   .

Blount and Fitz-Eustace rested still
With Lady Clare upon the hill;
On which (for far the day was spent)
The western sunbeams now were bent.
The cry they heard, its meaning knew,

Could plain their distant comrades view:
Sadly to Blount did Eustace say,
" Unworthy office here to stay!
No hope of gilded spurs to-day.—
But, see! look up,—on Flodden bent
The Scottish foe has fired his tent."—
    And sudden, as he spoke,
From the sharp ridges of the hill,
All downward to the banks of Till
    Was wreathed in sable smoke.
Volumed and vast, and rolling far,
The cloud enveloped Scotland's war,
    As down the hill they broke;
Nor martial shout, nor minstrel tone,
Announced their march; their tread alone,
At times their warning trumpet blown,
    At times a stifled hum,
Told England, from his mountain-throne
    King James did rushing come.—
Scarce could they hear or see their foes,
Until at weapon-point they close.—
They close in clouds of smoke and dust,
With sword-sway and with lance's thrust;
    And such a yell was there,
Of sudden and portentous birth,
As if men fought upon the earth
    And fiends in upper air:
O, life and death were in the shout,
Recoil and rally, charge and rout,
    And triumph and despair.
Long looked the anxious squires; their eye
Could in the darkness naught descry.

At length the freshening western blast
Aside the shroud of battle cast;
And, first, the ridge of mingled spears
Above the brightened cloud appears;
And in the smoke the pennons flew,
As in the storm the white sea-mew.
Then marked they, dashing broad and far,
The broken billows of the war,
And plumèd crests of chieftains bravè
Floating like foam upon the wave;
  But naught distinct they see:
Wide raged the battle on the plain;
Spears shook, and falchions flashed amain;
Fell England's arrow-flight like rain;
Crests rose, and stooped, and rose again,
  Wild and disorderly.
Amid the scene of tumult, high
They saw Lord Marmion's falcon fly:
And stainless Tunstall's banner white,
And Edmund Howard's lion bright,
Still bear them bravely in the fight;
  Although against them come
Of gallant Gordons many a one,
And many a stubborn Highlandman,
And many a rugged Border clan,
  With Huntley and with Home.

Far on the left, unseen· the while,
Stanley broke Lennox and Argyle;
Though there the western mountaineer
Rushed with bare bosom on the spear,
And flung the feeble targe aside,
And with both hands the broadsword plied,

'T was vain:—But Fortune, on the right,
With fickle smile, cheered Scotland's fight.
Then fell that spotless banner white,
   The Howard's lion fell;
Yet still Lord Marmion's falcon flew
With wavering flight, while fiercer grew
   Around the battle-yell.
The Border slogan rent the sky!
A Home! a Gordon! was the cry:
Loud were the clanging blows;
Advanced,—forced back,—now low, now high,
   The pennon sunk and rose;
As bends the bark's mast in the gale,
When rent are rigging, shrouds, and sail,
   It wavered mid the foes.
No longer Blount the view could bear:—
" By heaven and all its saints, I swear,
   I will not see it lost!
Fitz-Eustace, you with Lady Clare
May bid your beads, and patter prayer,—
   I gallop to the host."
And to the fray he rode amain,
Followed by all the archer train.
The fiery youth, with desperate charge,
Made, for a space, an opening large,—
   The rescued banner rose,
But darkly closed the war around.
Like pine-tree rooted from the ground,
   It sunk among the foes.
Then Eustace mounted too;—yet stayed,
As loath to leave the helpless maid,
   When, fast as shaft can fly,
Bloodshot his eyes, his nostrils spread,

The loose rein dangling from his head,
Housing and saddle bloody red,
　Lord Marmion's steed rushed by;
And Eustace, maddening at the sight,
　A look and sign to Clara cast,
　To mark he would return in haste,
Then plunged into the fight.

Ask me not what the maiden feels,
　Left in that dreadful hour alone:
Perchance her reason stoops or reels;
　Perchance a courage, not her own,
　Braces her mind to desperate tone.—
The scattered van of England wheels;—
　She only said, as loud in air
　The tumult roared, " Is Wilton there? "
They fly, or, maddened by despair,
　Fight but to die,—" Is Wilton there? "
With that, straight up the hill there rode
　Two horsemen drenched with gore,
And in their arms, a helpless load,
　A wounded knight they bore.
His hand still strained the broken brand;
His arms were smeared with blood and sand.
Dragged from among the horses' feet,
With dinted shield, and helmet beat,
The falcon-crest and plumage gone,
Can that be haughty Marmion! . . .
Young Blount his armor did unlace,
And, gazing on his ghastly face,
　Said,—" By Saint George, he 's gone!
That spear-wound has our master sped,—
And see the deep cut on his head!
　Good night to Marmion."—

" Unnurtured Blount! thy brawling cease:
He opes his eyes," said Eustace; " peace!"

When, doffed his casque, he felt free air,
Around 'gan Marmion wildly stare:—
" Where 's Harry Blount? Fitz-Eustace where?
Linger ye here, ye hearts of hare!
Redeem my pennon,—charge again!
Cry—' Marmion to the rescue!'—vain!
Last of my race, on battle-plain
That shout shall ne'er be heard again!—
Yet my last thought is England's:—fly,
    To Dacre bear my signet-ring:
    Tell him his squadrons up to bring:—
Fitz-Eustace, to Lord Surrey hie;
    Tunstall lies dead upon the field,
    His life-blood stains the spotless shield:
    Edmund is down;—my life is reft;—
    The Admiral alone is left.
Let Stanley charge with spur of fire,—
With Chester charge, and Lancashire,
Full upon Scotland's central host,
Or victory and England 's lost.—
Must I bid twice?—hence, varlets! fly!
Leave Marmion here alone—to die."
They parted, and alone he lay:
Clare drew her from the sight away,
Till pain rung forth a lowly moan,
And half he murmured,—" Is there none,
    Of all my halls have nurst,
Page, squire, or groom, one cup to bring,
Of blessèd water from the spring,
    To slake my dying thirst?"

O woman! in our hours of ease,
Uncertain, coy, and hard to please,
　And variable as the shade
By the light quivering aspen made;
When pain and anguish wring the brow,
A ministering angel thou!—
Scarce were the piteous accents said,
When, with the Baron's casque, the maid
　To the nigh streamlet ran;
Forgot were hatred, wrongs, and fears;
The plaintive voice alone she hears,
　Sees but the dying man.
She stooped her by the runnel's side,
　But in abhorrence backward drew;
For, oozing from the mountain's side,
Where raged the war, a dark-red tide
　Was curdling in the streamlet blue,
Where shall she turn!—behold her mark
　A little fountain cell,
Where water, clear as diamond-spark,
　In a stone basin fell.
Above, some half-worn letters say,
𝔇rink : weary : pilgrim : drink : and : pray :
𝔉or : the : kind : soul : of : 𝔖ybil : 𝔊ray :
　𝔚ho : built : this : cross : and : well :
She filled the helm, and back she hied,
And with surprise and joy espied
　A monk supporting Marmion's head;
A pious man whom duty brought
To dubious verge of battle fought,
　To shrive the dying, bless the dead.

Deep drank Lord Marmion of the wave,
And, as she stooped his brow to lave,—

" Is it the hand of Clare," he said,
" Or injured Constance, bathes my head? "
  Then, as remembrance rose,—
" Speak not to me of shrift or prayer!
  I must redress her woes.
Short space, few words, are mine to spare;
Forgive and listen, gentle Clare! "—
  " Alas! " she said, " the while,—
O, think of your immortal weal!
In vain for Constance is your zeal;
  She—died at Holy Isle."—
Lord Marmion started from the ground,
As light as if he felt no wound;
Though in the action burst the tide
In torrents from his wounded side.
" Then it was truth! " he said,—" I knew
That the dark presage must be true.—
I would the Fiend, to whom belongs
The vengeance due to all her wrongs,
  Would spare me but a day!
For wasting fire, and dying groan,
And priests slain on the altar stone,
  Might bribe him for delay.
It may not be!—this dizzy trance,—
Curse on yon base marauder's lance,
And doubly cursed my failing brand!
A sinful heart makes feeble hand."
Then, fainting, down on earth he sunk,
Supported by the trembling monk.

With fruitless labor, Clara bound,
And strove to stanch the gushing wound:
The monk, with unavailing cares,

Exhausted all the Church's prayers.
Ever, he said, that, close and near,
A lady's voice was in his ear,
And that the priest he could not hear,
  For that she ever sung,
"*In the lost battle, borne down by the flying,*
Where mingles war's rattle with groans of the
  dying!"
  So the notes rung:—
"Avoid thee, Fiend!—with cruel hand,
Shake not the dying sinner's sand!—
O, look, my son, upon yon sign
Of the Redeemer's grace divine:
  O, think on faith and bliss!—
By many a death-bed I have been,
And many a sinner's parting seen,
  But never aught like this."

The war, that for a space did fail,
Now trebly thundering swelled the gale,
  And STANLEY! was the cry:—
A light on Marmion's visage spread,
  And fired his glazing eye:
With dying hand above his head
He shook the fragment of his blade,
  And shouted "Victory!—
Charge, Chester, charge! On, Stanley, on!"
Were the last words of Marmion.

                              SIR WALTER SCOTT.

  21

THE BONNETS OF BONNIE DUNDEE.

[About 1688.]

To the lords of convention 't was Claverhouse
    spoke,
" Ere the king's crown shall fall, there are crowns
    to be broke;
So let each cavalier who loves honor and me
Come follow the bonnets of bonnie Dundee!"

Come fill up my cup, come fill up my can;
Come saddle your horses, and call up your men;
Come open the Westport and let us gang free,
And it 's room for the bonnets of bonnie Dundee!

Dundee he is mounted, he rides up the street,
The bells are rung backward, the drums they are
    beat;
But the provost, douce man, said, " Just e'en let
    him be,
The gude toun is well quit of that deil of Dun-
    dee!"

As he rode doun the sanctified bends of the Bow,
Ilk carline was flyting and shaking her pow;
But the young plants of grace they looked cowthie
    and slee,
Thinking, Luck to thy bonnet, thou bonnie Dun-
    dee!

With sour-featured whigs the Grass-market was
    thranged,
As if half the west had set tryst to be hanged;

There was spite in each look, there was fear in
    each ee,
As they watched for the bonnets of bonnie Dun-
    dee.

These cowls of Kilmarnock had spits and had
    spears,
And lang-hafted gullies to kill cavaliers;
But they shrunk to close-heads, and the causeway
    was free
At the toss of the bonnet of bonnie Dundee.

He spurred to the foot of the proud castle rock,
And with the gay Gordon he gallantly spoke:
" Let Mons Meg and her marrows speak twa
    words or three,
For the love of the bonnet of bonnie Dundee."

The Gordon demands of him which way he goes.
" Where'er shall direct me the shade of Montrose!
Your grace in short space shall hear tidings of me,
Or that low lies the bonnet of bonnie Dundee.

" There are hills beyond Pentland and lands be-
    yond Forth;
If there's lords in the Lowlands, there's chiefs
    in the north;
There are wild Duniewassals three thousand
    times three
Will cry ' Hoigh!' for the bonnet of bonnie Dun-
    dee.

" There's brass on the target of barkened bull-
    hide,

There 's steel in the scabbard that dangles be-
    side;
The brass shall be burnished, the steel shall flash
    free,
At a toss of the bonnet of bonnie Dundee.

" Away to the hills, to the caves, to the rocks,
Ere I own an usurper I 'll couch with the fox;
And tremble, false whigs, in the midst of your
    glee,
You have not seen the last of my bonnet and me."

He waved his proud hand, and the trumpets were
    blown,
The kettle-drums clashed, and the horsemen rode
    on,
Till on Ravelston's cliffs and on Clermiston's
    lea
Died away the wild war-notes of bonnie Dundee.

Come fill up my cup, come fill up my can;
Come saddle the horses, and call up the men;
Come open your doors and let me gae free,
For it 's up with the bonnets of bonnie Dundee!
                  SIR WALTER SCOTT.

LIBERTY TREE.

[1775.]

IN a chariot of light from the regions of day,
    The Goddess of Liberty came;
Ten thousand celestials directed the way,
    And hither conducted the dame.

A fair budding branch from the gardens above,
  Where millions with millions agree,
She brought in her hand as a pledge of her love,
  And the plant she named *Liberty Tree.*

The celestial exotic struck deep in the ground,
  Like a native it flourished and bore;
The fame of its fruit drew the nations around,
  To seek out this peaceable shore.
Unmindful of names or distinction they came,
  For freemen like brothers agree;
With one spirit endued, they one friendship pur-
    sued,
  And their temple was *Liberty Tree.*

Beneath this fair tree, like the patriarchs of old,
  Their bread in contentment they ate,
Unvexed with the troubles of silver and gold,
  The cares of the grand and the great.
With timber and tar they Old England supplied,
  And supported her power on the sea;
Her battles they fought, without getting a groat,
  For the honor of *Liberty Tree.*

But hear, O ye swains, 't is a tale most profane,
  How all the tyrannical powers,
Kings, Commons, and Lords, are united amain,
  To cut down this guardian of ours;
From the east to the west blow the trumpet to
    arms,
  Through the land let the sound of it flee,
Let the far and the near, all unite with a cheer,
  In defence of our *Liberty Tree.*

                              THOMAS PAINE.

HYMN:

SUNG AT THE COMPLETION OF THE CONCORD MONUMENT, APRIL 19, 1836.

By the rude bridge that arched the flood,
 Their flag to April's breeze unfurled,
Here once the embattled farmers stood,
 And fired the shot heard round the world.

The foe long since in silence slept;
 Alike the conqueror silent sleeps;
And Time the ruined bridge has swept
 Down the dark stream which seaward creeps.

On this green bank, by this soft stream,
 We set to-day a votive stone;
That memory may their deed redeem,
 When, like our sires, our sons are gone.

Spirit, that made those heroes dare
 To die, or leave their children free,
Bid Time and Nature gently spare
 The shaft we raise to them and thee.

RALPH WALDO EMERSON.

WARREN'S ADDRESS.*

Stand! the ground's your own, my braves!
Will ye give it up to slaves?
Will ye look for greener graves?
 Hope ye mercy still?

* General Joseph Warren, who fell at the battle of
Bunker Hill, June 17, 1775.

What 's the mercy despots feel?
Hear it in that battle-peal!
Read it on yon bristling steel!
    Ask it,—ye who will.

Fear ye foes who kill for hire?
Will ye to your *homes* retire?
Look behind you!—they 're afire!
    And, before you, see
Who have done it! From the vale
On they come!—and will ye quail?
Leaden rain and iron hail
    Let their welcome be!

In the God of battles trust!
Die we may,—and die we must:
But, O, where can dust to dust
    Be consigned so well,
As where heaven its dews shall shed
On the martyred patriot's bed,
And the rocks shall raise their head,
    Of his deeds to tell?

             JOHN PIERPONT.

"THE LONELY BUGLE GRIEVES."

FROM AN "ODE ON THE CELEBRATION OF THE
BATTLE OF BUNKER HILL, JUNE 17, 1825."

THE trump hath blown,
And now upon that reeking hill
Slaughter rides screaming on the vengeful ball;
While with terrific signal shrill,

The vultures from their bloody eyries flown,
    Hang o'er them like a pall.
Now deeper roll the maddening drums,
    And the mingling host like ocean heaves;
    While from the midst a horrid wailing
        comes,
And high above the fight the lonely bugle grieves!
                    GRENVILLE MELLEN.

NATHAN HALE.*

To drum-beat and heart-beat
    A soldier marches by:
There is color in his cheek,
    There is courage in his eye,
Yet to drum-beat and heart-beat
    In a moment he must die.

By starlight and moonlight,
    He seeks the Briton's camp;
He hears the rustling flag,
    And the armèd sentry's tramp;
And the starlight and moonlight
    His silent wanderings lamp.

With slow tread and still tread,
    He scans the tented line;
And he counts the battery guns
    By the gaunt and shadowy pine;
And his slow tread and still tread
    Gives no warning sign.

* Hanged as a spy by the British, in New York City,
September 22, 1776.

The dark wave, the plumed wave,
  It meets his eager glance;
And it sparkles 'neath the stars,
  Like the glimmer of a lance—
A dark wave, a plumed wave,
  On an emerald expanse.

A sharp clang, a steel clang,
  And terror in the sound!
For the sentry, falcon-eyed,
  In the camp a spy hath found;
With a sharp clang, a steel clang,
  The patriot is bound.

With calm brow, steady brow,
  He listens to his doom;
In his look there is no fear,
  Nor a shadow-trace of gloom;
But with calm brow and steady brow
  He robes him for the tomb.

In the long night, the still night,
  He kneels upon the sod;
And the brutal guards withhold
  E'en the solemn Word of God!
In the long night, the still night,
  He walks where Christ hath trod.

'Neath the blue morn, the sunny morn,
  He dies upon the tree;
And he mourns that he can lose
  But one life for Liberty;

And in the blue morn, the sunny morn,
  His spirit-wings are free.

But his last words, his message-words,
  They burn, lest friendly eye
Should read how proud and calm
  A patriot could die,
With his last words, his dying words,
  A soldier's battle-cry.

From Fame-leaf and Angel-leaf,
  From monument and urn,
The sad of earth, the glad of heaven,
  His tragic fate shall learn;
And on Fame-leaf and Angel-leaf
  The name of HALE shall burn!

                    FRANCIS MILES FINCH.

SONG OF MARION'S MEN.*

OUR band is few, but true and tried,
  Our leader frank and bold;
The British soldier trembles
  When Marion's name is told.
Our fortress is the good greenwood,
  Our tent the cypress-tree;
We know the forest round us,
  As seamen know the sea;
We know its walls of thorny vines,
  Its glades of reedy grass,

* General Francis Marion, of South Carolina, renowned
as a daring patriot partisan leader during the Revolution-
ary War.

Its safe and silent islands
  Within the dark morass.

Woe to the English soldiery
  That little dread us near!
On them shall light at midnight
  A strange and sudden fear;
When, waking to their tents on fire,
  They grasp their arms in vain,
And they who stand to face us
  Are beat to earth again;
And they who fly in terror deem
  A mighty host behind,
And hear the tramp of thousands
  Upon the hollow wind.

Then sweet the hour that brings release
  From danger and from toil;
We talk the battle over,
  And share the battle's spoil.
The woodland rings with laugh and shout,
  As if a hunt were up,
And woodland flowers are gathered
  To crown the soldier's cup.
With merry songs we mock the wind
  That in the pine-top grieves,
And slumber long and sweetly
  On beds of oaken leaves.

Well knows the fair and friendly moon
  The band that Marion leads,—
The glitter of their rifles,
  The scampering of their steeds.

'T is life to guide the fiery barb
  Across the moonlight plain;
'T is life to feel the night-wind
  That lifts his tossing mane.
A moment in the British camp—
  A moment—and away
Back to the pathless forest,
  Before the peep of day.

Grave men there are by broad Santee,
  Grave men with hoary hairs;
Their hearts are all with Marion,
  For Marion are their prayers.
And lovely ladies greet our band
  With kindliest welcoming,
With smiles like those of summer,
  And tears like those of spring.
For them we wear these trusty arms,
  And lay them down no more
Till we have driven the Briton
  Forever from our shore.

WILLIAM CULLEN BRYANT.

CARMEN BELLICOSUM.

In their ragged regimentals
Stood the old Continentals,
    Yielding not,
When the grenadiers were lunging,
And like hail fell the plunging
    Cannon-shot;
    When the files
    Of the isles,

From the smoky night encampment, bore the banner of the rampant
    Unicorn,
And grummer, grummer, grummer rolled the roll
    of the drummer,
    Through the morn!

Then with eyes to the front all,
And with guns horizontal,
    Stood our sires;
And the balls whistled deadly,
And in streams flashing redly
    Blazed the fires;
    As the roar
    On the shore,
Swept the strong battle-breakers o'er the green-
    sodded acres
    Of the plain;
And louder, louder, louder, cracked the black gun-
    powder,
    Cracking amain!

Now like smiths at their forges
Worked the red St. George's
    Cannoneers;
And the " villanous saltpetre "
Rung a fierce, discordant metre
    Round their ears;
    As the swift
    Storm-drift,
With hot sweeping anger, came the horseguards'
    clangor
    On our flanks;

Then higher, higher, higher, burned the old
    fashioned fire
      Through the ranks!

    Then the bare-headed colonel
    Galloped through the white infernal
      Powder-cloud;
    And his broad sword was swinging
    And his brazen throat was ringing
      Trumpet-loud.
    Then the blue
    Bullets flew,
And the trooper-jackets redden at the touch of the
    leaden
      Rifle-breath;
And rounder, rounder, rounder, roared the iron
    six-pounder,
      Hurling death!
              GUY HUMPHREY M'MASTER.

THE DANCE.

[Published soon after the surrender of Cornwallis.]

CORNWALLIS led a country dance,
    The like was never seen, sir,
Much retrogade and much advance,
    And all with General Greene, sir.

They rambled up and rambled down,
    Joined hands, then off they run, sir.
Our General Greene to Charlestown,
    The earl to Wilmington, sir.

Greene in the South then danced a set.
    And got a mighty name, sir,

Cornwallis jigged with young Fayette,
But suffered in his fame, sir.

Then down he figured to the shore,
Most like a lordly dancer,
And on his courtly honor swore
He would no more advance, sir.

Quoth he, my guards are weary grown
With footing country dances,
They never at St. James's shone,
At capers, kicks, or prances.

Though men so gallant ne'er were seen,
While sauntering on parade, sir,
Or wiggling o'er the park's smooth green,
Or at a masquerade, sir.

Yet are red heels and long-laced skirts,
For stumps and briars meet, sir?
Or stand they chance with hunting-shirts,
Or hardy veteran feet, sir?

Now housed in York, he challenged all,
At minuet or all 'amande,
And lessons for a courtly ball
His guards by day and night conned.

This challenge known, full soon there came
A set who had the bon ton,
De Grasse and Rochambeau, whose fame
Fut brillant pour un long tems.

And Washington, Columbia's son,
  Whom every nature taught, sir,
That grace which can't by pains be won,
  Or Plutus's gold be bought, sir.

Now hand in hand they circle round
  This ever-dancing peer, sir;
Their gentle movements soon confound
  The earl as they draw near, sir.

His music soon forgets to play—
  His feet can move no more, sir,
And all his bands now curse the day
  They jiggèd to our shore, sir.

Now Tories all, what can ye say?
  Come—is not this a griper,
That while your hopes are danced away,
  'T is you must pay the piper?

                              ANONYMOUS.

MONTEREY.

[Mexico, September 19, 1846.]

WE were not many,—we who stood
  Before the iron sleet that day;
Yet many a gallant spirit would
Give half his years if but he could
  Have been with us at Monterey.

Now here, now there, the shot it hailed
  In deadly drifts of fiery spray,

Yet not a single soldier quailed
When wounded comrades round them wailed
  Their dying shouts at Monterey.

And on, still on our column kept,
  Through walls of flame its withering way;
Where fell the dead, the living stept,
Still charging on the guns which swept
  The slippery streets of Monterey.

The foe himself recoiled aghast,
  When striking where he strongest lay,
We swooped his flanking batteries past,
And, braving full their murderous blast,
  Stormed home the towers of Monterey.

Our banners on those turrets wave,
  And there our evening bugles play;
Where orange boughs above their grave,
Keep green the memory of the brave
  Who fought and fell at Monterey.

We are not many,—we who pressed
  Beside the brave who fell that day;
But who of us has not confessed
He'd rather share their warrior rest
  Than not have been at Monterey?

                CHARLES FENNO HOFFMAN.

22

COMING.

[April, 1861.]

WORLD, art thou 'ware of a storm?
   Hark to the ominous sound;
How the far-off gales their battle form,
   And the great sea-swells feel ground!

It comes, the Typhoon of Death—
   Nearer and nearer it comes!
The horizon thunder of cannon-breath
   And the roar of angry drums!

Hurtle, Terror sublime!
   Swoop o'er the Land to-day—
So the mist of wrong and crime,
The breath of our Evil Time
   Be swept, as by fire, away!

       HENRY HOWARD BROWNELL.

IN STATE.

I.

O KEEPER of the Sacred Key,
And the Great Seal of Destiny,
Whose eye is the blue canopy,
Look down upon the warring world, and tell us
   what the end will be.

" Lo, through the wintry atmosphere,
On the white bosom of the sphere,

A cluster of five lakes appear;
And all the land looks like a couch, or warrior's
    shield, or sheeted bier.

" And on that vast and hollow field,
With both lips closed and both eyes sealed,
A mighty Figure is revealed,—
Stretched at full length, and stiff and stark, as
    in the hollow of a shield.

" The winds have tied the drifted snow
Around the face and chin; and lo,
The sceptred Giants come and go,
And shake their shadowy crowns and say: ' We
    always feared it would be so!'

" She came of an heroic race:
A giant's strength, a maiden's grace,
Like two in one seem to embrace,
And match, and bend, and thorough-blend, in her
    colossal form and face.

" Where can her dazzling falchion be?
One hand is fallen in the sea;
The Gulf Stream drifts it far and free;
And in that hand her shining brand gleams from
    the depths resplendently.

" And by the other, in its rest,
The starry banner of the West
Is clasped forever to her breast;
And of her silver helmet, lo, a soaring eagle is the
    crest.

" And on her brow, a softened light,
As of a star concealed from sight
By some thin veil of fleecy white,
Or of the rising moon behind the raining vapors
    of the night.

" The Sisterhood that was so sweet,
The Starry System sphered complete,
Which the mazed Orient used to greet,
The Four-and-Thirty fallen Stars glimmer and
    glitter at her feet.

" And over her,—and over all,
For panoply and coronal,—
The mighty Immemorial,
And everlasting Canopy and Starry Arch and
    Shield of All.

II.

" Three cold, bright moons have marched and
    wheeled;
And the white cerement that revealed
A Figure stretched upon a Shield,
Is turned to verdure; and the Land is now one
    mighty battle-field.

" And lo, the children which she bred,
And more than all else cherishèd,
To make them true in heart and head,
Stand face to face, as mortal foes, with their
    swords crossed above the dead.

" Each hath a mighty stroke and stride:
One true,—the more that he is tried;

The other dark and evil-eyed;—
And by the hand of one of them, his own dear
    mother surely died!

" A stealthy step, a gleam of hell,—
It is the simple truth to tell,—
The Son stabbed and the Mother fell:
And so she lies, all mute and pale, and pure and
    irreproachable!

" And then the battle-trumpet blew;
And the true brother sprang and drew
His blade to smite the traitor through;
And so they clashed above the bier, and the Night
    sweated bloody dew.

" And all their children, far and wide,
That are so greatly multiplied,
Rise up in frenzy and divide;
And choosing, each whom he will serve, unsheathe
    the sword and take their side.

" And in the low sun's bloodshot rays,
Portentous of the coming days,
The Two great Oceans blush and blaze,
With the emergent continent between them, wrapt
    in crimson haze.

" Now whichsoever stand or fall,
As God is great, and man is small,
The Truth shall triumph over all:
Forever and forevermore, the Truth shall triumph
    over all!

III.

" I see the champion sword-strokes flash;
I see them fall and hear them clash;
I hear the murderous engines crash;
I see a brother stoop to loose a foeman-brother's
    bloody sash.

" I see the torn and mangled corse,
The dead and dying heaped in scores,
The headless rider by his horse,
The wounded captive bayoneted through and
    through without remorse.

" I hear the dying sufferer cry,
With his crushed face turned to the sky,
I see him crawl in agony
To the foul pool, and bow his head into bloody
    slime, and die.

" I see the assassin crouch and fire,
I see his victim fall,—expire;
I see the murderer creeping nigher
To strip the dead.   He turns the head,—the face!
    The son beholds his sire!

" I hear the curses and the thanks;
I see the mad charge on the flanks,
The rents, the gaps, the broken ranks,
The vanquished squadrons driven headlong down
    the river's bridgeless banks.

"I see the death-gripe on the plain,
The grappling monsters on the main,

The tens of thousands that are slain,
And all the speechless suffering and agony of
    heart and brain.

" I see the dark and bloody spots,
    The crowded rooms and crowded cots,
    The bleaching bones, the battle blots,—
And writ on many a nameless grave, a legend of
    forget-me-nots.

" I see the gorgèd prison-den,
    The dead line and the pent-up pen,
    The thousands quartered in the fen,
The living-deaths of skin and bone that were the
    goodly shapes of men.

" And still the bloody Dew must fall!
    And His great Darkness with the Pall
    Of His dread Judgment cover all,
Till the Dead Nation rise Transformed by Truth
    to triumph over all! "

" And Last—and Last I see—The Dead."
    Thus saith the Keeper of the Key,
    And the Great Seal of Destiny,
    Whose eye is the blue canopy,
And leaves the Pall of His great Darkness over
    all the Land and Sea.

               FORCEYTHE WILLSON.

BROTHER JONATHAN'S LAMENT FOR SISTER CAROLINE.

[March 25, 1861, South Carolina having adopted the Ordinance of Secession.]

SHE has gone,—she has left us in passion and
    pride—
Our stormy-browed sister, so long at our side!
She has torn her own star from our firmament's
    glow,
And turned on her brother the face of a foe!

O Caroline, Caroline, child of the sun,
We can never forget that our hearts have been
    one,—
Our foreheads both sprinkled in Liberty's name,
From the fountain of blood with the finger of
    flame!

You were always too ready to fire at a touch;
But we said: "She is hasty—she does not mean
    much."
We have scowled when you uttered some turbulent
    threat;
But friendship still whispered: "Forgive and
    forget."

Has our love all died out? Have its altars grown
    cold?
Has the curse come at last which the fathers
    foretold?

Then Nature must teach us the strength of the
    chain
That her petulant children would sever in vain.

They may fight till the buzzards are gorged with
    their spoil,—
Till the harvest grows black as it rots in the soil,
Till the wolves and the catamounts troop from
    their caves,
And the shark tracks the pirate, the lord of the
    waves:

In vain is the strife! When its fury is past,
Their fortunes must flow in one channel at last,
As the torrents that rush from the mountains of
    snow
Roll mingled in peace in the valleys below.

Our Union is river, lake, ocean, and sky;
Man breaks not the medal when God cuts the die!
Though darkened with sulphur, though cloven
    with steel,
The blue arch will brighten, the waters will heal!

O Caroline, Caroline, child of the sun,
There are battles with fate that can never be won!
The star-flowering banner must never be furled,
For its blossoms of light are the hope of the world!

Go, then, our rash sister, afar and aloof,—
Run wild in the sunshine away from our roof;
But when your heart aches and your feet have
    grown sore,
Remember the pathway that leads to our door!

OLIVER WENDELL HOLMES.

JONATHAN TO JOHN.

It don't seem hardly right, John,
　When both my hands was full,
To stump me to a fight, John,—
　Your cousin, tu, John Bull!
Ole Uncle S., sez he, " I guess
　We know it now," sez he,
" The Lion's paw is all the law,
　Accordin' to J. B.,
　　Thet 's fit for you and me!"

You wonder why we 're hot, John?
　Your mark wuz on the guns,
The neutral guns, thet shot, John,
　Our brothers an' our sons:
Ole Uncle S., sez he, " I guess
　There 's human blood," sez he,
" By fits an' starts, in Yankee hearts,
　Though 't may surprise J. B.
　　More 'n it would you an' me."

Ef *I* turned mad dogs loose, John,
　On *your* front parlor stairs,
Would it just meet your views, John,
　To wait an' sue their heirs?
Ole Uncle S., sez he, " I guess,
　I on'y guess," sez he,
" Thet ef Vattel on *his* toes fell,
　'T would kind o' rile J. B.,
　　Ez wal ez you an' me!"

Who made the law thet hurts, John,
  Heads I win—ditto tails?
" J. B." was on his shirts, John,
  Onless my memory fails.
Ole Uncle S., sez he, " I guess
  (I 'm good at thet)," sez he,
" Thet sauce for goose ain't *jest* the juice
  For ganders with J. B.,
  No more 'n with you or me! "

When your rights was our wrongs, John,
  You didn't stop for fuss,—
Britanny's trident prongs, John,
  Was good 'nough law for us.
Ole Uncle S., sez he, " I guess
  Though physic 's good," sez he,
" It doesn't foller thet he can swaller
  Prescriptions signed ' J. B.'
  Put up by you an' me."

We own the ocean, tu, John,
  You mus'n' take it hard,
Ef we can't think with you, John,
  It 's jest your own back yard.
Ole Uncle S., sez he, " I guess
  Ef *thet 's* his claim," sez he,
" The fencin' stuff 'll cost enough
  To bust up friend J. B.
  Ez wal ez you an' me! "

Why talk so dreffle big, John,
  Of honor when it meant
You didn't care a fig, John,
  But jest for *ten per cent?*
Ole Uncle S., sez he, " I guess

He 's like the rest," sez he,
" When all is done, it 's number one
Thet 's nearest to J. B.,
Ez wal ez t' you an' me! "

We give the critters back, John,
Cos Abram thought 't was right;
It warn't your bullyin' clack, John,
Provokin' us to fight.
Ole Uncle S., sez he, " I guess
We 've a hard row," sez he,
" To hoe just now; but thet, somehow,
May happen to J. B.,
Ez well ez you an' me! "

We ain't so weak an' poor, John,
With twenty million people,
An' close to every door, John,
A school house an' a steeple.
Ole Uncle S., sez he, " I guess
It is a fact," sez he,
" The surest plan to make a Man
Is, think him so, J. B.,
Ez much ez you an' me! "

Our folks believe in Law, John;
An' it 's fer her sake, now,
They 've left the axe an' saw, John,
The anvil an' the plow.
Ole Uncle S., sez he, " I guess
Ef 't warn't fer law," sez he,
" There 'd be one shindy from here to Indy;
An' *thet* don't suit J. B.
(When 't ain't 'twixt you an' me!)"

We know we 've got a cause, John,
  Thet 's honest, just, an' true;
We thought 't would win applause, John,
  Ef nowhere else, from you.
Ole Uncle S., sez he, " I guess
  His love of right," sez he,
" Hangs by a rotten fibre o' cotton;
  There 's natur' in J. B.,
  Ez well ez you an' me!"

The South says, " *Poor folks down!* " John,
  An' " *All men up!* " say we,—
White, yaller, black, an' brown, John;
  Now which is your idee?
Ole Uncle S., sez he, " I guess
  John preaches wal," sez he;
" But, sermon thru, an' come to *du,*
  Why there 's the old J. B.
  A-crowdin' you an' me!"

Shall it be love or hate, John?
  It 's you thet 's to decide;
Ain't *your* bonds held by Fate, John,
  Like all the world's beside?
Ole Uncle S., sez he, " I guess
  Wise men fergive," sez he,
" But not ferget; an' some time yet
  Thet truth may strike J. B.,
  Ez wal ez you an' me!"

God means to make this land, John,
  Clear thru, from sea to sea,

Believe an' understand, John,
 The *wuth* o' bein' free.
Ole Uncle S., sez he, " I guess
 God's price is high," sez he;
" But nothin' else than wut he sells
 Wears long, an' thet J. B.
May larn, like you an' me ! "

JAMES RUSSELL LOWELL.

ALL QUIET ALONG THE POTOMAC.

" ALL quiet along the Potomac," they say,
 " Except now and then a stray picket
Is shot, as he walks on his beat, to and fro,
 By a rifleman hid in the thicket.
'T is nothing: a private or two, now and then,
 Will not count in the news of the battle;
Not an officer lost,—only one of the men,
 Moaning out, all alone, the death-rattle."

All quiet along the Potomac to-night,
 Where the soldiers lie peacefully dreaming;
Their tents in the rays of the clear autumn moon,
 Or the light of the watch-fires, are gleaming.
A tremulous sigh, as the gentle night-wind
 Through the forest leaves softly is creeping;
While stars up above, with their glittering eyes,
 Keep guard,—for the army is sleeping.

There 's only the sound of the lone sentry's tread
 As he tramps from the rock to the fountain,
And he thinks of the two in the low trundle-bed,
 Far away in the cot on the mountain.

His musket falls slack; his face, dark and grim,
　Grows gentle with memories tender,
As he mutters a prayer for the children asleep,
　For their mother,—may Heaven defend her!

The moon seems to shine just as brightly as then,
　That night when the love yet unspoken
Leaped up to his lips,—when low, murmured vows
　Were pledged to be ever unbroken;
Then drawing his sleeve roughly over his eyes,
　He dashes off tears that are welling,
And gathers his gun closer up to its place,
　As if to keep down the heart-swelling.

He passes the fountain, the blasted pine-tree,—
　The footstep is lagging and weary;
Yet onward he goes, through the broad belt of
　　light,
　Toward the shades of the forest so dreary.
Hark! was it the night-wind that rustled the
　　leaves?
　Was it moonlight so wondrously flashing?
It looked like a rifle: "Ha! Mary, good-bye!"
　And the life-blood is ebbing and plashing.

All quiet along the Potomac to-night,—
　No sound save the rush of the river;
While soft falls the dew on the face of the dead,—
　The picket's off duty forever.

ETHELINDA ELLIOTT BEERS.

THE COUNTERSIGN.

ALAS! the weary hours pass slow,
  The night is very dark and still,
And in the marshes far below
  I hear the bearded whippoorwill.
I scarce can see a yard ahead;
  My ears are strained to catch each sound;
I hear the leaves about me shed,
  And the spring's bubbling through the ground.

Along the beaten path I pace,
  Where white rags mark my sentry's track;
In formless shrubs I seem to trace
  The foeman's form, with bending back;
I think I see him crouching low—
  I stop and list—I stoop and peer,
Until the neighboring hillocks grow
  To groups of soldiers far and near.

With ready piece I wait and watch,
  Until my eyes, familiar grown,
Detect each harmless earthen notch,
  And turn guerrillas into stone;
And then amid the lonely gloom,
  Beneath the tall old chestnut trees,
My silent marches I resume,
  And think of other times than these.

"Halt!" who goes there?" my challenge cry,
  It rings along the watchful line;
"Relief!" I hear a voice reply—
  "Advance, and give the countersign!"

With bayonet at the charge I wait—
The corporal gives the mystic spell;
With arms aport I charge my mate,
Then onward pass, and all is well.

But in the tent that night awake,
I ask, if in the fray I fall,
Can I the mystic answer make,
When the angelic sentries call?
And pray that Heaven may so ordain,
Where'er I go, what fate be mine,
Whether in pleasure or in pain,
I still may have the countersign.

ANONYMOUS.

CIVIL WAR.

" RIFLEMAN, shoot me a fancy shot
Straight at the heart of yon prowling vidette;
Ring me a ball in the glittering spot
That shines on his breast like an amulet!"

" Ah, captain! here goes for a fine-drawn bead,
There's music around when my barrel's in
tune!"
Crack! went the rifle, the messenger sped,
And dead from his horse fell the ringing dra-
goon.

" Now, rifleman, steal through the bushes, and
snatch
From your victim some trinket to handsel first
blood;

23

A button, a loop, or that luminous patch
    That gleams in the moon like a diamond stud!"

" O captain! I staggered, and sunk on my track,
    When I gazed on the face of that fallen vidette,
For he looked so like you, as he lay on his back,
    That my heart rose upon me, and masters me
        yet.

" But I snatched off the trinket,—this locket of
        gold;
    An inch from the centre my lead broke its way,
Scarce grazing the picture, so fair to behold,
    Of a beautiful lady in bridal array."

" Ha! rifleman, fling me the locket!—'t is she,
    My brother's young bride, and the fallen dra-
        goon
Was her husband—Hush! soldier, 't was Heav-
        en's decree,
    We must bury him there, by the light of the
        moon!

" But hark! the far bugles their warnings unite;
    War is a virtue,—weakness a sin;
There 's a lurking and loping around us to-night,
    Load again, rifleman, keep your hand in!"

                    CHARLES DAWSON SHANLY.

THE TWO WIVES.

THE colonel rode by his picket-line
   In the pleasant morning sun,
That glanced from him far off to shine
   On the crouching rebel picket's gun.

From his command the captain strode
   Out with a grave salute,
And talked with the colonel as he rode:—
   The picket levelled his piece to shoot.

The colonel rode and the captain walked,—
   The arm of the picket tired;
Their faces almost touched as they talked,
   And, swerved from his aim, the picket fired.

The captain fell at the horse's feet,
   Wounded and hurt to death,
Calling upon a name that was sweet
   As God is good, with his dying breath.

And the colonel that leaped from his horse and
     knelt
   To close the eyes so dim,
A high remorse for God's mercy felt,
   Knowing the shot was meant for him.

And he whispered, prayer-like, under his breath,
   The name of his own young wife:
For Love, that had made his friend's peace with
     Death,
   Alone could make his with life.

            WILLIAM DEAN HOWELLS.

THREE HUNDRED THOUSAND MORE.

[September, 1861.]

WE are coming, Father Abraham, three hundred
    thousand more!
From Mississippi's winding stream and from New
    England's shore;
We leave our ploughs and workshops, our wives
    and children dear,
With hearts too full for utterance, with but a
    silent tear;
We dare not look behind us, but steadfastly be-
    fore:
We are coming, Father Abraham, three hundred
    thousand more!

If you look across the hill-tops that meet the north-
    ern sky,
Long moving lines of rising dust your vision may
    descry;
And now the wind, an instant, tears the cloudy
    veil aside,
And floats aloft our spangled flag in glory and in
    pride,
And bayonets in the sunlight gleam, and bands
    brave music pour:
We are coming, Father Abraham, three hundred
    thousand more!

If you look all up our valleys where the growing
    harvests shine,
You may see our sturdy farmer boys fast forming
    into line;

And children from their mother's knees are pull-
    ing at the weeds,
And learning how to reap and sow against their
    country's needs;
And a farewell group stands weeping at every cot-
    tage door:
We are coming, Father Abraham, three hundred
    thousand more!

You have called us, and we're coming, by Rich-
    mond's bloody tide
To lay us down, for Freedom's sake, our brothers'
    bones beside,
Or from foul treason's savage grasp to wrench
    the murderous blade,
And in the face of foreign foes its fragments to
    parade.
Six hundred thousand loyal men and true have
    gone before:
We are coming, Father Abraham, three hundred
    thousand more!

ANONYMOUS.

THE OLD MAN AND JIM.

OLD man never had much to say—
    'Ceptin' to Jim,—
And Jim was the wildest boy he had,
    And the old man jes' wrapped up in him!
Never heerd him speak but once
Er twice in my life,—and first time was
When the army broke out, and Jim he went,

The old man backin' him, fer three months;
And all 'at I heerd the old man say
Was jes' as we turned to start away,—
    " Well, good-bye, Jim:
    Take keer of yourse'f! "

'Peared like he was more satisfied
    Jes' *lookin'* at Jim
And likin' him all to hisse'f-like, see?—
    'Cause he was jes' wrapped up in him!
And over and over I mind the day
The old man come and stood round in the way
While we was drillin', a-watchin' Jim;
And down at the deepot a heerin' him say,—
    " Well, good-bye, Jim:
    Take keer of yourse'f! "

Never was nothin' about the farm
    Disting'ished Jim;
Neighbors all ust to wonder why
    The old man 'peared wrapped up in him:
But when Cap. Biggler, he writ back
'At Jim was the bravest boy we had
In the whole dern rigiment, white er black,
And his fightin' good as his farmin' bad,—
'At he had led, with a bullet clean
Bored through his thigh, and carried the flag
Through the bloodiest battle you ever seen,—
The old man wound up a letter to him
'At Cap. read to us, 'at said,—" Tell Jim
    Good-bye;
    And take keer of hisse'f! "

Jim come home jes' long enough
  To take the whim
'At he'd like to go back in the calvery—
  And the old man jes' wrapped up in him!
Jim 'lowed 'at he'd had sich luck afore,
Guessed he'd tackle her three years more.
And the old man give him a colt he'd raised,
And follered him over to Camp Ben Wade,
And laid around fer a week er so,
Watchin' Jim on dress-parade;
'Tel finally he rid away,
And last he heerd was the old man say,—
  "Well, good-bye, Jim:
  Take keer of yourse'f "

Tuk the papers, the old man did,
  A-watchin' fer Jim,
Fully believin' he'd make his mark
  Some way—jes' wrapped up in him!
And many a time the word 'ud come
'At stirred him up like the tap of a drum:
At Petersburg fer instunce, where
Jim rid right into their cannons there,
And tuk 'em, and p'inted 'em t' other way,
And socked it home to the boys in gray,
As they skooted fer timber, and on and on—
Jim a lieutenant,—and one arm gone,—
And the old man's words in his mind all day,—
  "Well, good-bye, Jim:
  Take keer of yourse'f! "

Think of a private, now, perhaps,
  We'll say like Jim,

'At 's clumb clean up to the shoulder-straps—
   And the old man jes' wrapped up in him!
Think of him—with the war plum' through,
And the glorious old Red-White-and-Blue
A-laughin' the news down over Jim,
And the old man, bendin' over him—
The surgeon turnin' away with tears
'At hadn't leaked fer years and years,
As the hand of the dyin' boy clung to
His Father's, the old voice in his ears,—
   "Well, good-bye, Jim:
   Take keer of yourse'f!"

JAMES WHITCOMB RILEY.

STONEWALL JACKSON'S WAY

COME, stack arms, men; pile on the rails;
   Stir up the camp-fire bright!
No growling if the canteen fails:
   We 'll make a roaring night.
Here Shenandoah brawls along,
There burly Blue Ridge echoes strong,
To swell the Brigade's rousing song,
   Of Stonewall Jackson's Way.

We see him now—the queer slouched hat,
   Cocked o'er his eye askew;
The shrewd, dry smile; the speech so pat,
   So calm, so blunt, so true.
The "Blue-light Elder" knows 'em well:
Says he, "That 's Banks; he 's fond of shell.—
Lord save his soul! we 'll give him—;" Well,
   That 's Stonewall Jackson's Way.

Silence! Ground arms! Kneel all! Caps off!
  Old Massa 's going to pray.
Strangle the fool that dares to scoff:
  Attention!—it 's his way.
Appealing from his native sod,
In forma paupcris to God.
" Lay bare Thine arm! Stretch forth Thy rod:
  Amen! "—That 's Stonewall 's Way.

He 's in the saddle now. Fall in!
  Steady! the whole brigade.
Hill 's at the ford, cut off; we 'll win
  His way out, ball and blade.
What matter if our shoes are worn?
What matter if our feet are torn?
Quick step! we 're with him before morn:
  That 's Stonewall Jackson's Way.

The sun's bright lances rout the mists
  Of morning; and—By George!
Here 's Longstreet, struggling in the lists,
  Hemmed in an ugly gorge.
Pope and his Dutchmen!—whipped before.
" Bay'nets and grape! " hear Stonewall roar.
Charge, Stuart! Pay off Ashby's score,
  In Stonewall Jackson's Way.

Ah, Maiden! wait and watch and yearn
  For news of Stonewall's band.
Ah, Widow! read, with eyes that burn,
  That ring upon thy hand.
Ah, Wife! sew on, pray on, hope on!

Thy life shall not be all forlorn.
The foe had better ne'er been born,
That gets in Stonewall's Way.

JOHN WILLIAMSON PALMER.

BARBARA FRIETCHIE.

UP from the meadows rich with corn,
Clear in the cool September morn,

The clustered spires of Frederick stand
Green-walled by the hills of Maryland.

Round about them orchards sweep,
Apple and peach trees fruited deep,

Fair as a garden of the Lord
To the eyes of the famished rebel horde,

On that pleasant morn of the early fall
When Lee marched over the mountain wall,—

Over the mountains, winding down,
Horse and foot into Frederick town.

Forty flags with their silver stars,
Forty flags with their crimson bars,

Flapped in the morning wind; the sun
Of noon looked down, and saw not one.

Up rose old Barbara Frietchie then,
Bowed with her fourscore years and ten;

Bravest of all in Frederick town,
She took up the flag the men hauled down;

In her attic-window the staff she set,
To show that one heart was loyal yet.

Up the street came the rebel tread,
Stonewall Jackson riding ahead.

Under his slouched hat left and right
He glanced: the old flag met his sight.

" Halt! "—the dust-brown ranks stood fast;
" Fire! "—out blazed the rifle-blast.

It shivered the window, pane and sash;
It rent the banner with seam and gash.

Quick, as it fell, from the broken staff
Dame Barbara snatched the silken scarf;

She leaned far out on the window-sill,
And shook it forth with a royal will.

" Shoot, if you must, this old gray head,
But spare your country's flag," she said.

A shade of sadness, a blush of shame,
Over the face of the leader came;

The nobler nature within him stirred
To life at that woman's deed and word:

" Who touches a hair of yon gray head
Dies like a dog! March on!" he said.

All day long through Frederick street
Sounded the tread of marching feet;

All day long that free flag tost
Over the heads of the rebel host.

Ever its torn folds rose and fell
On the loyal winds that loved it well;

And through the hill-gaps sunset light
Shone over it with a warm good-night.

Barbara Frietchie's work is o'er,
And the rebel rides on his raids no more.

Honor to her! and let a tear
Fall, for her sake, on Stonewall's bier.

Over Barbara Frietchie's grave,
Flag of freedom and union, wave!

Peace and order and beauty draw
Round thy symbol of light and law;

And ever the stars above look down
On thy stars below in Frederick town!

JOHN GREENLEAF WHITTIER.

CAVALRY SONG.

FROM "ALICE OF MONMOUTH."

OUR good steeds snuff the evening air,
Our pulses with their purpose tingle;
The foeman's fires are twinkling there;
He leaps to hear our sabres jingle!
HALT!
Each carbine send its whizzing ball:
Now, cling! clang! forward all,
Into the fight!

Dash on beneath the smoking dome:
Through level lightnings gallop nearer!
One look to Heaven! No thoughts of home:
The guidons that we bear are dearer.
CHARGE!
Cling! clang! forward all!
Heaven help those whose horses fall:
Cut left and right!

They flee before our fierce attack!
They fall! they spread in broken surges.
Now, comrades, bear our wounded back,
And leave the foeman to his dirges.
WHEEL!
The bugles sound the swift recall:
Cling! clang! backward all!
Home, and good night!

EDMUND CLARENCE STEDMAN.

CAVALRY SONG.

OUR bugles sound gayly. To horse and away!
And over the mountains breaks the day;
Then ho! brothers, ho! for the ride or the fight,
There are deeds to be done ere we slumber to-
    night!
   And whether we fight or whether we fall
   By sabre-stroke or rifle-ball,
   The hearts of the free will remember us yet,
   And our country, our country will never forget!

Then mount and away! let the coward delight
To be lazy all day and safe all night;
Our joy is a charger, flecked with foam,
And the earth is our bed and the saddle our home!
   And whether we fight, etc.

See yonder the ranks of the traitorous foe,
And bright in the sunshine bayonets glow!
Breathe a prayer, but no sigh; think for what
    you would fight;
Then charge! with a will, boys, and God for the
    right!
   And whether we fight, etc.

We have gathered again the red laurels of war;
We have followed the traitors fast and far;
But some who rose gayly this morn with the sun
Lie bleeding and pale on the field they have won!

But whether we fight or whether we fall
By sabre-stroke or rifle-ball,
The hearts of the free will remember us yet,
And our country, our country will never forget!

ROSSITER W. RAYMOND.

KEARNY AT SEVEN PINES.*

So that soldierly legend is still on its journey,—
    That story of Kearny who knew not to yield!
'T was the day when with Jameson, fierce Berry,
    and Birney,
    Against twenty thousand he rallied the field.
Where the red volleys poured, where the clamor
    rose highest,
    Where the dead lay in clumps through the
    dwarf oak and pine,
Where the aim from the thicket was surest and
    nighest,—
    No charge like Phil Kearny's along the whole
    line.

When the battle went ill, and the bravest were
    solemn,
    Near the dark Seven Pines, where we still held
    our ground,
He rode down the length of the withering column,
    And his heart at our war-cry leapt up with a
    bound;
He snuffed, like his charger, the wind of the pow-
    der,—

* Major-General Philip Kearny, killed at the battle of
Chantilly, September 1, 1862.

His sword waved us on and we answered the
   sign:
Loud our cheer as we rushed, but his laugh rang
   the louder,
   " There 's the devil's own fun, boys, along the
   whole line! "

How he strode his brown steed! How we saw
   his blade brighten
   In the one hand still left,—and the reins in his
   teeth!
He laughed like a boy when the holidays
   heighten,
   But a soldier's glance shot from his visor be-
   neath.
Up came the reserves to the mellay infernal,
   Asking where to go in,—through the clearing
   or pine?
" O, anywhere! Forward! 'T is all the same,
   Colonel:
   You 'll find lovely fighting along the whole
   line! "

O, evil the black shroud of night at Chantilly,
   That hid him from sight of his brave men and
   tried!
Foul, foul sped the bullet that clipped the white
   lily,
   The flower of our knighthood, the whole army's
   pride!
Yet we dream that he still,—in that shadowy
   region
   Where the dead form their ranks at the wan
   drummer's sign,—

Rides on, as of old, down the length of his legion,
And the word still is Forward! along the whole
line.

EDMUND CLARENCE STEDMAN.

THE GENERAL'S DEATH.

THE general dashed along the road
  Amid the pelting rain;
How joyously his bold face glowed
  To hear our cheers' refrain!

His blue blouse flapped in wind and wet,
  His boots were splashed with mire,
But round his lips a smile was set,
  And in his eyes a fire.

A laughing word, a gesture kind,—
  We did not ask for more,
With thirty weary miles behind,
  A weary fight before.

The gun grew light to every man,
  The crossed belts ceased their stress,
As onward to the column's van
  We watched our leader press.

Within an hour we saw him lie,
  A bullet in his brain,
His manly face turned to the sky,
  And beaten by the rain.

JOSEPH O'CONNOR.

24

DIRGE FOR A SOLDIER.*

Close his eyes; his work is done!
　What to him is friend or foeman,
Rise of moon or set of sun,
　Hand of man or kiss of woman?
　　Lay him low, lay him low,
　　In the clover or the snow!
　　What cares he? he cannot know;
　　Lay him low!

As man may, he fought his fight,
　Proved his truth by his endeavor;
Let him sleep in solemn night,
　Sleep forever and forever.
　　Lay him low, lay him low,
　　In the clover or the snow!
　　What cares he? he cannot know;
　　Lay him low!

Fold him in his country's stars,
　Roll the drum and fire the volley!
What to him are all our wars?—
　What but death-bemocking folly?
　　Lay him low, lay him low,
　　In the clover or the snow!
　　What cares he? he cannot know;
　　Lay him low!

Leave him to God's watching eye;
　Trust him to the hand that made him.

* Major-General Philip Kearny.

Mortal love weeps idly by;
   God alone has power to aid him.
    Lay him low, lay him low,
    In the clover or the snow!
    What cares he? he cannot know;
    Lay him low!

           GEORGE HENRY BOKER.

BAY BILLY.

[December 15, 1862.]

'T was the last fight at Fredericksburg,—
   Perhaps the day you reck,
Our boys, the Twenty-Second Maine,
   Kept Early's men in check.
Just where Wade Hampton boomed away
   The fight went neck and neck.

All day the weaker wing we held,
   And held it with a will.
Five several stubborn times we charged
   The battery on the hill,
And five times beaten back, re-formed,
   And kept our column still.

At last from out the centre fight
   Spurred up a general's aide.
" That battery must silenced be!"
   He cried, as past he sped.
Our colonel simply touched his cap,
   And then, with measured tread,

To lead the crouching line once more
  The grand old fellow came.
No wounded man but raised his head
  And strove to gasp his name,
And those who could not speak nor stir,
  " God blessed him " just the same.

For he was all the world to us,
  That hero gray and grim.
Right well we knew that fearful slope
  We 'd climb with none but him,
Though while his white head led the way
  We 'd charge hell's portals in.

This time we were not half-way up,
  When, midst the storm of shell,
Our leader, with his sword upraised,
  Beneath our bayonets fell.
And, as we bore him back, the foe
  Set up a joyous yell.

Our hearts went with him.   Back we swept,
  And when the bugle said
" Up, charge again ! " no man was there
  But hung his doggèd head.
" We 've no one left to lead us now,"
  The sullen soldiers said.

Just then before the laggard line
  The colonel's horse we spied,
Bay Billy with his trappings on,
  His nostrils swelling wide,
As though still on his gallant back
  The master sat astride.

Right royally he took the place
  That was of old his wont,
And with a neigh that seemed to say,
  Above the battle's brunt,
" How can the Twenty-Second charge
  If I am not in front? "

Like statues rooted there we stood,
  And gazed a little space,
Above that floating mane we missed
  The dear familiar face,
But we saw Bay Billy's eye of fire,
  And it gave us heart of grace.

No bugle-call could rouse us all
  As that brave sight had done,
Down all the battered line we felt
  A lightning impulse run.
Up! up the hill we followed Bill,—
  And we captured every gun!

And when upon the conquered height
  Died out the battle's hum,
Vainly mid living and the dead
  We sought our leader dumb.
It seemed as if a spectre steed
  To win that day had come.

And then the dusk and dew of night
  Fell softly o'er the plain,
As though o'er man's dread work of death
  The angels wept again,

And drew night's curtain gently round
A thousand beds of pain.

All night the surgeons' torches went,
The ghastly rows between,—
All night with solemn step I paced
The torn and bloody green.
But who that fought in the big war
Such dread sights have not seen?

At last the morning broke. The lark
Sang in the merry skies,
As if to e'en the sleepers there
It bade awake, and rise!
Though naught but that last trump of all
Could ope their heavy eyes.

And then once more with banners gay,
Stretched out the long brigade.
Trimly upon the furrowed field
The troops stood on parade,
And bravely mid the ranks were closed
The gaps the fight had made.

Not half the Twenty-Second's men
Were in their place that morn;
And Corporal Dick, who yester-noon
Stood six brave fellows on,
Now touched my elbow in the ranks,
For all between were gone.

Ah! who forgets that dreary hour
When, as with misty eyes,

To call the old familiar roll
  The solemn sergeant tries,—
One feels that thumping of the heart
  As no prompt voice replies.

And as in faltering tone and slow
  The last few names were said,
Across the field some missing horse
  Toiled up the weary tread.
It caught the sergeant's eye, and quick
  Bay Billy's name he read.

Yes! there the old bay hero stood,
  All safe from battle's harms,
And ere an order could be heard,
  Or the bugle's quick alarms,
Down all the front, from end to end,
  The troops presented arms!

Not all the shoulder-straps on earth
  Could still our mighty cheer;
And ever from that famous day,
  When rang the roll call clear,
Bay Billy's name was read, and then
  The whole line answered, " Here! "

FRANK H. GASSAWAY.

WOUNDED TO DEATH.

STEADY, boys, steady!
Keep your arms ready,
God only knows whom we may meet here.
Don't let me be taken;
I 'd rather awaken,

To-morrow, in—no matter where,
Than lie in that foul prison-hole—over there.
                    Step slowly!
                    Speak lowly!
              These rocks may have life.
              Lay me down in this hollow;
              We are out of the strife.
By heavens! the foemen may track me in blood,
For this hole in my breast is outpouring a flood.
No! no surgeon for me; he can give me no aid;
The surgeon I want is pickaxe and spade.
What, Morris, a tear?   Why, shame on ye, man!
I thought you a hero; but since you began
To whimper and cry like a girl in her teens,
By George! I don't know what the devil it means!
Well! well! I *am* rough; 't is a very rough school,
This life of a trooper,—but yet I 'm no fool!
I know a brave man, and a friend from a foe;
And, boys, that you love me I certainly know;
              But wasn't it grand
When they came down the hill over sloughing and
       sand!
But we stood—did we not?—like immovable rock,
Unheeding their balls and repelling their shock.
              Did you mind the loud cry
              When, as turning to fly,
Our men sprang upon them, determined to die?
              O, wasn't it grand!

God help the poor wretches that fell in that fight;
No time was there given for prayer or for flight;
They fell by the score, in the crash, hand to hand,

And they mingled their blood with the sloughing
    and sand.
             Huzza!
Great Heavens! this bullet-hole gapes like a grave;
A curse on the aim of the traitorous knave!
Is there never a one of ye knows how to pray,
Or speak for a man as his life ebbs away?
             Pray!
                Pray!

Our Father! our Father!... why don't ye proceed?
Can't you see I am dying? Great God, how I
    bleed!
Ebbing away!
        Ebbing away!
               The light of day
               Is turning to gray.
                    Pray!
                      Pray!
Our Father in Heaven,—boys, tell me the rest,
While I stanch the hot blood from this hole in
    my breast.
There's something about the forgiveness of sin—
Put that in! put that in!—and then
I'll follow your words and say an amen.

Here, Morris, old fellow, get hold of my hand;
And, Wilson, my comrade—O, wasn't it grand
When they came down the hill like a thunder-
    charged cloud!
Where's Wilson, my comrade?— Here, stoop
    down your head;
Can't *you* say a short prayer for the dying and
    dead!

"Christ God, who died for sinners all,
    Hear thou this suppliant wanderer's cry;
Let not e'en this poor sparrow fall
    Unheeded by thy gracious eye.

"Throw wide thy gates to let him in,
    And take him, pleading, to thine arms;
Forgive, O Lord! his life-long sin,
    And quiet all his fierce alarms."

God bless you, my comrade, for saying that hymn;
It is light to my path when my eye has grown dim.
I am dying—bend down till I touch you once
        more—
Don't forget me, old fellow,—God prosper this
        war!
Confusion to traitors!—keep hold of my hand—
And float the OLD FLAG o'er a prosperous land!
                        JOHN W. WATSON.

SOMEBODY'S DARLING.

INTO a ward of the whitewashed halls
    Where the dead and the dying lay,
Wounded by bayonets, shells, and balls,
    Somebody's darling was borne one day—
Somebody's darling, so young and brave;
    Wearing yet on his sweet pale face—
Soon to be hid in the dust of the grave—
    The lingering light of his boyhood's grace.

Matted and damp are the curls of gold
    Kissing the snow of that fair young brow;

Pale are the lips of delicate mould—
  Somebody's darling is dying now.
Back from his beautiful blue-veined brow
  Brush his wandering waves of gold;
Cross his hands on his bosom now—
  Somebody's darling is still and cold.

Kiss him once for somebody's sake,
  Murmur a prayer soft and low;
One bright curl from its fair mates take—
  They were somebody's pride, you know.
Somebody's hand hath rested here—
  Was it a mother's, soft and white?
Or have the lips of a sister fair
  Been baptized in their waves of light?

God knows best. He has somebody's love,
  Somebody's heart enshrined him there,
Somebody wafts his name above,
  Night and morn, on the wings of prayer.
Somebody wept when he marched away,
  Looking so handsome, brave, and grand;
Somebody's kiss on his forehead lay,
  Somebody clung to his parting hand.

Somebody 's watching and waiting for him,
  Yearning to hold him again to her heart;
And there he lies with his blue eyes dim,
  And the smiling, childlike lips apart.
Tenderly bury the fair young dead—
  Pausing to drop on his grave a tear.
Carve on the wooden slab o'er his head:
  " Somebody's darling slumbers here."

                         MARIA LA CONTE.

TRAMP, TRAMP, TRAMP.

In the prison cell I sit,
Thinking, mother dear, of you,
And our bright and happy home so far away,
And the tears they fill my eyes,
Spite of all that I can do,
Tho' I try to cheer my comrades and be gay.

Tramp, tramp, tramp, the boys are marching,
Oh, cheer up, comrades, they will come,
And beneath the starry flag we shall breathe the
air again,
Of freedom in our own belovèd home.

In the battle front we stood
When the fiercest charge they made,
And they swept us off a hundred men or more,
But before we reached their lines
They were beaten back dismayed,
And we heard the cry of vict'ry o'er and o'er.—

Chorus.

So within the prison cell
We are waiting for the day
That shall come to open wide the iron door,
And the hollow eye grows bright,
And the poor heart almost gay,
As we think of seeing friends and home once
more.

Tramp, tramp, tramp, the boys are marching,
Oh, cheer up, comrades, they will come,

And beneath the starry flag we shall breathe the
    air again,
Of freedom in our own belovèd home.

ANONYMOUS.

OUR ORDERS.

WEAVE no more silks, ye Lyons looms,
    To deck our girls for gay delights!
The crimson flower of battle blooms,
    And solemn marches fill the night.

Weave but the flag whose bars to-day
    Drooped heavy o'er our early dead,
And homely garments, coarse and gray,
    For orphans that must earn their bread!

Keep back your tunes, ye viols sweet,
    That poured delight from other lands!
Rouse there the dancer's restless feet:
    The trumpet leads our warrior bands.

And ye that wage the war of words
    With mystic fame and subtle power,
Go, chatter to the idle birds,
    Or teach the lesson of the hour!

Ye Sibyl Arts, in one stern knot
    Be all your offices combined!
Stand close, while Courage draws the lot,
    The destiny of human kind.

And if that destiny could fail,
  The sun should darken in the sky,
The eternal bloom of Nature pale,
  And God, and Truth, and Freedom die!

JULIA WARD HOWE.

WHEN THIS CRUEL WAR IS OVER.

DEAREST love, do you remember
  When we last did meet,
How you told me that you loved me
  Kneeling at my feet?
Oh, how proud you stood before me
  In your suit of blue,
When you vowed to me and country
  Ever to be true.

Chorus.—Weeping, sad and lonely,
      Hopes and fears, how vain;
      Yet praying
      When this cruel war is over,
      Praying that we meet again.

When the summer breeze is sighing
  Mournfully along,
Or when autumn leaves are falling,
  Sadly breathes the song.
Oft in dreams I see thee lying
  On the battle plain,
Lonely, wounded, even dying,
  Calling, but in vain.
Chorus.—Weeping, sad, etc.

If, amid the din of battle,
Nobly you should fall,
Far away from those who love you,
None to hear you call,
Who would whisper words of comfort?
Who would soothe your pain?
Ah, the many cruel fancies
Ever in my brain!
Chorus.—Weeping, sad, etc.

But our country called you, darling,
Angels cheer your way!
While our nation's sons are fighting,
We can only pray.
Nobly strike for God and country,
Let all nations see
How we love the starry banner,
Emblem of the free.

Chorus.—Weeping, sad and lonely,
Hopes and fears, how vain;
Yet praying
When this cruel war is over,
Praying that we meet again.

ANONYMOUS.

SHERIDAN'S RIDE.

[September 19, 1864.]

UP from the South at break of day,
Bringing to Winchester fresh dismay,
The affrighted air with a shudder bore,
Like a herald in haste, to the chieftain's door,

The terrible grumble and rumble and roar,
Telling the battle was on once more,
And Sheridan twenty miles away.

And wider still those billows of war
Thundered along the horizon's bar;
And louder yet into Winchester rolled
The roar of that red sea uncontrolled,
Making the blood of the listener cold
As he thought of the stake in that fiery fray,
With Sheridan twenty miles away.

But there is a road from Winchester town,
A good, broad highway, leading down;
And there, through the flash of the morning light,
A steed as black as the steeds of night
Was seen to pass as with eagle flight.
As if he knew the terrible need,
He stretched away with the utmost speed;
Hills rose and fell,—but his heart was gay,
With Sheridan fifteen miles away.

Still sprung from those swift hoofs, thundering
    South,
The dust, like smoke from the cannon's mouth;
Or the trail of a comet, sweeping faster and faster,
Foreboding to traitors the doom of disaster.
The heart of the steed and the heart of the master
Were beating, like prisoners assaulting their
    walls,
Impatient to be where the battle-field calls;
Every nerve of the charger was strained to full
    play,
With Sheridan only ten miles away.

Under his spurning feet, the road
Like an arrowy Alpine river flowed,
And the landscape sped away behind,
Like an ocean flying before the wind;
And the steed, like a bark fed with furnace ire,
Swept on, with his wild eyes full of fire;
But, lo! he is nearing his heart's desire,
He is snuffing the smoke of the roaring fray,
With Sheridan only five miles away.

The first that the General saw were the groups
Of stragglers, and then the retreating troops;
What was done,—what to do,—a glance told him
    both,
And, striking his spurs with a terrible oath,
He dashed down the line mid a storm of huzzas,
And the wave of retreat checked its course there,
    because
The sight of the master compelled it to pause.
With foam and with dust the black charger was
    gray;
By the flash of his eye, and his nostril's play,
He seemed to the whole great army to say,
" I have brought you Sheridan all the way
From Winchester down, to save the day! "

Hurrah, hurrah for Sheridan!
Hurrah, hurrah, for horse and man!
And when their statues are placed on high,
Under the dome of the Union sky,—
The American soldier's Temple of Fame,—
There with the glorious General's name
25

Be it said in letters both bold and bright:
" Here is the steed that saved the day
By carrying Sheridan into the fight,
From Winchester,—twenty miles away!"

THOMAS BUCHANAN READ.

LEFT ON THE BATTLE-FIELD.

WHAT, was it a dream? am I all alone
In the dreary night and the drizzling rain?
Hist!—ah, it was only the river's moan;
    They have left me behind with the mangled
        slain.

Yes, now I remember it all too well!
    We met, from the battling ranks apart;
Together our weapons flashed and fell,
    And mine was sheathed in his quivering heart.

In the cypress gloom, where the deed was done,
    It was all too dark to see his face;
But I heard his death-groans, one by one,
    And he holds me still in a cold embrace.

He spoke but once, and I could not hear
    The words he said for the cannon's roar;
But my heart grew cold with a deadly fear,—
    O God! I had heard that voice before!

Had heard it before at our mother's knee,
    When we lisped the words of our evening
        prayer!

My brother! would I had died for thee,—
    This burden is more than my soul can bear!

I pressed my lips to his death-cold cheek,
    And begged him to show me, by word or sign,
That he knew and forgave me: he could not
      speak,
    But he nestled his poor cold face to mine.

The blood flowed fast from my wounded side,
    And then for a while I forgot my pain,
And over the lakelet we seemed to glide
    In our little boat, two boys again.

And then, in my dream, we stood alone
    On a forest path where the shadows fell;
And I heard again the tremulous tone,
    And the tender words of his last farewell.

But that parting was years, long years ago,
    He wandered away to a foreign land;
And our dear old mother will never know
    That he died to-night by his brother's hand.

    .   .   .   .

The soldiers who buried the dead away
    Disturbed not the clasp of that last embrace,
But laid them to sleep till the judgment-day,
    Heart folded to heart, and face to face.

                  SARAH TITTLE BOLTON.

REQUIEM

FOR ONE SLAIN IN BATTLE.

BREATHE, trumpets, breathe
　　Slow notes of saddest wailing,—
Sadly responsive peal, ye muffled drums;
Comrades, with downcast eyes
　　　　And banners trailing,
　　　　Attend him home,—
The youthful warrior comes.

Upon his shield,
　　Upon his shield returning,
Borne from the field of honor
　　Where he fell;
Glory and grief, together clasped
　　In mourning,
His fame, his fate
　　With sobs exulting tell.

Wrap round his breast
　　The flag his breast defended,—
His country's flag,
　　In battle's front unrolled:
For it he died;
　　On earth forever ended
His brave young life
　　Lives in each sacred fold.
With proud fond tears,
　　By tinge of shame untainted,
Bear him, and lay him
　　Gently in his grave:

Above the hero write,—
   The young, half-sainted,—
His country asked his life,
   His life he gave!

GEORGE LUNT.

MUSIC IN CAMP.

Two armies covered hill and plain,
   Where Rappahannock's waters
Ran deeply crimsoned with the stain
   Of battle's recent slaughters.

The summer clouds lay pitched like tents
   In meads of heavenly azure;
And each dread gun of the elements
   Slept in its embrasure.

The breeze so softly blew, it made
   No forest leaf to quiver,
And the smoke of the random cannonade
   Rolled slowly from the river.

And now, where circling hills looked down
   With cannon grimly planted,
O'er listless camp and silent town
   The golden sunset slanted.

When on the fervid air there came
   A strain—now rich, now tender;
The music seemed itself aflame
   With day's departing splendor.

A Federal band, which, eve and morn,
  Played measures brave and nimble,
Had just struck up, with flute and horn
  And lively clash of cymbal.

Down flocked the soldiers to the banks,
  Till, margined by its pebbles,
One wooded shore was blue with " Yanks,"
  And one was gray with " Rebels."

Then all was still, and then the band,
  With movements light and tricksy,
Made stream and forest, hill and strand,
  Reverberate with " Dixie."

The conscious stream with burnished glow
  Went proudly o'er its pebbles,
But thrilled throughout its deepest flow
  With yelling of the Rebels.

Again a pause, and then again
  The trumpets pealed sonorous,
And " Yankee Doodle " was the strain
  To which the shore gave chorus.

The laughing ripple shoreward flew,
  To kiss the shining pebbles;
Loud shrieked the swarming Boys in Blue
  Defiance to the Rebels.

And yet once more the bugle sang
  Above the stormy riot;

No shout upon the evening rang—
  There reigned a holy quiet.

The sad, slow stream its noiseless flood
  Poured o'er the glistening pebbles;
All silent now the Yankees stood,
  And silent stood the Rebels.

No unresponsive soul had heard
  That plaintive note's appealing,
So deeply " Home, Sweet Home " had stirred
  The hidden fount of feeling.

Or Blue, or Gray, the soldier sees,
  As by the wand of fairy,
The cottage 'neath the live-oak trees,
  The cabin by the prairie.

Or cold, or warm, his native skies,
  Bend in their beauty o'er him;
Seen through the tear-mist in his eyes,
  His loved ones stand before him.

As fades the iris after rain
  In April's tearful weather,
The vision vanished, as the strain
  And daylight died together.

But memory, waked by music's art,
  Expressed in simplest numbers,
Subdued the sternest Yankee's heart,
  Made light the Rebel's slumbers.

And fair the form of Music shines,
That bright celestial creature,
Who still, 'mid war's embattled lines,
Gave this one touch of Nature.

                    JOHN RANDOLPH THOMPSON.

UNDER THE SHADE OF THE TREES.

[The last words of Stonewall Jackson * were: "Let us cross the river and rest under the shade of the trees."]

WHAT are the thoughts that are stirring his
    breast?
What is the mystical vision he sees?
—" Let us pass over the river, and rest
Under the shade of the trees."

Has he grown sick of his toils and his tasks?
    Sighs the worn spirit for respite or ease?
Is it a moment's cool halt that he asks
    Under the shade of the trees?

Is it the gurgle of water whose flow
    Ofttimes has come to him, borne on the breeze,
Memory listens to, lapsing so low,
    Under the shade of the trees?

Nay—though the rasp of the flesh was so sore,
    Faith, that had yearnings far keener than these,
Saw the soft sheen of the Thitherward Shore
    Under the shade of the trees;—

* Major-General Thomas J. Jackson, C. S. A., killed on a reconnoissance, May 10, 1863.

Caught the high psalm of ecstatic delight—
  Heard the harps harping, like soundings of
    seas—
Watched earth's assoiled ones walking in white
  Under the shade of the trees.

Oh, was it strange he should pine for release,
  Touched to the soul with such transports as
    these,—
He who so needed the balsam of peace,
  Under the shade of the trees?

Yea, it was noblest for him—it was best
  (Questioning naught of our Father's decrees),
There to pass over the river and rest
  Under the shade of the trees!
              MARGARET JUNKIN PRESTON.

THE BLACK REGIMENT.

[May 27, 1863.]

DARK as the clouds of even,
Ranked in the western heaven,
Waiting the breath that lifts
All the dead mass, and drifts
Tempest and falling brand
Over a ruined land,—
So still and orderly,
Arm to arm, knee to knee,
Waiting the great event,
Stands the black regiment.

Down the long dusty line
Teeth gleam and eyeballs shine;
And the bright bayonet,
Bristling and firmly set,
Flashed with a purpose grand,
Long ere the sharp command
Of the fierce rolling drum
Told them their time had come,
Told them what work was sent
For the black regiment.

" Now," the flag-sergeant cried,
" Though death and hell betide,
Let the whole nation see
If we are fit to be
Free in this land; or bound
Down, like the whining hound,—
Bound with red stripes of pain
In our cold chains again! "
O, what a shout there went
From the black regiment!

" Charge! " Trump and drum awoke;
Onward the bondmen broke;
Bayonet and sabre-stroke
Vainly opposed their rush.
Through the wild battle's crush,
With but one thought aflush,
Driving their lords like chaff,
In the guns' mouths they laugh;
Or at the slippery brands
Leaping with open hands,
Down they tear man and horse,

Down in their awful course;
Trampling with bloody heel
Over the crashing steel,—
All their eyes forward bent,
Rushed the black regiment.

" Freedom ! " their battle-cry,—
" Freedom ! or leave to die ! "
Ah ! and they meant the word,
Not as with us 't is heard,
Not a mere party shout ;
They gave their spirits out,
Trusted the end to God,
And on the gory sod
Rolled in triumphant blood.
Glad to strike one free blow,
Whether for weal or woe ;
Glad to breathe one free breath,
Though on the lips of death ;
Praying,—alas ! in vain !—
That they might fall again,
So they could once more see
That burst to liberty !
This was what " freedom " lent
To the black regiment.

Hundreds on hundreds fell ;
But they are resting well ;
Scourges and shackles strong
Never shall do them wrong.
O, to the living few,
Soldiers, be just and true !
Hail them as comrades tried ;

Fight with them side by side;
Never, in field or tent,
Scorn the black regiment!

GEORGE HENRY BOKER.

THE C. S. ARMY'S COMMISSARY.

I.—1863.

" WELL, this is bad!" we sighing said,
　While musing round the bivouac fire,
　And dwelling with a fond desire,
On home and comforts long since fled.

" How gayly came we forth at first!
　Our spirits high, with new emprise,
　Ambitious of each exercise,
And glowing with a martial thirst.

" Equipped as for a holiday,
　With bounteous store of everything
　To use or comfort minist'ring,
All cheerily we marched away.

" But as the struggle fiercer grew,
　Light marching orders came apace,—
　And baggage-wagon soon gave place
To that which sterner uses knew.

" Our tents—they went a year ago;
　Now kettle, spider, frying-pan
　Are lost to us, and as we can
We live, while marching to and fro.

" Our food has lessened, till at length,
    E'en want's gaunt image seems to threat—
    A foe to whom the bravest yet
Must yield at last his knightly strength.

" But while we 've meat and flour enough
    The bayonet shall be our spit—
    The ramrod bake our dough on it—
A gum-cloth be our kneading trough.

" We 'll bear privation, danger dare,
    While even these are left to us—
    Be hopeful, faithful, emulous
Of gallant deeds, though hard our fare! "

II.—1864.

" Three years and more," we grimly said,
    When order came to " Rest at will "
    Beside the corn-field on the hill,
As on a weary march we sped—

" Three years and more we 've met the foe
    On many a gory, hard-fought field,
    And still we swear we cannot yield
Till Fate shall bring some deeper woe.

" Three years and more we 've struggled on,
    Through torrid heat and winter's chill,
    Nor bated aught of steadfast will,
Though even hope seems almost gone.

" Ill fed, ill clad, and shelterless,
    How little cheer in health we know!

When wounds and illness lay us low,
How comfortless our sore distress!

" These flimsy rags, that scarcely hide
Our forms, can naught discourage us;
But Hunger—ah! it may be thus
That Fortune shall the strife decide.

" But while the corn-fields give supply
We'll take, content, the roasting-ear,
Nor yield us yet to craven fear,
But still press on, to do or die!"

ED. PORTER THOMPSON.

THE HIGH TIDE AT GETTYSBURG.

[July 3, 1863.]

A CLOUD possessed the hollow field,
The gathering battle's smoky shield.
Athwart the gloom the lightning flashed,
And through the cloud some horsemen dashed,
And from the heights the thunder pealed.

Then at the brief command of Lee
Moved out that matchless infantry,
With Pickett leading grandly down,
To rush against the roaring crown
Of those dread heights of destiny.

Far heard above the angry guns
A cry across the tumult runs,—
The voice that rang through Shiloh's woods

And Chickamauga's solitudes,
The fierce South cheering on her sons!

Ah, how the withering tempest blew
Against the front of Pettigrew!
A Khamsin wind that scorched and singed
Like that infernal flame that fringed
The British squares at Waterloo!

A thousand fell where Kemper led;
A thousand died where Garnett bled:
In blinding flame and strangling smoke
The remnant through the batteries broke
And crossed the works with Armistead.

"Once more in Glory's van with me!"
Virginia cried to Tennessee;
"We two together, come what may,
Shall stand upon these works to-day!"
(The reddest day in history.)

Brave Tennessee! In reckless way
Virginia heard her comrade say:
"Close round this rent and riddled rag!"
What time she set her battle-flag
Amid the guns of Doubleday.

But who shall break the guards that wait
Before the awful face of Fate?
The tattered standards of the South
Were shrivelled at the cannon's mouth,
And all her hopes were desolate.

In vain the Tennesseean set
His breast against the bayonet!
In vain Virginia charged and raged,
A tigress in her wrath uncaged,
Till all the hill was red and wet!

Above the bayonets, mixed and crossed,
Men saw a gray, gigantic ghost
Receding through the battle-cloud,
And heard across the tempest loud
The death-cry of a nation lost!

The brave went down! Without disgrace
They leaped to Ruin's red embrace.
They only heard Fame's thunders wake,
And saw the dazzling sun-burst break
In smiles on Glory's bloody face!

They fell, who lifted up a hand
And bade the sun in heaven to stand!
They smote and fell, who set the bars
Against the progress of the stars,
And stayed the march of Motherland!

They stood, who saw the future come
On through the fight's delirium!
They smote and stood, who held the hope
Of nations on that slippery slope
Amid the cheers of Christendom.

God lives! He forged the iron will
   That clutched and held that trembling hill.
God lives and reigns! He built and lent

The heights for Freedom's battlement
Where floats her flag in triumph still!

Fold up the banners! Smelt the guns!
Love rules. Her gentler purpose runs.
A mighty mother turns in tears
The pages of her battle years,
Lamenting all her fallen sons!

WILL HENRY THOMPSON.

LEE TO THE REAR.

[An incident in one of the battles in the Wilderness at the beginning of the campaign of 1864.]

DAWN of a pleasant morning in May
Broke through the Wilderness cool and gray;
While perched in the tallest tree-tops, the birds
Were carolling Mendelssohn's "Songs without
    Words."

Far from the haunts of men remote,
The brook brawled on with a liquid note;
And Nature, all tranquil and lovely, wore
The smile of the spring, as in Eden of yore.

Little by little, as daylight increased,
And deepened the roseate flush in the East—
Little by little did morning reveal
Two long glittering lines of steel;

Where two hundred thousand bayonets gleam,
Tipped with the light of the earliest beam,

26

And the faces are sullen and grim to see
In the hostile armies of Grant and Lee.

All of a sudden, ere rose the sun,
Pealed on the silence the opening gun—
A little white puff of smoke there came,
And anon the valley was wreathed in flame.

Down on the left of the Rebel lines,
Where a breastwork stands in a copse of pines,
Before the Rebels their ranks can form,
The Yankees have carried the place by storm.

Stars and Stripes on the salient wave,
Where many a hero has found a grave,
And the gallant Confederates strive in vain
The ground they have drenched with their blood,
    to regain.

Yet louder the thunder of battle roared—
Yet a deadlier fire on the columns poured;
Slaughter infernal rode with Despair,
Furies twain, through the murky air.

Not far off, in the saddle there sat
A gray-bearded man in a black slouched hat;
Not much moved by the fire was he,
Calm and resolute Robert Lee.

Quick and watchful he kept his eye
On the bold Rebel brigades close by,—
Reserves that were standing (and dying) at ease,
While the tempest of wrath toppled over the trees.

For still with their loud, deep, bull-dog bay,
The Yankee batteries blazed away,
And with every murderous second that sped
A dozen brave fellows, alas! fell dead.

The grand old graybeard rode to the space
Where Death and his victims stood face to face,
And silently waved his old slouched hat—
A world of meaning there was in that!

" Follow me! Steady! We 'll save the day!"
This was what he seemed to say;
And to the light of his glorious eye
The bold brigades thus made reply:

" We 'll go forward, but you must go back "—
And they moved not an inch in the perilous track:
" Go to the rear, and we 'll send them to hell!"
And the sound of the battle was lost in their yell.

Turning his bridle, Robert Lee
Rode to the rear. Like waves of the sea,
Bursting the dikes in their overflow,
Madly his veterans dashed on the foe.

And backward in terror that foe was driven,
Their banners rent and their columns riven,
Wherever the tide of battle rolled
Over the Wilderness, wood and wold.

Sunset out of a crimson sky
Streamed o'er a field of ruddier dye,

And the brook ran on with a purple stain,
From the blood of ten thousand foemen slain.

Seasons have passed since that day and year—
Again o'er its pebbles the brook runs clear,
And the field in a richer green is drest
Where the dead of a terrible conflict rest.

Hushed is the roll of the Rebel drum,
The sabres are sheathed, and the cannon are
    dumb;
And Fate, with his pitiless hand, has furled
The flag that once challenged the gaze of the
    world;

But the fame of the Wilderness fight abides;
And down into history grandly rides,
Calm and unmoved as in battle he sat,
The gray-bearded man in the black slouched hat.

             JOHN RANDOLPH THOMPSON.

DRIVING HOME THE COWS.

Out of the clover and blue-eyed grass
   He turned them into the river-lane;
One after another he let them pass,
   Then fastened the meadow bars again.

Under the willows, and over the hill,
   He patiently followed their sober pace;
The merry whistle for once was still,
   And something shadowed the sunny face.

Only a boy! and his father had said
   He never could let his youngest go;

Two already were lying dead
　Under the feet of the trampling foe.

But after the evening work was done,
　And the frogs were loud in the meadow-swamp,
Over his shoulder he slung his gun
　And stealthily followed the foot-path damp,

Across the clover and through the wheat
　With resolute heart and purpose grim,
Though cold was the dew on his hurrying feet,
　And the blind bat's flitting startled him.

Thrice since then had the lanes been white,
　And the orchards sweet with apple-bloom;
And now, when the cows came back at night,
　The feeble father drove them home.

For news had come to the lonely farm
　That three were lying where two had lain;
And the old man's tremulous, palsied arm
　Could never lean on a son's again.

The summer day grew cool and late,
　He went for the cows when the work was done;
But down the lane, as he opened the gate,
　He saw them coming one by one,—

Brindle, Ebony, Speckle, and Bess,
　Shaking their horns in the evening wind;
Cropping the buttercups out of the grass,—
　But who was it following close behind?

Loosely swung in the idle air
　The empty sleeve of army blue;
And worn and pale, from the crisping hair,
　Looked out a face that the father knew.

For gloomy prisons will sometimes yawn,
　　And yield their dead unto life again;
And the day that comes with a cloudy dawn
　　In golden glory at last may wane.

The great tears sprang to their meeting eyes;
　　For the heart must speak when the lips are
　　　　dumb;
And under the silent evening skies
　　Together they followed the cattle home.

KATE PUTNAM OSGOOD.

SHERMAN'S MARCH TO THE SEA.*

[May 4 to December 21, 1864.]

OUR camp-fires shone bright on the mountains
　　That frowned on the river below,
While we stood by our guns in the morning
　　And eagerly watched for the foe,

* This song was sung by thousands of Sherman's soldiers after the march, and had the honor of giving its
name to the campaign it celebrates. Its author had been
one of Sherman's army, and was captured at the battle of
Chattanooga. While a prisoner he escaped, disguised himself in a Confederate uniform, went to the Southern army,
and witnessed some of the fierce fighting about Atlanta.
He was discovered and sent back to prison at Columbia,
S. C., where he wrote the song. He soon escaped again,
rejoined Sherman's army, and for a time served on General Sherman's staff. From Cape Fear River he was sent
North with despatches to Grant and President Lincoln,
bringing the first news of Sherman's successes in the
Carolinas.

When a rider came out of the darkness
  That hung over the mountain and tree,
And shouted, " Boys, up and be ready!
  For Sherman will march to the sea."

Then cheer upon cheer for bold Sherman
  Went up from each valley and glen,
And the bugles re-echoed the music
  That came from the lips of the men;
For we knew that the stars in our banner
  More bright in their splendor would be,
And that blessings from Northland would greet
    us
  When Sherman marched down to the sea.

Then forward, boys, forward to battle,
  We marched on our wearisome way,
We stormed the wild hills of Resaca;
  God bless those who fell on that day!
Then Kenesaw, dark in its glory,
  Frowned down on the flag of the free,
But the East and the West bore our standards,
  And Sherman marched on to the sea.

Still onward we pressed, till our banners
  Swept out from Atlanta's grim walls,
And the blood of the patriot dampened
  The soil where the traitor flag falls;
Yet we paused not to weep for the fallen,
  Who slept by each river and tree;
We twined them a wreath of the laurel
  As Sherman marched down to the sea.

Oh! proud was our army that morning,
  That stood where the pine darkly towers,

When Sherman said: " Boys, you are weary;
　This day fair Savannah is ours!"
Then sang we a song for our chieftain,
　That echoed o'er river and lea,
And the stars in our banner shone brighter
　When Sherman marched down to the sea.

SAMUEL H. M. BYERS.

ARMY CORRESPONDENT'S LAST RIDE.

FIVE FORKS, APRIL 1, 1865.

Ho! pony.　Down the lonely road
　Strike now your cheeriest pace!
The woods on fire do not burn higher
　Than burns my anxious face;
Far have you sped, but all this night
　Must feel my nervous spur;
If we be late, the world must wait
　The tidings we aver:—
To home and hamlet, town and hearth,
　To thrill child, mother, man,
I carry to the waiting North
　Great news from Sheridan!

The birds are dead among the pines,
　Slain by the battle fright,
Prone in the road the steed reclines
　That never reached the fight;
Yet on we go,—the wreck below
　Of many a tumbled wain,—
By ghastly pools where stranded mules
　Die, drinking of the rain;

With but my list of killed and missed
   I spur my stumbling nag,
To tell of death at many a tryst,
   But victory to the flag!

"Halt! who comes there?　The countersign!"—
  "A friend."—"Advance!　The fight,—
How goes it, say?"—"We won the day!"—
  "Huzza! Pass on!"—"Good-night!"—
And parts the darkness on before,
   And down the mire we tramp,
And the black sky is painted o'er
   With many a pulsing camp;
O'er stumps and ruts, by ruined huts,
   Where ghosts look through the gloam,—
Behind my tread I hear the dead
   Follow the news toward home!

The hunted souls I see behind,
   In swamp and in ravine,
Whose cry for mercy thrills the wind
   Till cracks the sure carbine;
The moving lights, which scare the dark,
   And show the trampled place
Where, in his blood, some mother's bud
   Turns up his young, dead face;
The captives spent, whose standards rent
   The conqueror parades,
As at the Five Forks roads arrive
   The General's dashing aides.

O wondrous Youth! through this grand ruth
   Runs my boy's life its thread;

The General's fame, the battle's name,
  The rolls of maimed and dead
I bear, with my thrilled soul astir,
  And lonely thoughts and fears;
And am but History's courier
  To bind the conquering years;
A battle-ray, through ages gray
  To light to deeds sublime,
And flash the lustre of this day
  Down all the aisles of Time!

Ho! pony,—'t is the signal gun
  The night-assault decreed;
On Petersburg the thunderbolts
  Crash from the lines of Meade;
Fade the pale, frightened stars o'erhead,
  And shrieks the bursting air;
The forest foliage, tinted red,
  Grows ghastlier in the glare;
Though in her towers, reached her last hours,
  Rocks proud Rebellion's crest—
The world may sag, if but my nag
  Get in before the rest!

With bloody flank, and fetlocks dank,
  And goad, and lash, and shout—
Great God! as every hoof-beat falls
  A hundred lives beat out!
As weary as this broken steed
  Reels down the corduroys,
So, weary, fight for morning light
  Our hot and grimy boys;
Through ditches wet, o'er parapet
  And guns barbette, they catch

The last, lost breach; and I,—I reach
The mail with my despatch!

Sure it shall speed, the land to read,
As sped the happiest shell!
The shot I send strike the world's end;
This tells my pony's knell;
His long race run, the long war done,
My occupation gone,—
Above his bier, prone on the pier,
The vultures fleck the dawn.
Still, rest his bones where soldiers dwell,
Till the Long Roll they catch.
He fell the day that Richmond fell,
And took the first despatch!

GEORGE ALFRED TOWNSEND.

THE YEAR OF JUBILEE.*

SAY, darkeys, hab you seen de massa,
Wid de muffstash on he face,
Go long de road some time dis mornin',
Like he gwine leabe de place?
He see de smoke way up de ribber
Whar de Lincum gunboats lay;
He took he hat an' leff berry sudden,
And I spose he 's runned away.

* Sung by negro troops when entering Richmond.
George Cary Eggleston, in his collection of "American
War Ballads," says that it soon found favor among the
people and "was sung with applause by young men and
maidens in well-nigh every house in Virginia."

De massa run, ha, ha!
De darkey stay, ho, ho!
It mus' be now de kingdum comin',
An' de yar ob jubilo.

He six foot one way an' two foot todder,
An' he weigh six hundred poun' ;
His coat so big he couldn't pay de tailor,
An' it won't reach half way roun' ;
He drill so much dey calls him cap'n,
An he git so mighty tanned,
I spec he 'll try to fool dem Yankees,
For to tink he contraband.
De massa run, ha, ha!
De darkey stay, ho, ho!
It mus' be now de kingdum comin',
An' de yar ob jubilo.

De darkeys got so lonesome libb'n
In de log hut on de lawn,
Dey moved dere tings into massa's parlor
For to keep it while he gone.
Dar 's wine an' cider in de kitchin,
An' de darkeys dey hab some,
I spec it will be all fiscated,
When de Lincum sojers come.
De massa run, ha, ha!
De darkey stay, ho, ho!
It mus' be now de kingdum comin',
An' de yar ob jubilo.

De oberseer he makes us trubble,
An' he dribe us roun' a spell,

We lock him up in de smoke-house cellar,
  Wid de key flung in de well.
De whip am lost, de han'-cuff broke,
  But de massy hab his pay;
He big an' ole enough for to know better
  Dan to went an' run away.
    De massa run, ha, ha!
    De darkey stay, ho, ho!
    It mus' be now de kingdum comin',
    An' de yar ob jubilo.

ANONYMOUS.

THE CONQUERED BANNER.

FURL that Banner, for 't is weary;
Round its staff 't is drooping dreary:
    Furl it, fold it,—it is best;
For there 's not a man to wave it,
And there 's not a sword to save it,
And there 's not one left to lave it
In the blood which heroes gave it,
And its foes now scorn and brave it:
    Furl it, hide it,—let it rest!

Take that Banner down! 't is tattered;
Broken is its staff and shattered;
And the valiant hosts are scattered,
    Over whom it floated high.
Oh, 't is hard for us to fold it,
Hard to think there 's none to hold it,
Hard that those who once unrolled it
    Now must furl it with a sigh!

Furl that Banner—furl it sadly!
Once ten thousands hailed it gladly,
And ten thousands wildly, madly,
    Swore it should forever wave;
Swore that foeman's sword should never
Hearts like theirs entwined dissever,
Till that flag should float forever
    O'er their freedom or their grave!

Furl it! for the hands that grasped it,
And the hearts that fondly clasped it,
    Cold and dead are lying low;
And that Banner—it is trailing,
While around it sounds the wailing
    Of its people in their woe.

For, though conquered, they adore it,—
Love the cold, dead hands that bore it,
Weep for those who fell before it,
Pardon those who trailed and tore it;
And oh, wildly they deplore it,
    Now to furl and fold it so!

Furl that Banner! True, 't is gory,
Yet 't is wreathed around with glory,
And 't will live in song and story
    Though its folds are in the dust!
For its fame on brightest pages,
Penned by poets and by sages,
Shall go sounding down the ages—
    Furl its folds though now we must.

Furl that Banner, softly, slowly!
Treat it gently—it is holy,
    For it droops above the dead.

Touch it not—unfold it never;
Let it droop there, furled forever,—
  For its people's hopes are fled!
                    ABRAM JOSEPH RYAN.

ALL.

THERE hangs a sabre, and there a rein,
With a rusty buckle and green curb chain;
A pair of spurs on the old gray wall,
And a mouldy saddle—well, that is all.

Come out to the stable—it is not far;
The moss grown door is hanging ajar.
Look within! There 's an empty stall,
Where once stood a charger, and that is all.

The good black horse came riderless home,
Flecked with blood drops as well as foam;
See yonder hillock where dead leaves fall;
The good black horse pined to death—that 's all.

All? O, God! it is all I can speak.
Question me not—I am old and weak;
His sabre and his saddle hang on the wall,
And his horse pined to death—I have told you all.
                    FRANCIS ALEXANDER DURIVAGE.

THE CLOSING SCENE.

WITHIN the sober realm of leafless trees,
The russet year inhaled the dreamy air;
Like some tanned reaper, in his hour of ease,
When all the fields are lying brown and bare.

The gray barns looking from their hazy hills,
O'er the dun waters widening in the vales,
Sent down the air a greeting to the mills
On the dull thunder of alternate flails.

All sights were mellowed and all sounds subdued,
The hills seemed further and the stream sang
low,
As in a dream the distant woodman hewed
His winter log with many a muffled blow.

The embattled forests, erewhile armed with gold,
Their banners bright with every martial hue,
Now stood like some sad, beaten host of old,
Withdrawn afar in Time's remotest blue.

On slumb'rous wings the vulture held his flight;
The dove scarce heard its sighing mate's com-
plaint;
And, like a star slow drowning in the light,
The village church-vane seemed to pale and
faint.

The sentinel-cock upon the hillside crew,—
Crew thrice,—and all was stiller than before;

Silent, till some replying warden blew
    His alien horn, and then was heard no more.

Where erst the jay, within the elm's tall crest,
    Made garrulous trouble round her unfledged
        young;
And where the oriole hung her swaying nest,
    By every light wind like a censer swung;—

Where sang the noisy martens of the eaves,
    The busy swallows circling ever near,—
Foreboding, as the rustic mind believes,
    An early harvest and a plenteous year;—

Where every bird which charmed the vernal feast
    Shook the sweet slumber from its wings at
        morn,
To warn the reaper of the rosy east:—
    All now was sunless, empty, and forlorn.

Alone from out the stubble piped the quail,
    And croaked the crow through all the dreamy
        gloom;
Alone the pheasant, drumming in the vale,
    Made echo to the distant cottage-loom.

There was no bud, no bloom upon the bowers;
    The spiders moved their thin shrouds night by
        night,
The thistle-down, the only ghost of flowers,
    Sailed slowly by,—passed noiseless out of sight.
27

Amid all this—in this most cheerless air,
 And where the woodbine shed upon the porch
Its crimson leaves, as if the Year stood there
 Firing the floor with his inverted torch,—

Amid all this, the centre of the scene,
 The white-haired matron with monotonous tread
Plied the swift wheel, and with her joyless mien
 Sat, like a fate, and watched the flying thread.

She had known Sorrow,—he had walked with
 her,
 Oft supped, and broke the bitter ashen crust;
And in the dead leaves still she heard the stir
 Of his black mantle trailing in the dust.

While yet her cheek was bright with summer
 bloom,
 Her country summoned and she gave her all;
And twice War bowed to her his sable plume,—
 Re-gave the swords to rust upon the wall.

Re-gave the swords, but not the hand that drew
 And struck for Liberty the dying blow;
Nor him who, to his sire and country true,
 Fell mid the ranks of the invading foe.

Long, but not loud, the droning wheel went on,
 Like the low murmur of a hive at noon;
Long, but not loud, the memory of the gone
 Breathed through her lips a sad and tremulous
 tune.

At last the thread was snapped; her head was
    bowed;
Life dropt the distaff through his hands serene;
And loving neighbors smoothed her careful shroud,
    While Death and Winter closed the autumn
        scene.

THOMAS BUCHANAN READ.

THE MEN BEHIND THE GUNS.

[The Spanish-American War, 1898.]

A CHEER and salute for the Admiral, and here 's
    to the Captain bold,
And never forget the Commodore's debt when the
    deeds of might are told!
They stand to the deck through the battle's wreck
    when the great shells roar and screech—
And never they fear when the foe is near to prac-
    tise what they preach:
But off with your hat and three times three for
    Columbia's true-blue sons,
The men below who batter the foe—the men be-
    hind the guns!

Oh, light and merry of heart are they when they
    swing into port once more,
When, with more than enough of the " green-
    backed stuff," they start for their leave-o'-
        shore;
And you 'd think, perhaps, that the blue-bloused
    chaps who loll along the street

Are a tender bit, with salt on it, for some fierce
    " mustache " to eat—
Some warrior bold, with straps of gold, who
    dazzles and fairly stuns
The modest worth of the sailor boys—the lads
    who serve the guns.

But say not a word till the shot is heard that
    tells the fight is on,
Till the long, deep roar grows more and more
    from the ships of " Yank " and " Don,"
Till over the deep the tempests sweep of fire and
    bursting shell,
And the very air is a mad Despair in the throes
    of a living hell;
Then down, deep down, in the mighty ship, unseen
    by the midday suns,
You 'll find the chaps who are giving the raps—
    the men behind the guns!

Oh, well they know how the cyclones blow that
    they loose from their cloud of death,
And they know is heard the thunder-word their
    fierce ten-incher saith!
The steel decks rock with the lightning shock, and
    shake with the great recoil,
And the sea grows red with the blood of the dead
    and reaches for his spoil—
But not till the foe has gone below or turns his
    prow and runs,
Shall the voice of peace bring sweet release to the
    men behind the guns!

              JOHN JEROME ROONEY.

THE BATTLE OF MANILA.

A FRAGMENT.

[May 1, 1898.]

By Cavité on the bay
'T was the Spanish squadron lay;
And the red dawn was creeping
O'er the city that lay sleeping
To the east, like a bride, in the May.
There was peace at Manila,
In the May morn at Manila,—
When ho, the Spanish admiral
Awoke to find our line
Had passed by gray Corregidor,
Had laughed at shoal and mine,
And flung to the sky its banners
With " Remember " for the sign!

With the ships of Spain before
In the shelter of the shore,
And the forts on the right,
They drew forward to the fight,
And the first was the gallant Commodore;
In the bay of Manila,
In the doomed bay of Manila—
With succor half the world away,
No port beneath that sky,
With nothing but their ships and guns
And Yankee pluck to try,
They had left retreat behind them,
They had come to win or die!

.   .   .   .

For we spoke at Manila,
We said it at Manila,
Oh be ye brave, or be ye strong,
Ye build your ships in vain;
The children of the sea queen's brood
Will not give up the main;
We hold the sea against the world
As we held it against Spain.

Be warned by Manila,
Take warning by Manila,
Ye may trade by land, ye may fight by land,
Ye may hold the land in fee;
But not go down to the sea in ships
To battle with the free;
For England and America
Will keep and hold the sea!

RICHARD HOVEY.

IV.

PEACE.

———

ODE TO PEACE.

DAUGHTER of God! that sitt'st on high
Amid the dances of the sky,
And guidest with thy gentle sway
The planets on their tuneful way;
  Sweet Peace! shall ne'er again
The smile of thy most holy face,
From thine ethereal dwelling-place,
Rejoice the wretched, weary race
  Of discord-breathing men?
Too long, O gladness-giving Queen!
Thy tarrying in heaven has been;
Too long o'er this fair blooming world
The flag of blood has been unfurled,
  Polluting God's pure day;
Whilst, as each maddening people reels,
War onward drives his scythèd wheels,
And at his horses' bloody heels
  Shriek Murder and Dismay.

Oft have I wept to hear the cry
Of widow wailing bitterly;

To see the parent's silent tear
For children fallen beneath the spear;
   And I have felt so sore
The sense of human guilt and woe,
That I, in Virtue's passioned glow,
Have cursed (my soul was wounded so)
   The shape of man I bore!
Then come from thy serene abode,
Thou gladness-giving child of God!
And cease the world's ensanguined strife,
And reconcile my soul to life;
   For much I long to see,
Ere I shall to the grave descend,
Thy hand its blessèd branch extend,
And to the world's remotest end
   Wave Love and Harmony!

WILLIAM TENNANT.

END OF THE CIVIL WAR.

FROM KING RICHARD III., ACT I. SC. 1.

Now is the winter of our discontent
Made glorious summer by this sun of York,
And all the clouds that lowered upon our house
In the deep bosom of the ocean buried.
Now are our brows bound with victorious wreaths;
Our bruisèd arms hung up for monuments;
Our stern alarums changed to merry meetings,
Our dreadful marches to delightful measures.

Grim-visaged War hath smoothed his wrinkled
    front.
And now, instead of mounting barbèd steeds
To fright the souls of fearful adversaries,
He capers nimbly in a lady's chamber,
To the lascivious pleasing of a lute.

SHAKESPEARE.

DISARMAMENT.

"Put up the sword!" the voice of Christ once
    more
Speaks, in the pauses of the cannon's roar,
O'er fields of corn by fiery sickles reaped
And left dry ashes; over trenches heaped
With nameless dead; o'er cities starving slow
Under a rain of fire; through wards of woe
Down which a groaning diapason runs
From tortured brothers, husbands, lovers, sons
Of desolate women in their far-off homes,
Waiting to hear the step that never comes!
O men and brothers! let that voice be heard.
War fails, try peace; put up the useless sword!

Fear not the end. There is a story told
In Eastern tents, when autumn nights grow cold,
And round the fire the Mongol shepherds sit
With grave responses listening unto it:
Once on the errands of his mercy bent,
Buddha, the holy and benevolent,
Met a fell monster, huge and fierce of look,
Whose awful voice the hills and forests shook.

"O son of peace!" the giant cried, "thy fate
Is sealed at last, and love shall yield to hate."
The unarmed Buddha looking, with no trace
Of fear or anger, in the monster's face,
In pity said, " Poor fiend, even thee I love."
Lo! as he spake the sky-tall terror sank
To hand-breadth size; the huge abhorrence shrank
Into the form and fashion of a dove;
And where the thunder of its rage was heard,
Circling above him sweetly sang the bird:
" Hate hath no harm for love," so ran the song,
" And peace unweaponed conquers every wrong!"

JOHN GREENLEAF WHITTIER.

TUBAL CAIN.

OLD Tubal Cain was a man of might,
    In the days when earth was young;
By the fierce red light of his furnace bright,
    The strokes of his hammer rung:
And he lifted high his brawny hand
    On the iron glowing clear,
Till the sparks rushed out in scarlet showers,
    As he fashioned the sword and the spear.
And he sang: " Hurrah for my handiwork!
    Hurrah for the spear and the sword!
Hurrah for the hand that shall wield them well,
    For he shall be king and lord."

To Tubal Cain came many a one,
    As he wrought by his roaring fire,
And each one prayed for a strong steel blade
    As the crown of his desire:

And he made them weapons sharp and strong,
  Till they shouted loud for glee,
And gave him gifts of pearl and gold,
  And spoils of the forest free.
And they sang: "Hurrah for Tubal Cain,
  Who hath given us strength anew!
Hurrah for the smith, hurrah for the fire,
  And hurrah for the metal true!"

But a sudden change came o'er his heart,
  Ere the setting of the sun,
And Tubal Cain was filled with pain
  For the evil he had done;
He saw that men, with rage and hate,
  Made war upon their kind,
That the land was red with the blood they shed,
  In their lust for carnage blind.
And he said: "Alas! that ever I made,
  Or that skill of mine should plan,
The spear and the sword for men whose joy
  Is to slay their fellow-man!"

And for many a day old Tubal Cain
  Sat brooding o'er his woe;
And his hand forbore to smite the ore,
  And his furnace smouldered low.
But he rose at last with a cheerful face,
  And a bright courageous eye,
And bared his strong right arm for work,
  While the quick flames mounted high.
And he sang: "Hurrah for my handiwork!"
  And the red sparks lit the air;

"Not alone for the blade was the bright steel
  made,"—
 And he fashioned the first ploughshare.

And men, taught wisdom from the past,
 In friendship joined their hands,
Hung the sword in the hall, the spear on the wall,
 And ploughed the willing lands;
And sang: "Hurrah for Tubal Cain!
 Our stanch good friend is he;
And for the ploughshare and the plough
 To him our praise shall be.
But while oppression lifts its head,
 Or a tyrant would be lord,
Though we may thank him for the plough,
 We 'll not forget the sword!"

CHARLES MACKAY.

THE KNIGHT'S TOMB.

WHERE is the grave of Sir Arthur O'Kellyn?
Where may the grave of that good man be?—
By the side of a spring, on the breast of Helvellyn,
Under the twigs of a young birch-tree!
The oak that in summer was sweet to hear,
And rustled its leaves in the fall of the year,
And whistled and roared in the winter alone,
Is gone,—and the birch in its stead is grown.—
The knight's bones are dust,
And his good sword rust;—
His soul is with the saints, I trust.

SAMUEL TAYLOR COLERIDGE.

NOT ON THE BATTLE–FIELD.

"To fall on the battle-field fighting for my dear country,—that would not be hard."—*The Neighbors.*

O NO, no,—let me lie
Not on a field of battle when I die!
  Let not the iron tread
Of the mad war-horse crush my helmèd head;
  Nor let the reeking knife,
That I have drawn against a brother's life,
  Be in my hand when Death
Thunders along, and tramples me beneath
  His heavy squadron's heels,
Or gory felloes of his cannon's wheels.

  From such a dying bed,
Though o'er it float the stripes of white and red,
  And the bald eagle brings
The clustered stars upon his wide-spread wings
  To sparkle in my sight,
O, never let my spirit take her flight!

  I know that beauty's eye
Is all the brighter where gay pennants fly,
  And brazen helmets dance,
And sunshine flashes on the lifted lance;
  I know that bards have sung,
And people shouted till the welkin rung,
  In honor of the brave
Who on the battle-field have found a grave;
  I know that o'er their bones

How grateful hands piled monumental stones.
  Some of those piles I 've seen:
The one at Lexington upon the green
    Where the first blood was shed,
And to my country's independence led;
    And others, on our shore,
The " Battle Monument " at Baltimore,
    And that on Bunker's Hill.
Ay, and abroad, a few more famous still;
    Thy " tomb," Themistocles,
That looks out yet upon the Grecian seas,
    And which the waters kiss
That issue from the gulf of Salamis.
    And thine, too, have I seen,
Thy mound of earth, Patroclus, robed in green,
    That, like a natural knoll,
Sheep climb and nibble over as they stroll,
    Watched by some turbaned boy,
Upon the margin of the plain of Troy.
    Such honors grace the bed,
I know, whereon the warrior lays his head,
    And hears, as life ebbs out,
The conquered flying, and the conqueror's shout;
    But as his eye grows dim,
What is a column or a mound to him?
    What, to the parting soul,
The mellow note of bugles? What the roll
    Of drums? No, let me die
Where the blue heaven bends o'er me lovingly,
    And the soft summer air,
As it goes by me, stirs my thin white hair,
    And from my forehead dries
The death-damp as it gathers, and the skies

Seem waiting to receive
My soul to their clear depths! Or let me leave
The world when round my bed
Wife, children, weeping friends are gatherèd,
And the calm voice of prayer
And holy hymning shall my soul prepare
To go and be at rest
With kindred spirits,—spirits who have blessed
The human brotherhood
By labors, cares, and counsels for their good.

JOHN PIERPONT.

THE DAY IS COMING.

COME hither lads and hearken,
  for a tale there is to tell,
Of the wonderful days a-coming,
  when all shall be better than well.

And the tale shall be told of a country,
  a land in the midst of the sea,
And folk shall call it England
  in the days that are going to be.

There more than one in a thousand,
  in the days that are yet to come,
Shall have some hope of the morrow,
  some joy of the ancient home.

For then—laugh not, but listen
  to this strange tale of mine—
All folk that are in England
  shall be better lodged than swine.

Then a man shall work and bethink him,
   and rejoice in the deeds of his hand;
Nor yet come home in the even
   too faint and weary to stand.

Men in that time a-coming
   shall work and have no fear
For to-morrow's lack of earning,
   and the hunger-Wolf anear.

I tell you this for a wonder,
   that no man then shall be glad
Of his fellow's fall and mishap,
   to snatch at the work he had.

For that which the worker winneth
   shall then be his indeed,
Nor' shall half be reaped for nothing
   by him that sowed no seed.

Oh, strange new wonderful justice!
   But for whom shall we gather the gain?
For ourselves and for each of our fellows,
   and no hand shall labor in vain.

Then all Mine and all Thine shall be Ours,
   and no more shall any man crave
For riches that serve for nothing
   but to fetter a friend for a slave.

And what wealth then shall be left us,
   when none shall gather gold

To buy his friend in the market,
   and pinch and pine the sold?

Nay, what save the lovely city,
   and the little house on the hill,
And the wastes and the woodland beauty,
   and the happy fields we till;

And the homes of ancient stories,
   the tombs of the mighty dead;
And the wise men seeking out marvels,
   and the poet's teeming head;

And the painter's hand of wonder,
   and the marvellous fiddle-bow,
And the banded choirs of music:
   all those that do and know.

For all these shall be ours and all men's;
   nor shall any lack a share
Of the toil and the gain of living,
   in the days when the world grows fair.

Ah! such are the days that shall be!
   But what are the deeds of to-day,
In the days of the years we dwell in,
   that wear our lives away?

Why, then, and for what are we waiting?
   There are three words to speak:
We will it, and what is the foeman
   but the dream-strong wakened and weak?

28

Oh, why and for what are we waiting,
    while our brothers droop and die,
And on every wind of the heavens
    a wasted life goes by?

How long shall they reproach us,
    where crowd on crowd they dwell,—
Poor ghosts of the wicked city,
    the gold-crushed hungry hell?

Through squalid life they labored,
    in sordid grief they died,—
Those sons of a mighty mother,
    those props of England's pride.

They are gone; there is none can undo it,
    nor save our souls from the curse:
But many a million cometh,
    and shall they be better or worse?

It is we must answer and hasten,
    and open wide the door
For the rich man's hurrying terror,
    and the slow-foot hope of the poor.

Yea, the voiceless wrath of the wretched,
    and their unlearned discontent,—
We must give it voice and wisdom
    till the waiting-tide be spent.

Come then, since all things call us,
    the living and the dead,

And o'er the weltering tangle
  a glimmering light is shed.

Come then, let us cast off fooling,
  and put by ease and rest,
For the Cause alone is worthy
  till the good days bring the best.

Come, join in the only battle
  wherein no man can fail,
Where whoso fadeth and dieth,
  yet his deed shall still prevail.

Ah! come, cast off all fooling,
  for this, at least, we know:
That the dawn and the day is coming,
  and forth the banners go.
                              WILLIAM MORRIS.

THE GRAVE OF BONAPARTE.

ON a lone barren isle, where the wild roaring
    billows
  Assail the stern rock, and the loud tempests
    rave,
The hero lies still, while the dew-drooping wil-
    lows,
  Like fond weeping mourners, lean over the
    grave.
The lightnings may flash, and the loud thunders
    rattle:
  He heeds not, he hears not, he 's free from all
    pain;—

He sleeps his last sleep—he has fought his last
    battle!
No sound can awake him to glory again!

O shade of the mighty, where now are the legions
    That rushed but to conquer when thou led'st
        them on?
Alas! they have perished in far hilly regions,
    And all save the fame of their triumph is gone!
The trumpet may sound, and the loud cannon
    rattle!
    They heed not, they hear not, they 're free from
        all pain:
They sleep their last sleep, they have fought their
    last battle!
    No sound can awake them to glory again!

Yet, spirit immortal, the tomb cannot bind thee,
    For, like thine own eagle that soared to the
        sun,
Thou springest from bondage and leavest behind
    thee
    A name which before thee no mortal had won.
Though nations may combat, and war's thunders
    rattle,
    No more on the steed wilt thou sweep o'er the
        plain:
Thou sleep'st thy last sleep, thou hast fought thy
    last battle!
    No sound can awake thee to glory again!

                                LEONARD HEATH.

THE BATTLE OF BLENHEIM.

[In Bavaria, August 13, 1704, between the English and Austrians on one side, under the Duke of Marlborough and Prince Eugene, and the French and Bavarians on the other side, led by Marshal Tallart and the Elector of Bavaria. The latter party was defeated, and the schemes of Louis XIV. of France were materially checked.]

It was a summer evening,—
  Old Kaspar's work was done,
And he before his cottage door
  Was sitting in the sun;
And by him sported on the green
His little grandchild Wilhelmine.

She saw her brother Peterkin
  Roll something large and round,
Which he beside the rivulet,
  In playing there, had found;
He came to ask what he had found
That was so large and smooth and round.

Old Kaspar took it from the boy,
  Who stood expectant by;
And then the old man shook his head,
  And, with a natural sigh,—
" 'T is some poor fellow's skull," said he,
" Who fell in the great victory.

" I find them in the garden,
  For there 's many hereabout;

And often, when I go to plough,
   The ploughshare turns them out;
For many thousand men," said he,
" Were slain in the great victory."

" Now tell us what 't was all about."
   Young Peterkin he cries;
And little Wilhelmine looks up
   With wonder-waiting eyes,—
" Now tell us all about the war,
And what they fought each other for."

" It was the English," Kaspar cried,
   " Who put the French to rout;
But what they fought each other for
   I could not well make out;
But everybody said," quoth he,
" That 't was a famous victory.

" My father lived at Blenheim then,
   Yon little stream hard by;
They burnt his dwelling to the ground,
   And he was forced to fly;
So with his wife and child he fled,
Nor had he where to rest his head.

" With fire and sword the country round
   Was wasted far and wide;
And many a childing mother there,
   And new-born baby died;
But things like that, you know, must be
At every famous victory.

"They say it was a shocking sight
  After the field was won,—
For many thousand bodies here
  Lay rotting in the sun;
But things like that, you know must be
After a famous victory.

"Great praise the Duke of Marlborough won,
  And our good Prince Eugene."
"Why, 't was a very wicked thing!"
  Said little Wilhelmine.
"Nay, nay, my little girl!" quoth he,
"It was a famous victory.

"And everybody praised the duke
  Who this great fight did win."
"But what good came of it at last?"
  Quoth little Peterkin.
"Why, that I cannot tell," said he;
"But 't was a famous victory."

                              ROBERT SOUTHEY.

AT GIBRALTAR.

I.

ENGLAND, I stand on thy imperial ground
  Not all a stranger; as thy bugles blow,
  I feel within my blood old battles flow,—
The blood whose ancient founts are in thee found
Still surging dark against the Christian bound
  While Islam presses; well its peoples know

Thy heights that watch them wandering below:
I think how Lucknow heard their gathering
   sound.

I turn and meet the cruel, turbaned face.
   England! 't is sweet to be so much thy son!
I feel the conqueror in my blood and race;
   Last night Trafalgar awed me, and to-day
Gibraltar wakened; hark, thy evening gun
Startles the desert over Africa.

II.

Thou art the rock of empire set mid-seas
   Between the East and West, that God has built;
   Advance thy Roman borders where thou wilt,
While run thy armies true with his decrees;
Law, justice, liberty,—great gifts are these.
   Watch that they spread where English blood is
     spilt,
   Lest, mixed and sullied with his country's
     guilt
The soldier's life-stream flow, and Heaven dis-
   please!

Two swords there are: one naked, apt to smite,
   Thy blade of war; and, battle-storied, one
Rejoices in the sheath, and hides from light.
   American I am; would wars were done!
Now westward, look, my country bids good
   night,—
   Peace to the world, from ports without a gun!

               GEORGE EDWARD WOODBERRY.

THE BIVOUAC OF THE DEAD.

[Dedication of a monument to Kentucky volunteers,
killed at Buena Vista, Mexico.]

THE muffled drum's sad roll has beat
    The soldier's last tattoo;
No more on Life's parade shall meet.
    That brave and fallen few.
On Fame's eternal camping-ground
    Their silent tents are spread,
And Glory guards, with solemn round,
    The bivouac of the dead.

No rumor of the foe's advance
    Now swells upon the wind;
No troubled thought at midnight haunts
    Of loved ones left behind;
No vision of the morrow's.strife
    The warrior's dream alarms;
No braying horn nor screaming fife
    At dawn shall call to arms.

Their shivered swords are red with rust,
    Their plumèd heads are bowed;
Their haughty banner, trailed in dust,
    Is now their martial shroud.
And plenteous funeral tears have washed
    The red stains from each brow,
And the proud forms, by battle gashed,
    Are free from anguish now.

The neighing troop, the flashing blade,
  The bugle's stirring blast,
The charge, the dreadful cannonade,
  The din and shout, are past;
Nor war's wild note nor glory's peal
  Shall thrill with fierce delight
Those breasts that nevermore may feel
  The rapture of the fight.

Like the fierce northern hurricane
  That sweeps his great plateau,
Flushed with the triumph yet to gain,
  Came down the serried foe.
Who heard the thunder of the fray
  Break o'er the field beneath,
Knew well the watchword of that day
  Was " Victory or Death."

Long had the doubtful conflict raged
  O'er all that stricken plain,
For never fiercer fight had waged
  The vengeful blood of Spain;
And still the storm of battle blew,
  Still swelled the gory tide;
Not long, our stout old chieftain knew,
  Such odds his strength could bide.

'T was in that hour his stern command
  Called to a martyr's grave
The flower of his beloved land,
  The nation's flag to save.
By rivers of their fathers' gore
  His first-born laurels grew,

And well he deemed the sons would pour
  Their lives for glory too.

Full many a norther's breath has swept
  O'er Angostura's plain,
And long the pitying sky has wept
  Above its mouldered slain.
The raven's scream, or eagle's flight,
  Or shepherd's pensive lay,
Alone awakes each sullen height
  That frowned o'er that dread fray.

Sons of the Dark and Bloody Ground,
  Ye must not slumber there,
Where stranger steps and tongues resound
  Along the heedless air.
Your own proud land's heroic soil
  Shall be your fitter grave:
She claims from war his richest spoil—
  The ashes of her brave.

Thus 'neath their parent turf they rest,
  Far from the gory field,
Borne to a Spartan mother's breast
  On many a bloody shield;
The sunshine of their native sky
  Smiles sadly on them here,
And kindred eyes and hearts watch by
  The heroes' sepulchre.

Rest on, embalmed and sainted dead!
  Dear as the blood ye gave;

No impious footstep here shall tread
   The herbage of your grave;
Nor shall your glory be forgot
   While Fame her record keeps,
Or Honor points the hallowed spot
   Where Valor proudly sleeps.

Yon marble minstrel's voiceless stone
   In deathless song shall tell,
When many a vanished age hath flown,
   The story how ye fell;
Nor wreck, nor change, nor winter's blight,
   Nor Time's remorseless doom,
Shall dim one ray of glory's light
   That gilds your deathless tomb.

THEODORE O'HARA.

THE ARSENAL AT SPRINGFIELD.

THIS is the arsenal. From floor to ceiling,
   Like a huge organ, rise the burnished arms;
But from their silent pipes no anthem pealing
   Startles the villages with strange alarms.

Ah! what a sound will rise—how wild and
      dreary—
   When the death-angel touches those swift keys!
What loud lament and dismal miserere
   Will mingle with their awful symphonies!

I hear even now the infinite fierce chorus—
   The cries of agony, the endless groan,

Which, through the ages that have gone before
    us,
  In long reverberations reach our own.

On helm and harness rings the Saxon hammer;
  Through Cimbric forest roars the Norseman's
    song;
And loud amid the universal clamor,
  O'er distant deserts sounds the Tartar gong.

I hear the Florentine, who from his palace
  Wheels out his battle-bell with dreadful din;
And Aztec priests upon their teocallis
  Beat the wild war-drums made of serpents'
    skin;

The tumult of each sacked and burning village;
  The shout that every prayer for mercy drowns;
The soldiers' revels in the midst of pillage;
  The wail of famine in beleaguered towns;

The bursting shell, the gateway wrenched asunder,
  The rattling musketry, the clashing blade—
And ever and anon, in tones of thunder,
  The diapason of the cannonade.

Is it, O man, with such discordant noises,
  With such accursed instruments as these,
Thou drownest nature's sweet and kindly voices,
  And jarrest the celestial harmonies?

Were half the power that fills the world with ter-
    ror,

Were half the wealth bestowed on camps and
  courts,
Given to redeem the human mind from error,
  There were no need of arsenals nor forts;

The warrior's name would be a name abhorred;
  And every nation that should lift again
Its hand against a brother, on its forehead
  Would wear forevermore the curse of Cain!

Down the dark future, through long generations,
  The echoing sounds grow fainter and then
  cease;
And like a bell, with solemn, sweet vibrations,
  I hear once more the voice of Christ say,
  " Peace! "

Peace!—and no longer from its brazen portals
  The blast of war's great organ shakes the skies;
But, beautiful as songs of the immortals,
  The holy melodies of love arise.

HENRY WADSWORTH LONGFELLOW.

AN OLD BATTLE-FIELD.

THE softest whisperings of the scented South,
And rust and roses in the cannon's mouth;

And, where the thunders of the fight were born,
The wind's sweet tenor in the standing corn;

With song of larks, low-lingering in the loam,
And blue skies bending over love and home.

But still the thought: Somewhere,—upon the
   hills,
Or where the vales ring with the whip-poor-wills,

Sad wistful eyes and broken hearts that beat
For the loved sound of unreturning feet,

And, when the oaks their leafy banners wave,
Dream of the battle and an unmarked grave!
                              FRANK LEBBY STANTON.

THE BATTLE–FIELD.

ONCE this soft turf, this rivulet's sands,
   Were trampled by a hurrying crowd,
And fiery hearts and armèd hands
   Encountered in the battle-cloud.

Ah! never shall the land forget
   How gushed the life-blood of her brave,—
Gushed, warm with hope and courage yet,
   Upon the soil they fought to save.

Now all is calm and fresh and still;
   Alone the chirp of flitting bird,
And talk of children on the hill,
   And bell of wandering kine, are heard.

No solemn host goes trailing by
   The black-mouthed gun and staggering wain;
Men start not at the battle-cry,—
   O, be it never heard again!

Soon rested those who fought; but thou
  Who minglest in the harder strife
For truths which men receive not now,
  Thy warfare only ends with life.

A friendless warfare! lingering long
  Through weary day and weary year;
A wild and many-weaponed throng
  Hang on thy front and flank and rear.

Yet nerve thy spirit to the proof,
  And blench not at thy chosen lot;
The timid good may stand aloof,
  The sage may frown,—yet faint thou not.

Nor heed the shaft too surely cast,
  The foul and hissing bolt of scorn;
For with thy side shall dwell, at last,
  The victory of endurance born.

Truth, crushed to earth, shall rise again,—
  The eternal years of God are hers;
But Error, wounded, writhes in pain,
  And dies among his worshippers.

Yea, though thou lie upon the dust,
  When they who helped thee flee in fear,
Die full of hope and manly trust,
  Like those who fell in battle here!

Another hand thy sword shall wield,
  Another hand the standard wave,
Till from the trumpet's mouth is pealed
  The blast of triumph o'er thy grave.

WILLIAM CULLEN BRYANT.

HOW SLEEP THE BRAVE.

How sleep the brave who sink to rest
By all their country's wishes blest!
When Spring, with dewy fingers cold,
Returns to deck their hallowed mould,
She there shall dress a sweeter sod
Than Fancy's feet have ever trod.

By fairy hands their knell is rung
By forms unseen their dirge is sung;
There Honor comes, a pilgrim gray,
To bless the turf that wraps their clay;
And Freedom shall awhile repair,
To dwell a weeping hermit there!

WILLIAM COLLINS.

OUR FALLEN HEROES.

THE angel of the nation's peace
   Has wreathed with flowers the battle-drum;
We see the fruiting fields increase
   Where sound of war no more shall come.

The swallow skims the Tennessee,
   Soft winds play o'er the Rapidan;
There only echo notes of glee,
   Where gleamed a mighty army's van!

Fair Chattanooga's wooded slope
   With summer airs is lightly stirred,
29

And many a heart is warm with hope
Where once the deep-mouthed gun was heard.

The blue Potomac stainless rolls,
  And Mission Ridge is gemmed with fern;
On many a height sleep gallant souls,
  And still the blooming years return.

Thank God! unseen to outward eye,
  But felt in every freeman's breast,
From graves where fallen comrades lie
  Ascends at Nature's wise behest,

With springing grass and blossoms new,
  A prayer to bless the nation's life,
To freedom's flower give brighter hue,
  And hide the awful stains of strife.

O, Boys in Blue, we turn to you,
  The scarred and mangled who survive;
No more we meet in grand review,
  But all the arts of freedom thrive.

Still glows the jewel in its shrine,
  Won where the James now tranquil rolls;
Its wealth for all, the glory thine,
  O memory of heroic souls!

GEORGE BANCROFT GRIFFITH.

THE CAUSE OF THE SOUTH.

FROM "SENTINEL SONGS."

THE fallen cause still waits,—
　　Its bard has not come yet,
His song—through one of to-morrow's gates
　　Shall shine—but never set.

But when he comes—he 'll sweep
　　A harp with tears all stringed,
And the very notes he strikes will weep,
　　As they come, from his hand, woe-winged.

Ah! grand shall be his strain,
　　And his songs shall fill all climes,
And the Rebels shall rise and march again
　　Down the lines of his glorious rhymes.

And through his verse shall gleam
　　The swords that flashed in vain,
And the men who wore the gray shall seem
　　To be marshalling again.

But hush! between his words
　　Peer faces sad and pale,
And you hear the sound of broken chords
　　Beat through the poet's wail.

Through his verse the orphans cry—
　　The terrible undertone!

And the father's curse and the mother's sigh,
And the desolate young wife's moan.

. . . . .

I sing, with a voice too low
    To be heard beyond to-day,
In minor keys of my people's woe;
    And my songs pass away.

To-morrow hears them not—
    To-morrow belongs to fame:
My songs—like the birds'—will be forgot,
    And forgotten shall be my name.

And yet who knows! betimes
    The grandest songs depart,
While the gentle, humble, and low-toned rhymes
    Will echo from heart to heart.

                    ABRAM JOSEPH RYAN.

———

SENTINEL SONGS.

WHEN falls the soldier brave
    Dead—at the feet of wrong,—
The poet sings, and guards his grave
    With sentinels of song.

Songs, march! he gives command,
    Keep faithful watch and true;
The living and dead of the Conquered Land
    Have now no guards save you.

Grave Ballads! mark ye well!
    Thrice holy is your trust!

Go! halt! by the fields where warriors fell,
  Rest arms! and guard their dust.

List, Songs! your watch is long!
  The soldiers' guard was brief,
Whilst right is right, and wrong is wrong,
  Ye may not seek relief.

Go! wearing the gray of grief!
  Go! watch o'er the Dead in Gray!
Go guard the private and guard the chief,
  And sentinel their clay!

And the songs, in stately rhyme,
  And with softly sounding tread,
Go forth, to watch for a time—a time,
  Where sleep the Deathless Dead.

And the songs, like funeral dirge,
  In music soft and low,
Sing round the graves,—whilst hot tears surge
  From hearts that are homes of woe.

What though no sculptured shaft
  Immortalize each brave?
What though no monument epitaphed
  Be built above each grave?

When marble wears away,
  And monuments are dust,—
The songs that guard our soldiers' clay
  Will still fulfil their trust.

With lifted head, and steady tread,
   Like stars that guard the skies,
Go watch each bed, where rest the dead,
   Brave Songs! with sleepless eyes.

                    ABRAM JOSEPH RYAN.

ODE.

[Sung on the occasion of decorating the graves of the
Confederate dead, at Magnolia Cemetery, Charleston, S. C.]

SLEEP sweetly in your humble graves,—
   Sleep, martyrs of a fallen cause!
Though yet no marble column craves
   The pilgrim here to pause,

In seeds of laurel in the earth
   The blossom of your fame is blown,
And somewhere, waiting for its birth,
   The shaft is in the stone!

Meanwhile, behalf the tardy years
   Which keep in trust your storied tombs,
Behold! your sisters bring their tears,
   And these memorial blooms.

Small tributes! but your shades will smile
   More proudly on these wreaths to-day,
Then when some cannon-moulded pile
   Shall overlook this bay.

Stoop, angels, hither from the skies!
   There is no holier spot of ground

Than where defeated valor lies,
By mourning beauty crowned!

HENRY TIMROD.

THE BLUE AND THE GRAY.

[The women of Columbus, Mississippi, strewed flowers
alike on the graves of the Confederate and the National
soldiers.]

By the flow of the inland river,
Whence the fleets of iron have fled,
Where the blades of the grave-grass quiver
Asleep are the ranks of the dead;—
Under the sod and the dew,
Waiting the judgment-day;—
Under the one, the Blue;
Under the other, the Gray.

These in the robing of glory,
Those in the gloom of defeat,
All with the battle-blood gory,
In the dusk of eternity meet;—
Under the sod and the dew,
Waiting the judgment-day;—
Under the laurel, the Blue;
Under the willow, the Gray.

From the silence of sorrowful hours
The desolate mourners go,
Lovingly laden with flowers
Alike for the friend and the foe,—
Under the sod and the dew,
Waiting the judgment-day;—

Under the roses, the Blue;
Under the lilies, the Gray.

So with an equal splendor
    The morning sun-rays fall,
With a touch, impartially tender,
    On the blossoms blooming for all;—
        Under the sod and the dew,
            Waiting the judgment-day;—
        'Broidered with gold, the Blue;
            Mellowed with gold, the Gray.

So when the summer calleth,
    On forest and field of grain
With an equal murmur falleth
    The cooling drip of the rain;—
        Under the sod and the dew,
            Waiting the judgment-day;—
        Wet with the rain, the Blue;
            Wet with the rain, the Gray.

Sadly, but not with upbraiding,
    The generous deed was done;
In the storm of the years that are fading,
    No braver battle was won;—
        Under the sod and the dew,
            Waiting the judgment-day;—
        Under the blossoms, the Blue;
            Under the garlands, the Gray.

No more shall the war-cry sever,
    Or the winding rivers be red;
They banish our anger forever
    When they laurel the graves of our dead!

Under the sod and the dew,
  Waiting the judgment-day;—
Love and tears for the Blue,
  Tears and love for the Gray.

FRANCIS MILES FINCH.

CENTENNIAL HYMN.

[1876.]

OUR fathers' God! from out whose hand
The centuries fall like grains of sand,
We meet to-day, united, free,
And loyal to our land and Thee,
To thank Thee for the era done,
And trust Thee for the opening one.

Here, where of old, by Thy design,
The fathers spake that word of Thine
Whose echo is the glad refrain
Of rended bolt and falling chain,
To grace our festal time, from all
The zones of earth our guests we call.

Be with us while the New World greets
The Old World thronging all its streets,
Unveiling all the triumphs won
By art or toil beneath the sun;
And unto common good ordain
This rivalship of hand and brain.

Thou, who hast here in concord furled
The war flags of a gathered world,

Beneath our Western skies fulfil
The Orient's mission of good-will,
And, freighted with love's Golden Fleece,
Send back its Argonauts of peace.

For art and labor met in truce,
For beauty made the bride of use,
We thank Thee; but, withal, we crave
The austere virtues strong to save,
The honor proof to place or gold,
The manhood never bought nor sold!

Oh make Thou us, through centuries long,
In peace secure, in justice strong;
Around our gift of freedom draw
The safeguards of thy righteous law:
And, cast in some diviner mould,
Let the new cycle shame the old!

JOHN GREENLEAF WHITTIÉR.

HYMN OF THE WEST.*

WORLD'S FAIR, ST. LOUIS.

[1904.]

O Thou, whose glorious orbs on high
  Engird the earth with splendor round,
From out Thy secret place draw nigh
  The courts and temples of this ground;
      Eternal Light,
      Fill with Thy might

* Copyright 1904 by Robert Allan Reid.

These domes that in Thy purpose grew,
And lift a nation's heart anew!

Illumine Thou each pathway here,
  To show the marvels God hath wrought
Since first Thy people's chief and seer
  Looked up with that prophetic thought,
    Bade Time unroll
    The fateful scroll,
  And empire unto Freedom gave
From cloudland height to tropic wave.

Poured through the gateways of the North
  Thy mighty rivers join their tide,
And on the wings of morn sent forth
  Their mists the far-off peaks divide.
    By Thee unsealed,
    The mountains yield
  Ores that the wealth of Ophir shame,
And gems enwrought of seven-hued flame.

Lo, through what years the soil hath lain,
  At Thine own time to give increase—
The greater and the lesser grain,
  The ripening boll, the myriad fleece!
    Thy creatures graze
    Appointed ways;
  League after league across the land
The ceaseless herds obey Thy hand.

Thou, whose high archways shine most clear
  Above the plenteous western plain,
Thine ancient tribes from round the sphere
  To breathe its quickening air are fain;

And smiles the sun
To see made one
Their   brood   throughout   Earth's   greenest
space,
Land of the new and lordlier race!

EDMUND CLARENCE STEDMAN.

[The foregoing was the official hymn of the Louisiana
Purchase Exposition at St. Louis in 1904. It was written
upon invitation of the Exposition authorities, and was sung
at the opening of the Fair by a chorus of five hundred
voices, to music written for it, also upon official invitation,
by Professor John K. Paine, of Harvard University. It
fitly concludes the poems of Peace, in this volume of
" National Spirit."]

INDEX: AUTHORS AND TITLES.

461

INDEX OF AUTHORS AND TITLES.

For occupation, nativity, etc., of authors, and the American publishers of American poetical works, see General Index of Authors, Volume X.